Letters of Uncle Jonas Lawrence

An Early History Of Southern, Central,
Western New York, & Northern
And North Western Pennsylvania

1886

New York History Review
foreword by Diane Janowski
2022

Letters of Uncle Jonas Lawrence
By Jonas Lawrence
Edited by Diane Janowski

Copyright © 2022 New York History Review
Published by New York History Review Press
Elmira, New York

ISBN: 978-1-950822-10-2

Printed in the United States of America

"The unexamined life is not worth living."

— Socrates

Table of Contents

Foreward..9

Preview..13

Note..15

Rambles About Elmira................................18

Elmira's Development................................28

Personal Reminiscences............................36

Visit to Southport....................................54

Old Friends and Families..........................61

Historic Horseheads..................................70

The Tioga Valley......................................78

Blossburg and its Environs........................88

Hoytville and Arnot................................108

Morris Run and Fall Brook......................117

Tioga County Continued..........................137

Trip to Mansfield....................................149

Mansfield...161

Tioga and its Environs............................171

The Erie Railway....................................182

In Chemung County................................190

Corning's History....................................201

Newspapers and Businessmen..................207

A Railroad Center....................................213

The Fall Brook Company..........................220

Corning to Wellsboro..............................230

Wellsboro Past & Present.........................237

Wellsboro to Antrim................................245

Pine Creek & Jersey Shore.......................252

Williamsport to Elmira............................260

Political History......................................268

Formation of Counties............................275

Famous Campaigns..................................281

A Famous Struggle..................................288

A Charming Country................................295

The Last Trip..303

Foreward

As a historian, I hear "Elmira is not the same as it was." Yes, that is true, but every fifty years one can certainly notice the changes.

During the summer of 1885, The Elmira *Daily Advertiser* ran a 20-plus series of articles about Jonas Lawrence, who was born in Elmira, then called Newtown in 1805. "He grew to manhood in our little hamlet on the banks of the Chemung, was educated in the schools of that day and at a suitable age entered into active business as a merchant, lumber dealer, grain dealer, and shipper." Because of his business he knew most of the local citizens "up and down the Chemung River and north to the head of Seneca Lake." Jonas came home to Elmira for a visit after 44 years of being away. The changes in Elmira were significant to Jonas.

Back in his day, Jonas took an active part in the conception of the Chemung Canal in 1830s and also with the construction of the New York and Erie Railroad in 1839 and 1840. The railroad went bankrupt in 1841 and Jonas lost his money in the venture. He was forced to "close up his business as best he could, making large sacrifices, and went west to Ohio." Later he moved to young Chicago, Illinois. As Chicago grew and gained importance, "Uncle Jonas" as he was called, became more important and prosperous. Over time, his wife died and his children married, and his grandchildren "would climb in his lap" and ask for stories of the old times.

In 1885 Jonas was eighty years old. He loved to tell stories of his Elmira fifty or sixty years earlier. His memory afforded unerring accuracy.

Jonas came back to Elmira on Friday August 7, 1885 on the No. 12 train to spend several months at his childhood home to "look over familiar grounds and to search for old acquaintances. He is nicely quartered at the home of one of our best citizens (Harry Sampson) on West Water Street, who has promised to spend several months driving our streets, country roads, and visiting villages and towns in the surrounding country."

Jonas was a young business man when he left Elmira. The *Daily Advertiser* wished people to know that he was back in town to "make your acquaintance and to talk over bygones in a friendly manner."

Jonas first wanted to be directed to the corner of Lake and Water Streets. He remembered a tavern on the corner – the owner's name was Dunn. Dunn had built the first grist mill in Newtown around 1800 and the tavern in 1804. He remembered the tavern as being the most popular spot in town.

Jonas remember that John Arnot had a store on the opposite corner. Harry took Jonas farther down Water Street and showed him the Chemung Canal bank (today's Chemung County Historical Society). They talked about the Arnot family. Harry took him to the home of old friend Lyman Covell who was still alive.

Jonas noted that the old Mechanics' Hall had been replaced. He quoted, "There is not a single building standing here now that was here when I left." This included John Arnot's foundry on the corner of today's Lake and Market Streets. Also gone was Miles Cook's grocery store, and the old Mansion House hotel. All of these places were before photography came to Elmira so there are no photographs.

Harry told Jonas that the hotel had been destroyed by fire. They talked of the Advertiser newspaper and its history. They walked past the new Masonic temple (today's Hazlett building). Jonas had been a mason in Elmira in 1832. He remembered his initiation into the lodge as being a sleighing party of the masons where they had crossed Sing Sing Creek in Big Flats, and a sudden wind storm forced the entire group to seek shelter at a nearby farm. He remembered a brisk fire in the fireplace. Out came the "cider and red pepper" and doughnuts.

Upon reaching home in Newtown later in the evening a dinner with "extra fortitude" was taken. That evening continued with talks of raffles, shooting matches, fox and deer-hunts.

Jonas and Harry walked up Lake Street past the County buildings and the Arnot home (today's Arnot Art Museum). Jonas recalled that when he left Newtown in 1841 "none had predicted to see Newtown or Elmira as a city." He remembered "a big fight" between Newtown and Horseheads and who would get the county seat."

They walked up Church Street. Uncle Jonas was getting tired but he didn't want to quit. They looked at the First Presbyterian church. They walked down Railroad Avenue to the train station. Harry explained that four railroad companies used the station, the New York, Lake Erie and Western, the Lehigh Valley, the Northern Central and the Tioga and Elmira State Line.

They walked past Wisner Park and Jonas remembered it as a cemetery. They saw the Park Church. Jonas remembered Main Street as being called "the back road to Horseheads." He recalled the wheat fields along the road and "frequently you could hear the wolves howl."

They looked at the new Main Street bridge. Harry said, "Yes, Uncle Jonas, this is the Main Street bridge – and its free, too." Tolls were no longer charged. At this point they went home to Harry's for dinner.

At dinner, Harry explained that it was the railroads that made Elmira a real city. By the time that the railroad was completely finished, Jonas had been gone ten years. The completion of the rail line attracted a large number of persons to Elmira who became citizens. He remarked on those who became rich using the railroad to ship their goods nationwide. Harry told Jonas of the railroads south from Elmira to Pennsylvania with its coal mines and lumber.

The next morning Jonas and Harry walked down to the Lake Street bridge to "have a look at Clinton Island." Jonas recalled having some "good times down on the Island." "The grass was as soft as velvet and the shade in the summertime cool, the air refreshing, while the rippling of the waters furnished music that quieted the nerves and it was a resort to which the weary might take refuge." Harry explained that Clinton Island was gone. The owner of the land had cut down all the trees and hauled away its gravel.

Next they walked down East Water Street to Newtown Creek. They talked of the early settlers and their homes and stores in the vicinity. Jonas asked what the buildings on the hill were. Harry explained they were the Gleason Water Cure.

Jonas remembered the neighborhoods called Pigeon Point and Slabtown. Jonas remarked that "Elmira had erected elegant and substantial school buildings."

They looked at the Elmira Reformatory and the Rolling Mills along the railroad. Jonas remembered the Chemung Canal.

Then they got on a street car to see Elmira quicker. They went up to Horseheads that had been called Fairport when Jonas left. They went to Millport, Blossburg, Big Flats, Watkins Glen, and Mansfield.

The series of articles went along for about 20 weeks, and it just disappeared. It took me a while to figure out that the *Daily Advertiser* realized that the Jonas articles would work better as a book. The next year the newspaper published the Jonas articles *Letters of Uncle Jonas Lawrence* as a book that was given out free to its subscribers.

- Diane Janowski
Elmira City Historian
Elmira, New York

Preview

Letters of Uncle Jonas Lawrence

An Early History Of Southern, Central, Western New York, And Northern And North Western Pennsylvania

COMPRISING

Counties of Chemung, Tioga, Tompkins, Broome, Chenango, Cortland, Cayuga, Seneca, Schuyler, Steuben, Yates, Ontario, Allegany, Cattaraugus, Monroe, Chautauqua, Orleans, Bradford, Northumberland, Tioga, Lycoming, Potter, and McKean, giving descriptions of old-time customs, hunting, and fishing, raisings, political campaigns, etc., together with descriptions of mountain scenery, coal mines, canals, railroads, villages, towns, cities, and many other interesting reminiscences.

Among the Railroads described are the New York, Lake Erie and Western, with the Tioga Branch; the Corning, Cowanesque and Antrim; the Syracuse, Geneva and Corning; the Jersey Shore and Pine Creek; the Northern Central; the Lehigh Valley; the Delaware, Lackawanna and Western; the Elmira, Cortland, and Northern; Addison and Northern Pennsylvania, and the Southern Central.

This is one of the most valuable and interesting routes and sketchbooks ever offered to the public and is presented gratis to the subscribers of the Elmira *Weekly Advertiser*.

NOTE.

Seventy-five years ago, Jonas Lawrence was born in the village of New-town, now the city of Elmira. He grew to manhood in the little hamlet on the banks of the Chemung, was educated in the schools of that day, and at a suitable age entered into active business as a merchant, lumber dealer, grain dealer, and shipper. His business brought him in contact with the citizens of Newtown and all the surrounding country and gave him a very extensive acquaintance up and down the Chemung River, north to the head of the Seneca Lake, and northeast to Owego, Spencer, Ithaca, Binghamton, and westward to Big Flats, Painted Post, Bath, Addison and Hornellsville, and southward up Seeley creek, across the Pennsylvania line to Burlington, Troy, Alba, Canton and Williamsport, and also on the Tioga River at Lawrenceville, Willardsburg (now Tioga) and upon the Cowanesque at Beecher's Island, Elkland, Deerfield, Knoxville, and Westfield.

Jonas Lawrence took an active part in agitating the construction of the Chemung canal and witnessed its completion. He also was a warm friend and advocate of the construction of the New York and Erie railroad in the years 1839 and 1840 and took a great interest in its construction, which commenced in the valley of the Chemung in the year 1840. But when the company failed in 1841, and work ceased, and the whole country was in a state of bankruptcy, Jonas Lawrence closed up his business as best he could, making enormous sacrifices, took a few hundred dollars, and turned his face towards the west. The farmlands of Ohio and Illinois were then the objective points towards which the people of the east were directing their attention. Mr. Lawrence went to Ohio and remained there temporarily and from thence to Illinois, settling in the outskirts of Chicago, then a mere village, and purchasing a quarter section of land. For a few years, he and his family struggled against malaria and adverse circumstances; but the tide eventually turned in their favor. Chicago commenced to increase in population and become a more central point. Every year the possessions of Mr. Lawrence became more valuable. Chicago spread out wider and wider and continued to lay deeper and deeper the foundation of her present and future prosperity. Although Uncle Jonas, as he is now familiarly called, generally prospered, still there were "times in his history when the financial shadows cast a cloud over his affairs. But he was successful upon the whole. His wife, Harriet, about five years ago, was laid tenderly to rest in the silent tomb. His children were married, the older ones many years ago, and grandchildren have come, in whose young life the venerable man renews his youth.

His nephew resided with him many years and called him Uncle Jonas, and thus was that title bestowed upon him. Uncle Jonas is now in his seventy-fifth year, hale, hearty and strong. Age sits lightly upon his person, and with a memory remarkable for one of his years, he can revert to the inhabitants who dwelt in and about Elmira fifty or sixty years ago with almost unerring accuracy. He came to Elmira not long ago to spend a few months in the home of his childhood, look over familiar grounds, search for old acquaintances, and mark the changes that have taken place in southern New York and northern Pennsylvania. He is comfortably ensconced in the home of one of our best citizens on West Water Street, who has promised to spend several months with him in driving our principal streets, country roads, and visiting villages and towns in the surrounding country. The readers of the *Advertiser* will, therefore, permit us without further ceremony to introduce to them Uncle Jonas Lawrence, a former honored citizen of Elmira, one of the early businessmen of this valley, "who has come among them to make their acquaintance and to talk over bygones in a friendly manner. His friend, Harry Sampson, needs no introduction. He will usually accompany Uncle Jonas in his walks and drives and assist him in locating the homes of his old-time friends and imparting such information concerning them as we hope will prove interesting to the readers of the *Advertiser*.

RAMBLES ABOUT ELMIRA.
SOME OF THE EARLY SETTLERS AND THEIR WORKS. —
CHANGES AND IMPROVEMENTS.

"This, Uncle Jonas, is the corner of Lake Street and Water Street, the place you said you wanted to be directed to."

"Oh, yes, Harry. Well, in my first recollection of these corners, William Dunn, the father of the Dunn boys, Charles, James, and William, kept a tavern on that corner. He had formerly resided in Bath and was the first sheriff of Steuben county in 1796. He went to Bath under the auspices of General Williamson and was appointed sheriff when Steuben county was organized from Ontario. He came to Newtown about the year 1800 and built the first grist mill in Newtown, and about the year 1804 opened a tavern on that corner. After his death, his widow married the late John Davis, and the stand thereafter was known as the John Davis stand.

When I left here, Harry, it was still occupied as a tavern, and one of the most popular in the village. Where that fine structure is now, on the opposite corner, John Arnot occupied a brick store and was engaged in selling goods. However, he was quite a large stockholder in the Chemung Canal bank, which was established soon after the completion of the Chemung Canal.

The Hon. John McDowell, of Chemung, I think, was the president of the institution and the Hon. William Maxwell cashier. Harry, I recollect well when the bridge across the river was first built." There has been three bridges here, Uncle Jonas. The one you refer to was rebuilt about the year 1845, and that one was replaced by the present structure a few years ago."

"Oh, yes, so I have been told.

"Well, Harry," continued Uncle Jonas, "down the river, below the bridge, Miles Covell had a store and shipping dock. He and his brother Lyman Covell, were formerly associated in the mercantile business. But they dissolved partnership and Miles continued the old store, where William Roberts is now located, and Lyman opened a store next to John Arnot, on Water street. I see Harry that the old Chemung Canal bank building is still occupied."

"Yes, Uncle Jonas, soon after you left Elmira, John Arnot got the control of the institution, placed it upon a sound and reliable financial foundation, and continued the principal owner of its stock until the time of his death in November 1873. He became one of the most prominent financiers in southern New York, and was largely interested in the New York and Erie Railroad, having with him four other gentlemen: John Magee, Constant Cook, Charles Cook, I. S. Stranahan, who built the road from Binghamton to Hornellsville, in the years 1848-50. He also constructed the Junction Canal from Elmira, connecting with the North Branch canal at Athens, and was largely interested in real estate in Elmira and in coal mines at Arnot, in Tioga County, Pennsylvania, and elsewhere. He left the care and management of his very large estate to his sons, Stephen, John, Jr., and Mathias, who have added to their patrimony."

"Yes, yes, Harry, I recollect him well, also his father-in-law, the late Stephen Tuttle."

"Your old friend Lyman Covell, Uncle Jonas, still lives at the advanced age of ninety-two."

"Is that possible, Harry? I remember him as one of the most energetic businessmen in all this country. Quick and impulsive, but with a kind and warm heart. Before I return I must call on him. But let us walk up to the old stand of E. Jones - I want to see how it looks up there. We will take it slow, for I want to witness the changes. Well, the old Mechanics' Hall I see has been replaced; in fact, there is not a single building standing here now that was here when I left. Over yonder where that large four-story building is located was the site of Colonel William R. Judson's harness shop; the opera house stands on the site of the John Arnot foundry. Miles Cook's grocery has vanished also.

"Here! Whose magnificent building is this? John M, Robinson's, I'm glad to see it! Here used to stand a low wooden building. What, does this mean, Harry? Here is where Elijah Jones used to hold forth in the Mansion House. The *Advertiser* association, is it? Well, that's good."

"Let us rest here a moment. Uncle Jonas, on these cast-iron lions, and I will give you a brief history of this place since you left Elmira forty -four years ago."

THE OLD HOTEL CORNER —
MASONIC REMINISCENCES.

"After you left Elmira, Uncle Jonas, your old friend, E. Jones, kept the hotel for several years, entertaining some of the most distinguished lawyers and jurists in the state, as well as many others less distinguished. He was succeeded by Silas Haight and Mathew Sly, who enlarged the building and made many improvements. After a few months this hotel was destroyed by fire and upon the same site this building was erected by a stock company, consisting of such gentlemen as the late William Maxwell, Samuel G. Hathaway, Jr., Silas Haight, William T. Reeder and others, and Silas Haight and William T. Reeder installed as landlords. You must recollect Silas Haight, Uncle Jonas?"

"Oh, yes, Harry, I recollect him as a merchant, hotel-keeper, superintendent of the Chemung Canal, an energetic businessman."

"Mr. Reeder, Uncle Jonas, was a son of one of your old Big Flats friends, the late William H. Reeder. He was for many years the constable and collector in the town of Big Flats, canal collector at Horseheads, deputy sheriff and sheriff of Chemung County. Messrs. Haight and Reeder purchased; a majority of the stock and controlled the house for several years, making it one of the most popular hotels in the southern tier. They finally sold out their interests to Col. Samuel G. Hathaway, Jr.,and it was for some time known as the Hathaway House and considered as the headquarters of the democracy of the city and county. The Hon. John G. McDowell presented the ship of state you see suspended in the vestibule, to the house, and where it has since remained. The *Advertiser* association is the outgrowth of the *Advertiser* founded by the late Charles G. Fairman, in the year 1853. It has increased in strength and usefulness, merging into a strong financial stock association, known as the *Advertiser* association in the year 1870, which now owns the entire building. At some future time, Uncle Jonas, I will give a more extended history of the *Advertiser*.

"What building is that on the corner, where Riggs Watrous and Daniel Stephens formerly had a blacksmith shop?"

"That Uncle Jonas is the Masonic temple. The cornerstone was laid with Masonic ceremonies, September 5, 1878. There were present: Clinton F. Paige, the grandmaster of the masonic fraternity of the state; C. N. Shipman, deputy grandmaster; John D. Williams, grand warden; Sutherland Dewitt, grand junior warden; F. A. Phillips, grand treasurer; Griff D. Palmer, grand secretary; W. P. Burdick, grand senior deacon; Stephen McDonald, grand junior deacon; P. D. Ramsdell, grand steward; Cyrus Barlow, grand steward, and Brother E. A. Swan, representative for the grand architect; the Rev. George H. McKnight, grand chaplain.

Addresses were made on that occasion by the Rev. George H. McKnight and Jesse L. Cooley. Those who were largely instrumental in bringing this matter to a successful issue were Jesse L. Cooley, son of Levi J. Cooley; John D. Williams, son of your friend William Williams, the tanner; and Sutherland Dewitt, Maurice Levy, and Chauncey Shipman. In about a year thereafter, the temple was completed and dedicated."

"Speaking of masonry, Harry reminds me of my initiation in the year 1832. Old Newtown Lodge had suspended operations in the year 1828 by reason of the Morgan excitement. At Big Flats there was a masonic lodge in working order, or working under special dispensation. The place of meeting was kept a profound secret for many years. The lodge room was in the garret of Captain George Gardiner's inn. The members at Big Flats that I recollect were George Gardiner, Abram Bennett, John Huey, Isaac Watrous, Henry McCormick, Abram McCormick, Erastus Beard, Nicholas Winans, Charles Reynolds, Orange Chapman. It was arranged that we should have a sleighing party and quietly invite some of our Elmira friends, among whom were the late Thomas Maxwell, and go up to Big Flats.

The night was one of the most bitterly cold nights that had been known in many years. However, reinforced by some of John Davis's best, we set out. Still, as we crossed the Sing Sing Creek near the David Reynold's farm, the wind came down the valley from the northwest with such fury that we were obliged to turn in and seek shelter with our Pennsylvania German friend, David Van Gorder. A brisk fire was blazing in the old-fashioned fireplace, which soon melted the frost from our whiskers and faces. Uncle David brought in some cider and red pepper, and after refreshing ourselves with the cider and eating a half-dozen doughnuts and a half-circle of mince pie each, we bade our worthy host a good night and reached Captain Gardiner's in a few minutes.

A number of the townsmen were sitting in the bar-room, and some of them were outspoken anti-masons, and all due circumspection was required in order not to betray the object of our meeting.

A side issue was planned immediately. One of the leading anti-masons was very fond of raffling for turkeys and chickens. The captain ordered his colored man to take a half-dozen chickens and a few turkeys and go down to Benjamin Farwell's cabinet shop and announce "a raffle," instructing him to call into the bar room with his poultry before going to the shop. The colored man was in his element, and was enthusiastic in his work. In less than ten minutes, he rushed into the bar room with a fluttering, squawking lot of poultry and announced a raffle, *"seven pennies in the pot, three shakes for sixpence, and de most heads win de rooster."* This announcement had the desired result.

The bar room was soon cleared, and, one by one, we escaped to the garret or lodge room. We, I say, but I mean that all my friends went, and left me sitting solitary and alone in the bar room. They had gone before me, to get the gridiron good and hot. After waiting for about ten minutes I was invited upstairs. I noticed that my friend was armed with a long sword, which came down nearly to the floor, and that he had to raise it up to keep it from hitting the steps as we ascended. At last we reached the garret, and I was suitably prepared and made my entrance, and took the entered apprentice degree, when we took some refreshments. I was again prepared and was given the Fellowcraft degree, when more refreshments followed. The brethren then urged me to summon all of my fortitude for the grand finale. An extra refreshment was taken, upon the strength of that information, and I was ready for the master's degree. My friends entered into the spirit of the work before them and I presume no other man had in years gone through with a more impressive ceremony. A supper followed in the dining room below, and we were just sitting down to the table, when the anti-masons returned from the raffle loaded with poultry. We gave them an invitation to join us, which some of them accepted, little dreaming that we had been engaged in the business of making Freemasons.

Had our business been known, we would have been accused of every vile action, and in the chance of having been mobbed before we left the village. But Tommy Maxwell adroitly turned the topic of conversation to raffling, shooting matches, fox and deer hunts, which occupied our time at the table. The chief anti-mason had been very successful as a "raffler," and our party purchased his booty for one dollar and a half. And as we were driving off, he called out to us, that when we came again, he would try and get up another raffle for our benefit. Well, Harry, this may not interest you much now in these days, when it is no disgrace, but an honor, to be a Freemason, but fifty years ago no such magnificent temple would have been permitted to have been erected by the Freemasons of this state.

Let us stroll along up the Lake Road or Lake Street, and I should have said. I see new buildings have been erected on the site of the court-house and county clerk's office.

"Well, Harry, we will talk about them at some future time. Yes; here is the residence of the late John Arnot. I remember well when it was built. By some, it was thought that Mr. Arnot made a mistake in erecting so fine a residence so far uptown. That seems highly absurd now but you see fifty years ago nobody expected to see Newtown, Elmira, a city, A few predicted it but we thought they were visionary. When the Chemung Canal was completed in 1833, we thought Elmira would then grow into a city in a few years. But I waited eight years and it only took a spasmodic spring even after the county was formed in 1836, and Elmira chosen as the county seat, in preference, to the rival claim of our neighboring village of Horseheads, now North Elmira. I tell you, Harry, that was a big fight between Horseheads and Elmira for the county seat of Chemung County. But we out-generaled them. The Westlakes, Bentleys, Conklins, Sayres, Jacksons, of Horseheads, were no mean adversaries. Then they had the help of such men as William Bentley, John Dean, Jabez Bradley, Elijah Sexton, Sylvester Sexton, Sylvander Sexton, Daniel Parsons, Erastus Crandall, Doctor Seaman of Veteran, and Charles Cook, Guy Hinman, Elijah Hinman, William Skellinger, Dr. Watkins and others of Catharine, Hiram White of Cayuta, the Crawfords, and Green and Charlie Bennett, of Dix. The indifference of Catlin and Big Flats was all that saved us. I tell you, Harry, it was a close thing. Horseheads, I am told, still maintains her position as the political center of the county, where all conventions are held. "

"Yes, that is so, Uncle Jonas. But they surrendered gracefully to us last winter when they consented to obliterate the name of Horseheads and substitute North Elmira."

"Here is the residence. Uncle Jonas, of the late David H. Tuthill, you must remember him."

"Certainly, Harry, certainly. He was a merchant engaged in selling general merchandise. His place of business was on Water Street. At one time, he had associated with him B. C. Wickham, who subsequently located at Williardsburg, now Tioga, in Pennsylvania. Mr. Tuthill had the confidence of the businessmen of Elmira and the inhabitants of the surrounding country to as great an extent as any man who lived in Elmira during the thirty years that I resided here. But what street is this, Harry?"

"This is Church Street."

"Oh, yes. Whose elegant residence is that over the way?"

"That is the residence of Stephen T. Reynolds. He is the son of the late Charles Reynolds, of Big Flats."

"Oh, yes. I knew Charles Reynolds well. He was a very enterprising businessman at Big Flats many years ago. He died in the prime of his in March 1837. Suppose we take a streetcar and go home. We can go down Lake to Water, up Water to Main, and then we will have only a few steps to walk."

"Nonsense, Harry. We can go up Church Street and out to Main, as you call it, in less time than we are talking about it, besides I am not fatigued in the least."

"Just as you say, Uncle Jonas. But we won't stop to make any observations on the way. Here is the First Presbyterian Church." "This, I see, has kept pace with the progress of Elmira. This congregation or church, Harry, was instituted as early as 1795. Its a noble structure now. And this is Baldwin street. Over there was your old friend Solomon L. Gillett."

"Is that so. Well, I shall have to call on him at the first opportunity I have."

"This is Railroad Avenue. Look out, uncle, yonder comes the Lehigh train. There are four railroads using these tracks, the New York, Lake Erie & Western, the Lehigh Valley, the Northern Central, and the Tioga & Elmira State Line."

"Harry, on this corner, there was when I left Elmira an Episcopal church, but I see it is turned into a foundry and boiler manufactory owned by Reid & Cooper."

"That nice cozy little brick on the opposite corner is owned by the Young Men's Railway Christian Association, one of the very best associations in Elmira. Some day we will drop in and look it over. This is the Baptist church, and this park or lawn is where the old Elmira graveyard was. The bodies have been removed."

"Oh, yes, Harry, I recollect this well. Here was where some of the first citizens of Elmira were buried."

"This building on the opposite side of the street is a memorial erected by one of the late John Arnot's daughters. The church on the corner is an Episcopal church. That massive structure of stone out yonder is Park Church. The Rev. Thomas K. Beecher is the pastor of this church. I tell you, Uncle Jonas, there are a great many interesting places in Elmira which we must visit, and then if you desire we will go out into the country and drive over all the old haunts you used to be familiar with."

"Well, well, Harry, I am thoroughly in earnest in this business. I do not want to do too much in one day, so long as I have months before me, but I came here to enjoy myself in this way instead of going to the seashore or some fashionable watering-place, and I am enjoying it very much. What did you say this was Harry?"

"This is Main Street, Uncle Jonas."

"Oh, yes, I see. This is what we used to call the "back road" to Horseheads, that went up past Covell's, Wisner's, McCann's, Suffern's, Rockwell's, and McConnell's. When I was a boy, Harry, the deer would come into the wheat fields along the road, and frequently you could hear the wolves howl up on the hill west of Wisner's."

"Suppose we turn down Main Street to Water Street. Uncle Jonas."

"Just as you say, Harry. I recognize this corner as being the spot where Judge Theodore North's residence formerly stood. When I was a young man, Judge North's residence, although composed of wood, was thought to be one of the most elegant dwellings in the village. Now a huge pile of brick occupies its place. What! Is that a bridge across the river?"

"Yes, Uncle Jonas, that is called the Main Street Bridge — and free, too." "Harry this is a great improvement, I assure you."

ELMIRA'S DEVELOPMENT.
THE GREAT BENEFIT CONFERRED BY RAILROADS —
HISTORY OF THEIR GROWTH.

"It is raining, Uncle Jonas, and we can't go out this afternoon, and that will give me an opportunity of answering your question at the dinner table: 'What was the chief cause in the development of Elmira into a city? My answer to that question. Uncle Jonas, is briefly, railroads; and I will tell you why and give you a short history of their construction. You will bear in mind that the Erie Railroad was chartered April 24, 1832, and opened from Piermont to Goshen, New York, nine years after, or in the year 1841. You resided here in Elmira in 1840 when the company undertook to construct the road from Goshen to Erie simultaneously upon piles driven into the ground and timbers to be placed upon them and held together by cross-ties, the state guaranteeing their bonds to the amount of $3,000,000. You recollect how each county through which the proposed line of the railroad would pass insisted that the money should be expended in those counties because their representatives had been instrumental in securing the appropriation or the endorsement of the bonds of the company, and how instead of commencing the road and expending their own money and that which the state had given them, in completing the road section by section in one continuous chain, that the company spread their money over the entire road from Piermont to Erie, and only had a few miles of road completed and in running order, when the money was exhausted, the road uncompleted and the company bankrupt. That Uncle Jonas, you recollect, was the condition in which the affairs of the Erie company were in when you left Elmira in the year 1841. It was a matter in which the people of the southern tier of counties of New York and the northern counties of Pennsylvania were deeply interested. The southern tier counties in New York

28

were more personally interested, but the citizens of Susquehanna, Bradford, Tioga, Potter, McKean, Warren and Erie counties of Pennsylvania, would be materially benefited by the construction of the road, for it would have a tendency to open up an eastern market for their lumber and coal. After several years of financing, the railroad company was reorganized, and a new set of men controlled the management of affairs.

As I told you this morning, the late John Arnot, of Elmira, the Hon. John Magee, of Bath; the Hon. Charles Cook, of Havana; Constance Cook and I. S. Stranahan of New York City, took hold of the enterprise and constructed the road from Binghamton to Hornellsville. The road was finally constructed and reached Lake Erie on May 14, 1851. To recapitulate, the road was constructed from Piermont to Goshen in September 1841, to Middletown in June 1843, to Port Jervis January 1848, to Binghamton December 1848, to Elmira October 1849, to Corning January 1850, and to Dunkirk, on Lake Erie, in May 1851, the event being celebrated all along the line and by an excursion over the road, accompanied by the president, Millard Fillmore, the secretary of state, Daniel Webster, and other distinguished men of this state and nation. It was indeed a proud and grand day for Elmira. The president and secretary of state remained in Elmira overnight, Daniel Webster making a speech from the balcony of the Brainard or Rathbun house.

The completion of the road and the consequent and attendant expenses connected with its building attracted a large number of persons to Elmira to engage in business and become permanent residents. In anticipation of the completion of the Erie, a railroad company was formed early in the year 1849 known as the "Chemung Railroad Company," composed chiefly of enterprising citizens of Elmira, Horseheads, Veteran, Havana, and Watkins, who constructed during that year (1849) a railroad from Elmira to Watkins Glen, at the head of Seneca Lake, and a company soon after formed continued the road on north to Canandaigua and Niagara Falls. In the year 1853, the Elmira & Williamsport Railroad Company constructed a railroad from Elmira to Williamsport, seventy-eight miles in length, and had it in operation in 1854.

Thus, Elmira had an eastern outlet two ways, one by the Chemung Canal to Albany and the Hudson River, and by the Erie Railroad to Piermont on the Hudson, and also through New Jersey to New York. She also had two southern outlets, one by the Chemung River and the other by the Elmira & Williamsport Railroad, which at the latter place made connections as far south as Baltimore. Elmira, while she gained much in population, lost some of her best citizens by the construction of the Elmira & Williamsport Railroad, who went to Williamsport and engaged extensively in the manufacture of lumber. It was, however, only an exchange of citizenship, for Elmira gained a number of enterprising Pennsylvanians. The western outlet from Elmira was to Corning and thence to Rochester, (for the Cohocton Valley Railroad was completed in the year 1855) and on the west from Corning to Lake Erie. At Corning, a railroad ran south up into the Tioga Valley to Blossburg, the center of the semi-bituminous coal regions of Northern Pennsylvania, which was quite an advantage to the citizens of Elmira. The northward outlet reaches up to the shores of Lake Ontario — intersecting the Central railroad at Canandaigua.

Thus matters stood for two or three years, Elmira increasing in wealth and population and spreading out wider and wider, laying the foundation on a permanent basis for her present position.

There was a little enterprise that contributed largely to the business of Elmira, which I have omitted to name. It was the building of a plank road from Elmira southwest to the Pennsylvania State the upon Seeley Creek, which enabled the lumbermen of that section as well as the farmers to get their products to an Elmira market. It was a good investment in every respect. The farmers and lumbermen could well afford to pay toll over the road and haul two or three thousand feet of lumber at a load instead of worrying through the mud axle-deep with eight hundred or a thousand feet. I have not the figures just handy here. Uncle Jonas, but I believe the plank road was built about the year 1848 or 1849. I remember I assisted in its construction, but my books are upstairs in the garret, and we will let this pass.

The people in Bradford County, Pennsylvania, were anxious to extend their canal system from Towanda to Athens, PA on the New York state line, and there connect with a canal, which should be constructed either by the state of New York or by private enterprise or by a company. Pennsylvania had opened up valuable coal mines at Barclay, southwest from Towanda, and they wanted to get an outlet for it northward. The matter was tallied over in Elmira, and the result was the construction of the Junction canal, the capital furnished chiefly by the late John Arnot. In fact, it was called John Arnot's canal. This canal gave the Pennsylvanians an opportunity of shipping northward their semi-bituminous coal of Bradford County and the anthracite coal of Luzerne County, and the citizens of Elmira to ship their lumber, grain and other products southward to Philadelphia if necessary.

Public improvements remained for a time, as your old legal friend, James Robinson, would express it, "in status quo," giving the people time to erect suitable dwellings, public buildings, churches, schools, and colleges, commensurate with the dignity and importance of the place, and to establish increased facilities for the dissemination of news, and herald to the world the central position of Elmira and its extraordinary location for the transaction of business.

Right nobly did the Elmira *Daily and Weekly Advertiser,* and the Elmira *Daily and Weekly Gazette* respond to the wants of the prospective city. The war came on. Elmira was made a military rendezvous and also a military prison for the safekeeping of rebel prisoners. For four years did she enjoy the distinction, in the meantime increasing her wealth and population and improving her streets and extending the boundaries of her corporate limits. Her sons had distinguished themselves in battle, in the halls of legislation, upon the floors of Congress and the councils of the nation. Her Divens, Hathaways, Hoffmans, Beechers, Robinsons, and a host of others had made a splendid record. Elmira was divesting herself of her quiet village manners and assuming city airs. Before the war was closed, she was incorporated as a city and the Hon. John Arnot, Jr., elected the first mayor in April 1804.

In 1866 the Elmira & Williamsport Railroad and the Chemung Railroad and the Canandaigua & Watkins Glen branch were leased by a Pennsylvania company and had since been know under the general head as the Northern Central. The citizens of Elmira desired railroad connections with Ithaca, Cortland, DeRuyter, Cazenovia, and Utica. They wanted a road that would connect Elmira by rail with these points more directly instead of taking the roundabout way to Canandaigua, thence east via Geneva, Auburn Syracuse and Rome to Utica. The late Dr. Eldridge and other citizens from Elmira, seconded by that persevering and indefatigable worker, Joseph Rodburn, of Breesport, succeeded in constructing a railroad under the title of Utica, Ithaca & Elmira Railroad, which reached Elmira in the year 1875, thus adding one more outlet from Elmira and increasing its central position for shipments. In the meantime, the Lehigh Valley Railroad, under the direction of that mastermind, the Hon. Asa Packer, deceased, had extended the line of that road from Easton on the Delaware River, up the Lehigh via Bethlehem, Allentown, Mauch Chunk and White Haven, crossed over the mountain between the Lehigh and the north branch of the Susquehanna, penetrated the beautiful valley of the

Wyoming and continued and connected his hue via Wilkesbarre, Pittston, Tunkhannock, Wyalusing, Wysox, Towanda to Waverly, where he had made the connection with the Erie and thus reached Elmira, using the Erie depot for his passenger traffic, but erecting a commodious freight depot for the discharge and reception of freight. This added materially to the shipping facilities and business interests of Elmira.

The citizens of Elmira were not contented with their almost unlimited facilities for shipping north and south, east and west; but conceived the idea of constructing a railroad from Elmira southwest through the town of Southport up Seeley Creek, thence westward, scaling the mountains intervening between the Chemung Valley in New York and the Tioga Valley in Pennsylvania, making connections with the Tioga Railroad and the semi-bituminous coal mine at Arnot, in the Blossburg region. The citizens of Elmira subscribed liberally towards this enterprise, and in the year 1876, the road was constructed, and its completion celebrated in fine style. This has proved to be one of the best investments of the kind for the city of Elmira, according to the capital employed, that she has engaged in for years. It puts the businessmen of Elmira in close contact with the farmers of Tioga County, Pennsylvania, and businessmen generally of that county, while it literally places a coal mine at the very gates of the city, as well as a great lumber yard; Tioga County being distinguished for her forests of valuable timber, as well as for her coal, likewise for her agricultural products, her butter, and cheese, her wheat, corn, oats, buckwheat, and tobacco. As you will perceive. Uncle Jonas, this centennial road as it is termed by some because it was built in that year, added another spoke in the wheel of Elmira's prosperity and added more to her fame as a central point and increased her facilities for manufacturing.

Three years ago, another railroad reached our city from Pennsylvania. This one, the Delaware, Lackawanna & Western Railroad, came here from New York, by way of the anthracite coal regions of Pennsylvania and entering the eastern portion of the city and thence westward by way of Corning and Bath to Buffalo. It is a strong company with elegant rolling stock and a faultless roadbed.

Elmira, you perceive, has been continually increasing in wealth and population attracting to it railroads from all points of the compass. While it cannot boast of rapid and phenomenal growth as some of your western cities, Uncle Jonas, she has steadily reached out right and left and annually increased in strength. But Uncle Jonas, the things have not come to her without an effort. She has not sat down and folded her hands and quietly waited for these events to take place. Oh, no! It has taken brains, money, energy, skill, patience, and enterprise. I don't want to say too much, Uncle Jonas, to one who thinks there is no place so progressive as the great west, but I do believe that there is not an inland city in the east, (out of compliment to you I won't say the west,) that can compare with Elmira today in facilities for manufacturing and shipping, either for glass, iron, boots and shoes, clothing, tobacco, cigars, the malting and brewing business, the milling of flour and feed, the manufacture of cloth, the manufacture of stoves and foundry and machine work generally, including that of engines and locomotives, the construction of freight and passenger cars, the manufacture of saws and edge tools, the wholesaling of goods of every description, for the reason railroad freights are cheap in all directions, and competition between rival lines brisk. We are substantially at the outlet of mines of bituminous and anthracite coal, near the great iron deposits, near the glass-sand rock, the forests of timber, the center of a great wool and tobacco trade, the center of railroads, requiring cars of all descriptions. We are near the great cokeries of Tioga County, PA., where the best coke is made in America for the manufacture of iron and steel and the tempering of edged tools, and with plenty of elbow room to spread out up to North Elmira, or down to

Wellsburg, or up the river to Dan Fitch's old place. We have schools and colleges, churches and printing presses; we have street railways, water and gas works, and a fair system of sewerage: we have broad streets well protected by shade trees; we have professional men eminent in their work, and, taken altogether, one of the most desirable places for a residence in the country."

PERSONAL REMINISCENCES.
RECOLLECTIONS OR INCIDENTS IN THE LIVES
OF THE EARLY RESIDENTS.

"Did you say, Harry, that the house was situated on the "Billy Hoffman" farm?"

"Yes, Uncle Jonas." "I can remember Mr. Hoffman as far back as sixty years ago. He was a hatter and furrier by trade and was considered one of the best in the country. He was a Pennsylvanian by birth, born I think in the county of Northumberland. He was one of nature's noblemen, honest and square in his dealings, kind and hospitable. He carried on business on Water street, and was finally succeeded by the late Nelson W. Gardner, and then devoted his entire time and attention to farming. As he was distinguished as a hatter, he also became distinguished as a farmer, producing the finest wheat, corn, and oats in the country, as well as raising the finest steers and young cattle for the market. Soon after you left Elmira, he erected one of the finest barns in the Chemung Valley and painted it yellow. His place was known far and wide. The plain, brick house, and the mammoth yellow barn, were landmarks by which his farm was described.

The completion of the Erie Railroad to Elmira, in 1849, stimulated the sale of village lots. Mr. Hoffman about that time commenced laying out lots and selling them, until his fine farm of about 200 acres was covered over, not with waving fields of grain nor herds of neat cattle, but cottages and costly dwellings. The yellow barn was torn down to make room for the habitations of men, women, and children, instead of being the site where the fruits of the field were garnered or the herds of the farm sheltered. He died July 4, 1867, aged ninety years, as sincerely mourned as any man who had ever resided in the Chemung Valley.

His son, Colonel Henry C. Hoffman, distinguished himself in the war for the preservation of the union, commanding the gallant 23rd Regiment of New York state volunteers, and died quite suddenly at Horseheads about two years ago. He resided on and owned the farm where the old pioneer, John Breese, first settled in the year 1788. The colonel had erected upon it a fine mansion, a creamery, and was a stock breeder of fine cattle. He had twice represented the county of Chemung in the popular branch of the legislature and was a gentleman highly esteemed. His age was about fifty-four, and physically he was one of the finest proportioned men in the southern tier."

"Harry, let us walk down the street this morning. Now you must put on your 'thinking cap,' for I shall, no doubt, ask you a great many questions. Since I have got Uncle Billy Hoffman's place located, I think I can locate the rest along the road. Yes, over there is where Billy Williams had his tannery. This is where the Goulds built their grist mill, and on this site is where Silas Billings lived, and here is the Judge North corner. Down below this Main Street bridge, of which, Harry, you promised to give me a history, is the old ark yard, and a little lower down is where Ben Vail had a cabinet shop."

"How can you locate these places so well, Uncle Jonas?"

"Because, Harry, I had traveled this road or street more than a thousand times when there were not more than a dozen buildings between the Whittington Sayre place or tavern upon the corner of what you now call State street up to Billy Hoffman's. I can recollect, Harry, when there were fields of grain growing where these piles of brick are now laid up. Let us move along, Harry, down to the Eagle."

"Who is that old gentleman in the carriage, looking this way?"

"That, Uncle Jonas, is Judge Gray."

"What, Hiram Gray?"

"Yes, Uncle Jonas."

"Well, I declare, he is well preserved. He is about ten years older than I am. He must, therefore, be in his eighty-fifth year. Why do you call him a judge, Harry? He was practicing law when I left with such men as Andrew K. Gregg, John W. Wisner, Samuel G. Hathaway, Jr., James Dunn, Thomas Maxwell, Aaron Konkle, Ariel S. Thurston, William Maxwell, Elijah P. Brooks, as members of the bar from Elmira." "Let us rest a moment here in this easy seat in the reception room of the Rathbun House, and I will tell you. You recollect, Uncle Jonas, that two years before you left Elmira, Mr. Gray had been elected to congress and had associated with him the young and rising lawyer Samuel G, Hathaway, Jr. The partnership was a very fortunate combination. Hiram Gray was a cool, logical lawyer. At the same time, Hathaway was a smooth, polished, and accomplished gentleman, not then so deeply versed in law, but a fine scholar, excellent manners, fluent in speech, and almost irresistible before a jury. Gray and Hathaway were both graduates of Union College, Schenectady, presided over by the famous Dr. Nott, so distinguished for his scholarly attainments, and particularly for his faculty of imparting to his students the science of elocution and rhetoric. When a client applied to the firm, Hiram Gray looked up the law and the decisions in the case, and Colonel Hathaway selected in addition to the law which Gray referred to him, the points upon which he might enlist the sympathy of the judge or jury, and if necessary in trying the case, made his plea, conform to the equity instead of the law in the premises. No man excelled Colonel Hathaway in trying a case in the court of common pleas, where the case should have been decided according to law, and before the judge or jury were aware of it, deciding it a case of equity. I say Uncle Jonas it was a fortunate combination, Hiram Gray having a clear judicial mind, which was capable of grasping and presenting all the points at issue, calculated to call forth the better feelings of the judge and the jury. In 1845, or about that time, Alexander S. Diven, now known as General Diven, who had been a student with Hiram Gray, became a member of the firm. In 1816 Mr. Gray was appointed by Governor Silas Wright one of the judges of the supreme court and in the year 1847, the office being abolished by the new constitution, Judge Gray was elected one of the justices of the supreme court in June of that year and served eight years in that capacity. In the year 1867, Union College conferred upon him the degree of doctor of laws, and in 1870 he was appointed as one of the commissioners of appeals, and, old as he is now, many cases of great importance are yet submitted to him."

"Well, Harry, we will call on him and renew our acquaintance. But what of Hathaway and Diven?"

"After Judge Gray went upon the bench the law firm was 'Diven & Hathaway,' and was additionally strengthened by the accession of James L. Woods, a great student, and a careful counselor, when the firm became 'Diven, Hathaway & Woods,' and was one of the most trusted firms in Southern New York. Colonel Hathaway was elected a member of the legislature and was several times a candidate for congress, but was not elected. He was one of the most polished democratic campaign speakers in the state.

During the rebellion, he raised a regiment and went gallantly to the front. The climate of the south was fatal to him. He contracted a disease, resigned his commission and returned to his old home at Solon, Cortland County, NY, where he died April 16, 1864, in the fifty-fifth year of his age, one year before the close of the war. He was a gentleman greatly beloved and respected. Alexander S. Diven continued as a member of the firm above referred to until the year 1861 — in the meantime having acted as a director in the Erie railroad and been instrumental in its construction, had also been conspicuously connected with the building of the Elmira & Williamsport Railroad, had served a term in the state senate and was elected to congress in the year 1860 as a Republican.

In 1862 he assisted in raiding the 107th regiment of New York state volunteers and went into service as its lieutenant-colonel, where he discharged his duty with courage and fidelity. He was subsequently appointed provost marshal, with headquarters at Elmira, which duties he discharged with eminent ability and satisfaction. He is still living and is about one year your senior, Uncle Jonas, being seventy-six years old. He resides in a beautiful home on the southern portion of the old Carpenter farm, on the road to Horseheads, and has a winter residence in Florida. His son, George M. Diven, is a prominent attorney of this city now. James L. Woods, the junior member of the firm of Diven Hathaway & Woods, still resides in the city. As a counselor, he stands pre-eminent in his profession. I recollect him well when he was a student in the office of Gray & Hathaway, Jimmy Woods, as he was then called boarded with Judge Gray, who about the year 1843, purchased a stony farm on the ridgeback from the River Road, near the Colonel John Hendy farm, and built himself a large stone residence made of round cobblestones which were found on his farm. The mansion stood back from the road in the fields and scrub oak and yellow pine brush. Judge Gray caused the course of the old highway leading from Elmira to Big Flats, which, at this point, ran along near the riverbank, to be changed and straightened, so that it would run within a few rods of the mansion. It was situated about two miles from the office. Regular as the sun, Jimmy Woods, then a pale, slender youth, could be seen walking from the office to Judge Gray's for his meals and returning to the office again. In this manner, he obtained exercise, gave himself time for reflection and thought, and developed into a strong man physically and mentally and became a perfect dictionary or encyclopedia of law and court decisions. He resides near us, Uncle Jonas, and sometime when it is convenient, we may call on him.

"Harry, I want to go down again to the Lake Street bridge and take a look at Clinton Island. I have spent many a happy hour upon it."

"Uncle Jonas, there is no Clinton Island now."

"What, no Clinton Island; what has become of it?"

"Oh, it has been entirely obliterated, not by floods, but by the hand of man. The ownership of it finally was vested in a gentleman, who cut down the trees, dug out the stumps and hauled away the gravel and earth of which it was composed, to pave our streets."

"What desecration, Harry. I have often thought in my western home, as I would occasionally hear from Elmira, that she was making splendid progress, that the corporation would purchase Clinton Island, protect its banks from washing away by the construction of suitable docks and piers, and make a public park of it. Nature had done her part in planting those magnificent buttonball, butternut, maple, and other forest trees. The grass was as soft as velvet, and the shade in summertime cool, the air refreshing. At the same time, the rippling of the waters furnished music that quieted the nerves and made it a resort to which the weary might take refuge when overburdened with the cares, the noise and the tumult of the busy street. Yes, Harry, I have often thought of Clinton Island, the picnics, the parties, the celebrations, and the quiet walks I had enjoyed upon that beautiful island. But if it is now in the condition you describe, I do not wish to look at it; I do not wish to mar the remembrance of its former beauty and loveliness by gazing now upon its deformity. I want to cherish its memory.

"There is one thing, Harry, that I have remarked in my travels over this city, and particularly along Water Street and Lake Street, that there is only one business sign hanging out here today, and but few names in the business directory, that were to be seen or read when I left Elmira. The sign on the Chemung Canal bank is the same, and the business is being carried on by the same parties or their descendants now that were then. In the directory, I find the names of Partridge, Collingwood, Arnot, Baldwin, Post, Gillett, Dunn, Hart, Goldsmith, Ayers, Haight, Cooley, Gray, Thurston, Purdy, Perry, Satterlee, Hall, Preswick, and a few others, but the old names are substantially gone, and others have taken their places.

"Harry, I am getting into a melancholy and reflective mood, and let us go down Water Street to Newtown Creek. It is quite a distance, yet I am strong and feel well, and we will take our time."

They pass down Water Street. Uncle Jonas was pointing out the old business places between Baldwin and Lake Streets and making comments. They go on down by the Chemung Canal bank, the residence of Lyman Covell, chatting about old times until they reached Madison Avenue. Uncle Jonas thought of his old friends, the Greggs, turned up the Avenue admiring the beautiful residence of Dr. Flood, and made their way to the Gregg homestead. How small the mansion appeared in comparison with some of the present residences in Elmira. In its day, it was a residence of no mean proportions.

"Here, Harry, resided a family who was great friends of mine, and with whom I exchanged many courtesies in a business and social way. They were of Irish descent and connected with some of the best families in central Pennsylvania and southern New York. Ex-Governor Curtin, the great war governor of Pennsylvania, was a relative of them. The head of the family settled in Northumberland County, Pennsylvania, during or soon after the revolutionary war. His name was Andrew Gregg, and his son, Andrew K. Gregg, was born in Elmira and was about ten years my senior. I think he was born in 1799 and I in 1810. He studied law and was admitted to practice, and in 1835 was chosen district attorney for the county of Tioga, before the county of Chemung was formed, and also after it was formed, acting in that capacity as late as 1841. His house was the center of a refined and cultivated circle. Two of his children, I recollect well, Isaac B. and Mary. Isaac studied law with his father and was admitted to practice, but soon thereafter, I learn, obtained a position in the custom-house in New York City, and remained there for many years. In 1857 Andrew K. Gregg severed his business relations with the people of Chemung County and went west, locating at Chippewa Falls, Wisconsin, where he died about ten years later, April 5, 1868, aged sixty-nine years. He was distinguished for his honesty, his legal acquirements, and his social qualities.

"Harry, what are those buildings upon the hillside beyond New-town Creek?"

"Those, Uncle Jonas, are the Elmira Water Cure. This cure has been established for twenty-five years or more."

"And what are those yonder?"

"The Elmira woolen mills. Uncle Jonas."

"Yes, I see. I must acknowledge, Harry, that Elmira has spread out over a wider territory than I expected."

"But, Uncle Jonas, you have not seen yet how the Southport side of the city is settled. We will look that over at some future time."

"Harry, I want to return home by "Pigeon Point," or "Slabtown," as we called it years ago. I can recollect when the ground where we are now was covered with black alders and water with thousands of frogs in the summertime, making the night hideous with their croakings. What a change, what a change. Come on, Harry, I know the "lay of the land" here even if it is built up with fine residences, schools, churches, and manufacturing establishments."

"This, Uncle Jonas, is the Delaware & Lackawanna Railroad, which I told you about yesterday. See what a perfect roadbed."

"Harry, we can build in the west railroads very much cheaper than you can here in the east."

"Yes, I admit it, Uncle Jonas."

"I see. Harry, that there are still a great many colored people here at the 'Point.'"

"Yes, but Uncle Jonas, they have improved very much in their habits and character since you left. Now, these colored people have erected churches and chapels, have regular ministers of their own color, support and maintain Sunday-schools, and have taken commendable steps to advance in morals and education."

"I am glad of it, Harry. I see that your city has erected elegant and substantial school buildings, yet no section of the United States excels in our western and northwestern cities in their school buildings and the apparatus and appliances necessary for imparting information. Yonder, Harry, is one of the old landmarks of Elmira, the late residence of the Hon. William Maxwell. How small it looks comparatively. When I lived here, I thought it was large enough for the president of the United States. It was erected a few years before I went west and considered the finest residence in Chemung County."

"You must have been acquainted with 'Billy' Maxwell, Uncle Jonas?"

"Very well, Harry. He was a son of one of the pioneers of Chemung County at Elmira, was a lawyer and one of the first officers of the Chemung Canal Bank, was prominently connected with the early trials and struggles of the New York & Erie Railroad. Oh, yes, Harry, I knew him well."

"There is an incident connected with his history. Uncle Jonas, after you left Elmira which I wish to relate: You must recollect, Uncle Jonas, the great struggle of the citizens of Southern New York to prevail upon the legislature of the state of New York to pass the bill for the construction of the Chemung Canal, and the sympathy and assistance that Tioga and Bradford counties in Pennsylvania rendered in that event. You must recollect that

Chemung County sent a committee of its citizens, one of whom I believe was Judge Gray, as early as 1825 to go to Blossburg, in Tioga County, PA, and examine the coal and iron beds, and how one of the enterprising citizens of Horseheads, then the town of Elmira, Vincent Conklin, went to Blossburg with his team and drew a load of the coal in a wagon to Albany to show the members of the legislature what mineral existed in the mountains just over the state line in Pennsylvania, besides showing the immense growth of valuable pine timber there was in Chemung and Steuben Counties which would be manufactured and taken eastward if the proposed canal was constructed. You must also recollect that prominent among those who opposed the construction of the canal was Colonel Samuel Young, of Saratoga County, who was a member of the legislature of New York, made an adverse report, using the term 'sturdy beggars' to those who petitioned and advocated the construction of the canal. Well, in 1846, five years after you left Elmira, a constitutional convention was called to revise the constitution of the state, and delegates from each assembly district were selected to sit in the convention. The democratic party of the state was then divided into two factions, one was styled the Hunkers, and the other, the Barnburners, two not very euphonious names. Colonel Young wished to be a member of that convention, or at least his friends did. Colonel Young, it was determined, after a careful canvass of Saratoga County, could not be elected from that county. He was a Barnburner, and the hunker or conservative wing of the democratic party was too strong for him there. A county convention of democrats was held in Horseheads in February of that year (1846) to recommend to the canal board suitable persons to be appointed as superintendent and collector of the canal, in Chemung County, and in the call for the convention, there was no mention made or authority given to the convention to nominate a person to represent Chemung County in the constitutional convention which would convene in Albany, June 1,

1816. The county convention was convened at Horseheads. The Superintendent and collector were recommended, and the convention adjourned,
and a large portion of the delegates left the hall. The convention was composed of both factions, but they had agreed to 'pool their issues" and recommend the others above referred to. The Barnburner portion of the convention remained in the hall by a secret understanding, and as soon as their
friends the hunkers had substantially vacated, a motion was made that the
resolution to adjourn be reconsidered, which was carried, of course — a
few of the hunkers rushing back into the hall and protesting vehemently,
but of no avail. The convention was restored to life, and Colonel Young, of
Saratoga, was put in nomination as a suitable person to represent Chemung
County in the constitutional convention. To say that the hunker portion
of the democratic party was indignant is too mild a term. The old version
of the scriptures was then orthodox, and the hunker portion used King
James English in a vociferous manner. The Barnburners were evidently in
the majority in the county, that is, they outnumbered the hunkers, but they
did not outnumber the whigs and hunkers combined. It was claimed that
there had never been such an insult offered to the intelligence and dignity
of the county as the nomination of such a person as Colonel "Sam" Young
to represent a section of the state to whom he had applied the opprobrious
epithet of "sturdy beggars"; that it was a virtual acknowledgment that the
county had no one capable of representing her in the convention which
would meet to revise her organic law. A paper was drawn up whose reput-
ed author was General Alexander S. Diven, setting forth the facts and circumstances under which Colonel Young received the nomination, to be
signed by the voters of the county requesting the Hon. William Maxwell to
accept the nomination for delegate to the convention. This paper received
the names of such men as Lyman Covell, Colonel Samuel G. Hathaway,
Jr., Alexander S. Diven, Levi J. Cooley, Thomas Maxwell, Hiram Gray, of

Elmira; Moderica Rickey, Legrand Barlow, of Horseheads; Elijah Sexton, Chauncey Taylor, Daniel Parsons, of Veteran, the Hon. George B. Guinnip, Simeon L. Rood and others in the northern portion of the county, and by Judge James Hughson, Judge John L. Sexton, U. Hampton Davy, John W. Hughson, Lorenzo D. Hughson, George A. Gardiner of Big Flats; the Hon. John G. McDowell, of Chemung, and hundreds of others throughout the county. The hunkers had no newspaper in the county to advocate then cause but were supported by the Albany Argus at the capital. The Elmira Gazette was then owned by George W. Mason and William C. Rhodes, and it supported Colonel Young. I tell you. Uncle Jonas, I have been familiar with the political contests in Chemung county since its organization, and I have never witnessed a more bitter and stubborn contest than that. Mr. Maxwell accepted the nomination; the whigs made no nomination, but as a general thing sympathized with the hunkers and desired to rebuke the insult and voted for Mr. Maxwell, thus securing his election by about 800 majority. He ably represented the county in the convention, was a gentleman of pleasing address, well versed in the fundamental principles of organic law, and knew the necessity of the revision of the constitution of the state, and the necessity of reorganizing the judiciary and eliminating many of the old and crude forms of procedure which had been handed down and continued from colonial times. Mr. Maxwell was elected next year member of the assembly and served with distinction. He died in the year 1858 of paralysis, aged about fifty-six years. He left no children."

"What large buildings are those, Harry, away across yonder on the back road? "

"That, Uncle Jonas, is the Elmira state reformatory prison. We will call there someday in the near future and go through the institution."

"Very well. Is that a rolling mill over there by the canal?"

"Yes, that is what is known as 'The Elmira Iron & Steel Rolling

Mill.' It was originally chartered August 7, 1860, as 'The Elmira Rolling Mill Company,' but has since changed its title. The officers were: Asher Tyler, president; Edwin Eldridge, vice-president; H. W. Rathbone, secretary, and treasurer.   It is now one of the strongest manufacturing companies in southern New York. It has from time to time added to its original plant, erecting furnaces and plate mills. Did you know General Ransom Rathbone, of Rathboneville, Steuben county, Uncle Jonas?"

"Oh, yes."

"Well, his son, Henry W. Rathbone, is now chief stockholder and manager of this concern. Then there is Jesse L. Cooley, son of your old friend, Levi J. Cooley, and John D. Williams, son of your old friend, William Williams, hold responsible positions there. They have been with the company since it first organized.

"Is that so Harry! I should be pleased to make their acquaintance."

"Yonder, Uncle Jonas, is the depot of the Delaware Lackawanna & Western Railway, and that long building down there is the freight depot of the Lehigh Valley Railroad, and that new building you see down this track is the depot of the Elmira, Cortland, & Northern Railway, formerly the Utica, Ithaca, and Elmira. That building up this track is a tobacco warehouse under the charge of Reuben Lovell & Son. Reuben Lovell is a son of your old friend Levi Lovell, of Big Flats."

"I declare, Harry, this is like Chicago in some respects. When I left here, this was swampy land, and in the spring of the year, there were a million blackbirds (is that blackbirds enough, Harry), singing in the alders and willows along the canal here. Why it reminds me of Chicago is that a large portion of it when I first went there was swampy and wet. But now it is one of the finest portions of the city."

"This, Uncle Jonas, is the business office of the Northern Central Railroad! Although the structure is an unpretending one, there is still a great amount of business done there. As you will recollect, this road extends from Niagara Falls via. Canandaigua, Elmira, Troy, Williamsport, Northumberland, Sunbury, Harrisburg, to Baltimore. It is a very important line. Now look out, Uncle Jonas, when crossing here. There are so many cars arriving and departing here that one has to keep a sharp lookout, or he will be run over. We are safely over, and suppose we take a walk down the avenue to the Union depot. Of course, we can't stop to talk over every place we pass; we must reserve that business for days when the weather is bad, and we can't go out. This building belongs to Andrew Hathorn, son of your old friend, John Hathorn, who lived on the back road from Richardson's mill to Big Flats, just beyond McConnell's."

"Oh, yes, I remember John Hathorn. He was a prominent farmer. Near his house, there was an oak grove, where camp meetings were held by the Methodists; that is now called West Junction, or North Elmira [Elmira Heights]. The grove has been cut down since 1850, soon after the Erie Railroad passed through it. Here, Uncle Jonas, was the tobacco warehouse of the John Brand estate, and this is a grist mill, and that is the warehouse of the Hon. John I. Nicks, a prominent tobacconist who came to Elmira about forty years ago, and opened a little shop on Water Street near the bridge. I recollect well, Uncle Jonas, when he first came to Elmira. He was a rosy-cheeked, well-informed young man of about twenty-two years of age. He commenced business with a small capital, was industrious, frugal, saving, sober and punctual in his dealings, and soon grew into prominence in a financial and political way. He was elected as a republican, the second mayor of the city of Elmira in the year 1865, to the senate the same year, taking his seat in that body January 2, 1866. He was also for a long term of years United States revenue collector for the district and receiving other confidences of the people and the government. He is truly a self-made man, energetic, thorough, and practical in all his undertakings."

"This, Uncle Jonas, is the Union passenger depot, which is used by the old line, the New York, Lake Erie & Western, as it is now called, the Lehigh Valley, the Northern Central, and the Tioga Elmira & State Line Railroads. Robert B. Cable is superintendent of the Susquehanna division of the New York, Lake Erie & Western, together with the Tioga, Elmira & State Line Railroad, which is now a branch of the Erie. He is a gentleman well calculated to discharge the responsible duties devolved upon him. William C. Buck, son of your old friend, the Hon. George W. Buck, or more familiarly known as "Wash" Buck, of Chemung, is a general freight agent for the Susquehanna division, the Tioga branch, and another branch leading into the hard coal regions. His father, the Hon. George W. Buck was prominently connected with the old Erie, when it was completed in 1849, as an appraiser of damages in the "right of way." His son William C. possesses in an eminent degree the characteristics of his father, in transacting a great amount of business with accuracy and discretion, and evidently has a bright future before him. Over that network of iron, rails are the Erie car shops which were established by the Erie company soon after the road was completed to Elmira, about the year 1851, with William E. Rutter as manager and superintendent. It has been destroyed by fire several times. Mr. Rutter, Uncle Jonas, was an accomplished gentleman and a kind-hearted man. He was the father of the late James H. Rutter, president of the New York Central & Hudson River railroad. He had another bright son, William, who was injured fatally about the year 1854 while running to a fire. He occupied the position of secretary of the "Young America Fire Company," which was organized on September 25, 1854. His funeral was largely attended and greatly mourned by the citizens of Elmira, who sympathized deeply with the affliction of Mr. and Mrs. Rutter. I attended his funeral. Uncle Jonas. The fire department turned out in a body, led by the celebrated William Wisner brass band, who discoursed a most solemn dirge on occasion.

"We had better take a streetcar. Uncle Jonas."

"Just as you say, Harry."

"It is one of your old friends, Timothy Satterlee's sons, who occupy the store on the corner. That is the residence of the Hon. Ariel S. Thurston. His sisters, you recollect, conducted a seminary for young ladies there for years. This is Dr. William C. Wey's residence on the west side of the street, and that over yonder is Henry W. Rathbone's, of whom we talked in connection with the Elmira Rolling Mill, and that is Charles J. Langdon's, son of your old friend, Jervis Langdon whom you recollect lived in Millport, NY, but subsequently moved to Elmira and engaged extensively in the lumber trade and finally in the coal trade.

"Charley, as he is familiarly called, has large investments in coal property in Pennsylvania and is increasing the patrimony left him. This is Park Church. It is the outgrowth of an independent Congregational church, established in 1845, Thomas B. Covell and Stephen H. Henford, deacons, and with about forty members, principally from the First Presbyterian church. The Rev. T. W. Graves was established minister in charge in the year 1846 in the month of February and continued until November of that year, was succeeded by the Rev. Messrs. A. M. Ball, E. H. Fairchild, William Bement, and Thomas K. Beecher, the latter commencing his pastorate in June 1854, thirty-one years ago. The church edifice was taken down in 1872 to make room for the elegant and durable structure. It is a church home containing an auditorium, session room, parlor, dining room, kitchen, and other rooms for the convenience of the pastor and his people. It was chiefly designed by Mr. Beecher. Under his ministration, the church has annually increased in strength and usefulness. There have never been any serious disagreements between pastor and flock, and for the past thirty- one years a harmony and unity of purpose have been the characteristics of the church. Mr. Beecher numbers among his flock some of the most wealthy and influential citizens of Elmira. By some, he is called eccentric, but there is one thing certain Uncle Jonas, his eccentricity has carried joy, peace and happiness into many a family, the high, the low, the rich and the poor, and scattered broadcast the doctrine of peace on earth and goodwill to men." His hand has always been open to the poor, and his voice always heard pleading for the oppressed."

"This, Uncle Jonas, is the residence of the late Hon. Asher Tyler, who came to Elmira in the year 1848, during the construction of the New York & Erie railroad. He was their general land agent. He was a native of the county of Oneida, in this state, and was born in the year 1798, receiving a collegiate education, studied law, and was admitted to the bar. He formerly resided in Cattaraugus County, New York, and had been largely interested in real estate in that county and had represented his district in congress. He was the very personification of a gentleman of the old school — kind, courteous, and obliging. During his early life in Oneida county and his later life in western New York, he had come in contact with the red man and had studied their traits of character, their history, and traditions. After the railroad was completed to Dunkirk and the titles for the right of way and other real estate were completed, he identified himself with several of the then young industries of Elmira. He was one of the originators of the company formed under the title of the Elmira Rolling Mill Company, and for a period, was the president of the company. Physically, he was a man about six feet in height and well proportioned, walking erect and dressed with care. As a conversationalist, he excelled in attracting his hearers by his fine diction and descriptive powers. In a company of friends, they seemed to have no desire to speak, content to listen to his pleasing and entertaining conversation. I have often thought, Uncle Jonas, that the Hon. Asher Tyler and the Hon. Horatio Seymour must have been instructed by the same model teacher; the two resemble each other so much in their excellent manners and gifted conversational powers. Mr. Tyler died ten years ago the first of this month (August), leaving this beautiful residence to his wife and daughters. We are most down to Water Street, Uncle Jonas, and I will pull the bell-rope."

VISIT TO SOUTHPORT.

"Harry, after I have looked over the newspapers a few minutes suppose we drive over to Southport Corners — I mean over to the place where so many of the Jones family and Charley Evans formerly resided. I want to see what improvements have been made on the south side of the river. You say that Elmira has absorbed quite a portion of Southport, and the probabilities are that she will in time, absorb more territory."

"All right, Uncle Jonas, I will be around with the carriage in a few minutes. This, Uncle Jonas, is the Main street bridge. A company was organized in the year 1853 and constructed a bridge here, and in 1862 the company became involved in the bridge was sold at sheriff's sale. Moses Cole, of Millport, NY was the builder. In the great freshet of March 17, 1865, the trestling over Clinton Island was carried away. The damage was repaired. In 1866 the first span was burned. In 1865 the Lake street, or old bridge company and the Main street company consolidated, both companies charging tolls. This toll business was a tax upon every farmer who came to Elmira from Southport to sell the products of his farm or make purchases of dry goods and groceries and a general interchange of commodities, the burden of which fell upon the house-holder who purchased of the farmer, for the toll was added to every farm product that was purchased by the grocer and retailed to the consumer. The consequence was that the subject of free bridges was agitated for several years and resulted in the abandonment of the toll system, and an act of the legislature authorizing the city of Elmira to expend one hundred and twenty thousand dollars in the construction of two iron bridges in lieu of the old wooden structures, which should be free. After the work had progressed for a season, it was ascertained that the sum of one hundred and twenty thousand dollars was inadequate to complete them, and the sum of thirty thousand dollars was authorized by an act of the legislature of 1874 to finish the work, the actual cost being $149,321.

Thus was Elmira ten years ago released from the restriction of trade and commerce by means of the abandonment of the toll system. The tax to pay for the construction of the bridges was more equally levied, and the result has been highly beneficial to all parties concerned. The Rev. Thomas K. Beecher took an active part in bringing about this most desirable object. I tell you, Uncle Jonas, it was quite an effort to get the people awakened fully to the necessity of the outlay of one hundred and fifty thousand dollars, but even those who opposed it are now proud of them and point with pride to these splendid pieces of mechanism. Their construction increased the wealth and population of both sides of the river. This, Uncle Jonas, is the residence of the late Dr. Edwin Eldridge, of whom I will tell you more hereafter."

"Keep quiet for a moment, Harry. I want to see if I can discover any old landmarks. Since that beautiful island is destroyed, I have quite lost my reckoning. Oh! I see yonder is Mount Zoar. It is all right now. As we drive along, I will tell you Harry about the times we used to have chasing deer with hounds from Mount Zoar into Seeley Creek, or into the river just above the point of Clinton Island, opposite the late residence of Uncle Billy Hoffman. All along where we are driving now were woods then growing down to the river bank. Along the Lake Street or Southport road to Wellsburg, NY, it was cleared, of course, but this land along here was the rear end of the farms, covered with a thick growth of timber. The Gulp and Loop boys, Dr. Jotham Purdy, E. Jones, myself and a few others, would take our dogs in the fall of the year, say in September or October, and send a trusty man with them up to Mount Zoar or Spanish Hill and distribute ourselves along the river and in the road between here and Simeon R. Jones's or Solly Smith's and then wait for the coming game. By and by, we would hear, as

Dr. Purdy used to express it, the heavenly music, the barking of the hounds in pursuit of the deer. Some would lead off to the south and west, while others would come straight for the point of the island, and if the hunter failed to kill his buck, which was frequently the case, the deer would swim across the river, crossing West Water street, going between Billy Hoffman's and Dr. Thesus Brook's place and along across the fields a little west of Park Church, dash across to where the union depot now is and off into the alders and willows by the Chemung Canal described this morning with its million blackbirds, and if not captured would bound away across Newtown Creek on to East Hill, passing between the late residence of the Hon. William Maxwell and the present residence of General A. S. Diven. Sometimes our party would capture three or four fine deer, and, then again, we would steal away home one by one, without a single trophy. This hurrying throng of people along on these walks would scarcely believe that the man now lives, who has seen this section covered with forest trees and thickly populated with wild animals. Harry, did you ever hunt raccoons? Well, this flat here and away down the river bank on the Sly Flats, these mischievous animals were plenty. I think, Harry, I have had really more fun to the square inch hunting those thieves, than in any other sport I ever engaged in. Perhaps it was not the capturing and killing of those animals that constituted the fun. Still, the associates and the necessary concomitants of the chase — the midnight supper, with green corn, harvest apples and spring chickens in the buttonwoods, the songs sang and the stories told around the big campfire, may have added some to the sport. Really, Harry, you have quite a city on this side of the river. What is that large building that we see down yonder across the railroad track? "

"It is the La France steam fire engine manufactory, Uncle Jonas. That is one of the manufacturing industries of which Elmira is proud. The sons of General Alexander S. Diven are largely interested in the work. That cluster of brick buildings you see farther to the south and west are the shops of the Northern Central Railroad Company. A large number of men are given steady employment, and quite a number of them are owners of houses and lots in this vicinity. The establishment is nominally in the town of Southport, but perhaps it will be but a few years before they will be embraced in the city of Elmira."

"What are those farther to the east?"

"They are the shops of B. W. Payne & Sons. They have recently been removed from Corning, NY. The firms are large founders and manufacturers of steam engines, and desirous of obtaining more room and more advantageous shipping facilities, they were induced to locate there. They also give employment to quite a large number of men."

"I suppose, Harry, that almost all, if not quite all, of the persons with whom I was acquainted within this town are dead, I recollect Solomon L. Smith, Philo B. Jones, the Rev. Simeon R. Jones, Richmond Jones, William Jenkins, Jacob Miller, George W. Miller, James Griswold, Wilham Wells, T. O. Scudder, Richard Baker, Charles Evans, Seth Marvin, John Marvin, Miller McHenry, Abram Stryker, William Lowe, William T. Knapp, Ezra Canfield, William Brown, John L. Smith, William Webb, Archibald Jenkins, --- Dalrymple, Hiram Middaugh, Hiram Roushey, John W. Knapp, Samuel Middaugh, John Fitzsimmons, Almon Kenyon, Nathaniel Knapp, Thomas Maxwell, James B. Goff, Samuel Strong, Platt Bennett, John Bovier, Isaac L. Wells, Thomas Comfort, Jeremiah Coleman, Judge Baker, Abram Miller, and no doubt there were many others whose names have escaped my memory at the present whom I would recall were they mentioned. There is nothing here that I recall at the corner, so drive on. Along this road, Harry, when I left Elmira, was a great forest of white pine timber. I see that it has all been cut down, and even the stumps pulled up and burned or made into a fence. What little hamlet is this that we are approaching, Harry?"

"That, Uncle Jonas, is Pine City."

"About forty years ago, an attack was made on the white pine timber that stood in this vicinity. Allen, Lyman, Samuel, and W. L. Gibson, then of Elmira, Seth Marvin, and the Webbs, commenced the attack. Allen S. Gibson removed here with his family from Elmira and erected a large lumber shanty and remained for several years and then removed back to Elmira, purchasing the lot upon which the female college is now located, and afterward purchasing lots on the corner of Main and Church Streets, where the parsonage, memorial chapel, and Episcopal parsonage are now located. Samuel C. Gibson opened a store above this place and subsequently removed to Big Flats and engaged in the sale of merchandise there. Lyman and William L. Gibson, soon after, established themselves upon Baldwin Street, above the First Presbyterian Church, in the lumber and mercantile business, purchasing and shipping lumber to Albany, Troy, and New York City. Their store was called 'The Lumbermen's Store.' Of the four brothers only one is now alive, W. L. Gibson, who still resides on Baldwin street, near where the Lumbermen's Store was located. His wife was Betsy Jones, daughter of Elijah Jones, who formerly owned the hotel where the building of the Elmira *Advertiser* association is now located. The Gibsons were good hunters and fond of spending now and then a day in hunting and fishing. If I were addicted to telling fishing and hunting stories, Harry, I could relate some that were true and yet in this day would seem improbable and entirely overwrought. It was no extraordinary event fifty or sixty years ago, when I was a boy, to see half a dozen fishermen take a seine and go to the river and catch a wagon box full of pickerel, shad, bass, perch and other fish in less than half a day. After they had got their wagon load, they would drive to some central point, select a grassy plat where there was plenty of shade, unload the fish and divide them.

Uncle Johnny owned the land near the best fishing point, had no share in the seine, but would always, in consideration of his locality, claim a share in the fish. Uncle Johnny could be easily excited, and hated suckers, mullets, and chubs as most people do rattlesnakes. The fishing party understood the animosity of Uncle Johnny and would proceed to lay in one pile the pickerel, in another the bass and perch, and thus distribute all the most desirable fish by themselves, while the inferior class, such as chubs, suckers, and mullets, would be placed in a pile for the benefit of Uncle Johnny, and in order to excite his ire. While this assorting process was going on, Uncle Johnny would be kept busy sampling the wet groceries extracted from a gallon jug. When everything was in readiness, one of the party would turn his back to the piles of fish lying on the grass, and another would call out to him, 'Who shall have that pile of fish? The answer would be, 'Philo Jones.' That pile would be a splendid lot of pickerel and perch, or bass and perch, the man would then turn his back, and the query would then be repeated with slight variations, 'who shall have this pile of fish? The answer would be, 'Uncle Johnny.' The calling of his name would attract his attention, and Uncle Johnny, who had hitherto been kept busy sampling the contents of the jug, would make a rush to examine his pile of fish. Then was when the ball would open, and the grand march takes place. Johnny always carried a strong heavy cane and was usually accompanied by a large and ferocious brindle dog, who would take delight in masticating any offender whom Johnny would point out. Johnny would walk around, take an extra chew of pigtailed or lady twist Cavendish tobacco, and commence breathing like a bellows, for the moment too full for utterance. At last, he would break out in a volley of oaths that would literally shake the thorn apples from the trees, or the rocks from then' beds, ending in a peremptory order for everyone to leave that place immediately and calling on brindle Bose to enforce the order. Bose would make a dash; some would take to the wagon and others to the trees, leaving Uncle Johnny and his brindle companion in possession of the field with all the fish, good, bad, and indifferent. Someone would attempt to negotiate with Uncle Johnny on a peace basis. The one most skilled in diplomacy would be selected. A flag of truce accompanied by the jug would then be sent into the camp of the victor. By and by Johnny would order Bose to be down, the parties would descend from the trees and wagon, and a new distribution agreed to. The second distribution perhaps would meet with no better success than the first. Instead of Johnny getting all chub and suckers as he did on the first distribution, by this and that process, he would get all perch, excellent fish but hard to prepare for the pan. The second opening of hostilities would commence, and the same means of attack and escape resorted to.

What Johnny wanted was pickerel, or at least his share of them. By the same course of diplomacy, peace would once again prevail. A new umpire would be chosen, a fairer distribution would be made, and a final and satisfactory division of the fish takes place. Uncle Johnny loaded down with pickerel and bass, and filled to the brim with wet groceries, accompanied with his faithful Bose, would take their departure — while the jolly fishermen would laugh with great glee at the farce of dividing the fish. I declare Harry; we are almost back to Elmira again!"

OLD FRIENDS AND FAMILIES.
UNCLE JONAS BRINGS FORWARD SOME
INTERESTING FACTS.

"Good morning, Uncle Jonas. We are storm-stayed, no riding or walking out today. But we can enjoy ourselves at home, and I will tell you about your old friends in Elmira."

"That will please me, Harry. Go on."

"To commence with your old friend, Aaron Konkle, you, of course, knew that he studied law in the office of Mathews & Edwards, and in the year 1826 was appointed by Governor Dewitt Clinton district attorney for Tioga county, then embracing the territory composed now of the counties of Tioga, a portion of Broome, a portion of Tompkins, a portion of Schuyler and the entire portion of Chemung County, holding the office for three successive terms. He was also appointed supreme court commissioner, and upon the resignation of the Hon. John W. Wisner was appointed in the year 1850 judge of Chemung County, Ariel S. Thurston succeeded him in that position. Judge Konkle died October 13, 1861, aged seventy-five years. As you recollect, he was a very modest and unassuming man, always dressed neatly, very dignified in manner, a ripe scholar and a safe counselor. Were you acquainted, Uncle Jonas, with Judge Thurston?"

"Do you mean Ariel S. Thurston?"

"Yes."

"Oh, I recollect him well. He was a young attorney then, just coming into prominence, and a law partner of John W. Wisner."

"Since you went away. Uncle Jonas, he was, in 1851, elected county judge, serving four years in that capacity. In 1859 he was appointed state assessor, serving three years in that office, and in 1876 he was appointed one of the managers of the state reformatory prison at Elmira. The judge has been quite successful financially, securing a competency for his old age. He and Judge Gray are the only members of the Chemung County bar who were admitted to practice at the Tioga County bar before the county of Chemung was formed, in 1836. Their certificate of admission to the bar ante-date the organization of the county and are the connecting links, yet unbroken, m the chain binding the old with the new, reflecting honor upon their profession and the bar of Chemung County. You, of course, recollect, Uncle Jonas, Judge James Dunn?"

"Oh, yes, Harry."

"Well, in 1844 he became county judge, serving two years in that capacity, with great satisfaction. He, however, preferred active practice to the dull routine of the bench, and became one of the leading advocates and attorneys in the county. He was a genial and social companion, hospitable and charitable in its broadest sense. He had the faculty of making friends and retaining them. He died May 1, 1877, in the seventy-third year of his age. Of course. Uncle Jonas, you were acquainted with Major Levi J. Cooley?"

"Yes; he was one of my very warmest friends."

"Well the major, when you left Elmira, was engaged extensively in the various stage lines leading into Elmira, with Mr. Maxwell, his brother-in-law, under the firm name of Cooley & Maxwell. He continued in that business until stage coaching was superseded by the locomotive. He was a polished gentleman and warm friend. He died June 4, 1874, in the seventy-third year of his age. Benjamin Vail was one of your old friends. Uncle Jonas. Well, he came to Elmira in the early days and engaged in the manufacture of cabinet ware upon a small scale, also the manufacture of coffins. He resided in Elmira and its immediate vicinity fifty-eight years, occupying the same dwelling for forty-four years located in Elmira. He was ever the same honest, companionable, upright mechanic, citizen, and neighbor. He was married to Miss Eliza Smith on February 27, 1823, and celebrated his golden wedding February 27, 1873. The marriage ceremony was performed in 1823 by the Rev. Simeon R. Jones, the pioneer minister. Uncle Benjamin Vail died July 12, 1873, in the seventy-fifth year of his age."

"Riggs Watrous, another of your old friends, son of Isaac Watrous, of Big Flats, came to Elmira in the year 1849 and engaged in the manufacture of tinware, nearly opposite the present site of the Elmira *Advertiser* association building, and gradually increased his business so that in 1842 he removed to Water street and added the hardware line to his former pursuits. In these branches, he prospered, until he became the foremost hardware dealer and tinner, in southern New York. During his thirty-five years of active business life, he met with several severe reverses but always came out of them with honor and credit. He was prominently connected in the establishment and maintenance of the Baptist church. He several times held offices of trust and responsibility, which he discharged with fidelity. Still, he preferred to bend his energies upon his chosen pursuit rather than accept the political or official distinction. He died on September 11, 1883, aged sixty-three years, two months, and twenty-five days.

"I have incidentally mentioned, Uncle Jonas, the name of John Arnot, with whom you were acquainted, and I will now give you a brief history of Elmira's foremost man after you left here. Mr. Arnot, as you recollect, came to Elmira in the year 1819, and engaged in mercantile pursuits and was very successful. At one time, he had a branch store at Painted Post in Steuben County. In the year 1824, he was married to Miss Harriet Tuttle, daughter of Stephen Tuttle. In the year 1830, he erected the first brick store in Elmira, which stood on the northwest corner of Lake and Water Streets, where the present elegant block is now situated. The year previous in 1829, he erected a foundry upon the site of the present opera house and set up the first steam engine in southern New York. In 1836 he became a stockholder in the Chemung Canal bank. In 1812 he sold out his stock of goods, becoming cashier of the Chemung Canal bank, with the late Hon. Charles Cook, of Havana, NY, president. In 1848, 1849, 1850, he and the late Hon. John Magee, Charles Cook, Constance Cook, and I. S. Stranahan constructed the New York & Erie Railroad from Binghamton to Hornellsville. In 1854 he was largely interested in the construction of what was known as the Junction Canal. In 1858 he was prevailed upon to accept the nomination for congress in a district that held 3,000 majority against him. So popular was he and such confidence had the people in his integrity that he was only defeated by about 300 votes. Had he made a personal canvass, there is no doubt that he would have been elected. At this time, he was president of the Chemung Canal bank, having been chosen in the year 1852. He had previously been interested in the construction of the railroad from Elmira to Watkins and from Elmira to Williamsport, PA, in fact, in every enterprise calculated to benefit the people at large or the village of Elmira. He was also interested in the construction of gas works for the proper illumination of the village. In the year 1866, he became largely interested in the coal lands and railroads in Tioga County, PA, and the founding of a prosperous mining town, which was named Arnot, in his honor, and which today is the most populous village in that county. His death occurred November 17, 1873, aged eighty years, regretted and mourned by people in all sections of the country."

"I declare, Uncle Jonas, the storm has abated, and I think the weather will be fine this afternoon. Suppose we take a drive up to Horseheads, or North Elmira, as it is now called."

"Well, Harry, that will suit me."

"Which road shall we take."

"Take the old Lake Road, Harry; I want to see how it looks, and we will return by the back way, perhaps, or down the Avenue, you told me about."

In a short time, Uncle Jonas and Harry are seated in the carriage on their way to North Elmira.

"What is this, Harry?"

"A street railway is running from here to North Elmira. It is a worthy enterprise. This, Uncle Jonas, is the residence of General A. S. Diven. See how nicely he has fitted up the old place. He has resided there about thirty years, or it is about that time since he purchased it, and perhaps more than thirty. Time slips away so fast one really can't tell without referring to dates how rapidly it has passed."

"These lands along here, Harry, when I was a boy, were covered with scrub oak and dwarf pitch pines, and so stony that many farmers said they would not take the land as a gift. But they made a great mistake. They are warm and quick. See how well that corn looks."

"This is the Carpenter estate. John Carpenter, who recently died, lived here for many years and kept a hotel. This place here on the right is what is known as the Hugh O'Hanlon farm, and here is the old Richardson property. Over yonder is the late residence of Richard Hetfield."

"Oh, yes; I recollect Richard Hetfield well. He was a natural landlord. Could make his guests feel at home. Mrs. Hetfield was well calculated for a landlady and acted well her part."

"Charley Kline lived in that house for many years. You must recollect him, Uncle Jonas?"

"Very well, indeed."

"This is the David McConnell farm. He has been dead some years. This is the Increase Mather farm."

"He must have come here after I left."

"This is the Sayre property."

"Why, what has become of the Canal? Oh, I forgot, Harry, that it was abandoned,"

"That dwelling out there on the left is the late residence of the Hon. Charles Hullett."

"Oh, I remember him. He formerly lived in Veteran, NY. Yonder is where Vincent Conklin's distillery stood when I left. Horseheads has brightened up very much since I last saw it. There are no old landmarks that I recognize."

"Well, Uncle Jonas, when we get home tonight, I will tell you all about it."

"Harry, let us drive about the town and take a view of it and return by the avenue, and when we get home, we will talk the matter over. I can make inquiries of you and I rather like the way you converse upon these old people, and those that have taken their places."

Harry drives north as far as the late residence of John Westlake, then returns and goes west as far as the late residence of Joseph Livesay, noting the churches, the schools, the depots, manufacturing establishments, banking institutions, hotels, private dwellings, and returns by the way of the avenue, down by the state fairgrounds, Eldridge Park, to Elmira and home to dinner.

"You may think your old uncle a little lazy, Harry, but these afternoon dinner naps are very refreshing. We have taken a splendid trip today, and I could not, as we passed along, refrain from silently contrasting the appearance of the country now, and when I first went over the road more than sixty-five years ago. I was a lad then of ten years. My father sent me on horseback up to Judge Darius Bentley's, who lived a few miles north of Horseheads, and who was a surveyor. It was in the month of August, about the tenth I should judge. The valley between Newtown (we called it Newtown then) and Horseheads was completely enshrouded in smoke, arising from the burning at fallows. The fallows were burning here on the Hoffman farm, on the Robert Covell farm, on the Wisner and McCann farms on the back road, and on the Lake Road a fallow was being burnt where, a few days ago, you pointed out to me the residence of Stephen T. Reynolds. The lands at the head of Baldwin Street and Pigeon Point were being cleared off and great brush and log heaps were on fire. The alders had been cut down by the roadside between where the late Hon. William Maxwell erected his fine residence fifteen years later, and where General A. S. Diven now resides, and the heaps set on fire. They were so close to the road and made such a hot fire that it was almost impossible to pass, even on horseback at a smart gallop. When I got to the stony ridge on the Carpenter estate, long windrows of brush were piled up and ran west to where the Chemung canal was afterwards constructed. Just before I arrived there, the torch was applied to them and great waves of fire twenty or thirty feet high were rolling down toward the highway, driving me out into the timber on the east side of the road. I took a cow path that led around to a little flat on the banks of the Newtown Creek, and by a circuitous route reached the highway again half a mile further northward. The wind lifted the smoke for a short time and I could look away to the westward and see fallows burning on the John Suffern, William Rockwell, John McConnell, and John Hathorn farms, the great volumes of black smoke rising up reminding me of the pictures I had seen of the eruptions of Mount Vesuvius. Fallows was on fire along my path on the Hetfield and Sayre farms, the Gildersleeve and Breese farms, the Le Homiden reserves, and on small lots in Horseheads. East of Horseheads, I could see the smoke rising from the fallows on fire up Newton Creek, but to the northward, there was only one small clearing on lands subsequently owned by John E. Westlake, until you reached Judge Bentley's on the marsh. Judge Bentley subsequently erected a very fine residence on higher ground, in which he resided when I left the country. At length I reached Judge Bentley's, my eyes swimming with water, from the heat and smoke which I had passed through. The Judge was away from home and did not return until it was nearly dark. I transacted my business with him and after partaking of a hearty supper I started for home. The air was full of smoke and falling cinders. When I arrived at Conkling's tavern at Horseheads and looked down the valleys toward Newtown, the sky was illuminated by a hundred fires, set ablaze. Vincent Conkling then was the landlord and knew my father, and tried to persuade me to remain overnight, as it was dangerous for me to undertake to ride through these columns of fire. But I knew that my father and mother would not rest until I came. I determined to go on. I stated this fact to Mr. Conkling, and he said to me: "Jonas, if that is the case, you must have an escort." I thanked him, told him that I did not need any, as I had taken supper at Judge Bentley's. I shall never forget the look that Mr. Conkling gave me when I told him that. After a moment, he said: "Jonas, an escort is not anything to eat; it means a guard, a companion. I mean to send my man Hawkins with you down as far as Carpenter's, and from there, you can get along safely enough. And he did. Hawkins was a man of all work about the hotel, a person given to large and miraculous stories. While he assisted me in avoiding dangerous fires, he tuned up my nerves to the highest pitch, by relating hair-breadth escapes from panthers, wolves, catamounts and bears. Some of the stories made every hair on my head as large as a rope, and fairly lifted my cap from its place. We parted company at Carpenter's, near the present Diven mansion, and I arrived home safely. But Hawkins had so filled me with terror in the recital of his extravagant and fictitious stories that I expected every moment a huge wolf or panther would sally out from the woods and make a meal of me, and I did not breathe freely until I got down to Captain Grant Baldwin's. After I reached home and went to bed, I could see those long lines of fire, like so many columns of soldiers, advancing with an irresistible fury. Now and then there would appear a single blaze in the top of some large tree flashing out in the darkness like a signal; then would appear a solid column advancing from the west, while in the east broken columns in platoons and divisions were making great exertions to escape. Here and there in the darkness would appear a faint and flickering light, where at one time the battle had waged in its fiercest fury, then again the columns would mass their strength, sending up high in air huge pillars of fire and smoke reflecting their light upon a broad field of blackened and charred fragments of the contest. I have seen, Harry, great lakes of fire in mountain waves, sweep over the prairies of the west, which were a grand spectacle to behold! but their march was onward and steady and lacked that variety of scenery of a hundred fallow fires skirted by forest, and encircled by hills and mountains as seen sixty-five years ago along the valley of Newtown Creek."

HISTORIC HORSEHEADS.
THE EARLY SETTLERS— MEN OF STRONG CHARACTER —
THE RESULTS OF THEIR WORK.

"The pioneer settlers of Horseheads were nearly all living, Harry, when I was a boy, and I am thus enabled to give you an outline history of that village from its first settlement in 1789. I was also acquainted with a revolutionary soldier who lived at Big Flats by the name of William Mapes, who accompanied General Sullivan on his expedition against the Indians in the year 1779 and was present when the cavalry and artillery horses were killed by Sullivan's order in October of that year. Some of the horses' heads and bones were to be seen lying around on the surface of the ground as late as 1830. John Breese and his brother-in-law, Asa Gildersleeve, were the first settlers, Breese locating in 1779, and Gildersleeve a few months later. They were succeeded by John Winkler, David Powers, Christopher Vandeventer, Jonathan S. Conkling, James Sayre, Ebenezer Sayre, John Parkhurst, Israel Catlin, Seneca Roland, Nathan Teal, Caleb Bentley, Britton Payne, Solomon Moore, Jacob Powell, John Jackson, who settled in Horseheads and its immediate vicinity. Mordecai Rickey, John Tenbrook and Gershom Livesay settled some two or three miles to the westward, but in the town of Horseheads. Darius Bentley, afterward known as Judge Bentley, settled to the northward about three miles, and John Jackson to the eastward, and on the 'back road,' was the McConnells and William Rockwell. The Westlakes were early settlers. John E. Westlake, Samuel Westlake, and Jacob Westlake, the latter known as Colonel Jacob Westlake, represented Chemung County in the assembly of the State the first year after the county was formed, with much honor to himself and satisfaction of his constituents. He was a man of more than ordinary ability, and one of the most pleasing and effective public speakers in the southern tier."

"As soon as the early pioneers had secured a shelter over their heads, they employed a teacher to instruct their children. As early as 1793, Miss Amelia Parkhurst, daughter of John Parkhurst, was thus engaged. The Rev. Daniel Thatcher, a Presbyterian clergyman of Newtown, held services in the new settlement (which it was voted to christen Horseheads) as early as the year 1798. The Rev. Roswell Goff, a Baptist minister, also held services as early as 1807. The Methodists held services as early as 1815, the Rev. Benjamin Westlake officiating. So you will perceive, Harry, that Horseheads did not want in schools or church instruction. The Quakers, or society of friends, led by such reliable citizens as J. Marshall, and assisted by David Coddington, Francis Bowman, Benjamin Palmer, Richardson Cornell, Amos Crandall, Josiah Cornell, Stephen Estes, Abel Shute, and Richard Wild, gave additional facilities to worship God according to the dictates of conscience. As soon as the bill was passed for the construction of the Chemung Canal in April 1829, large accessions were made to the population of Horseheads. It was certain that the canal would pass through Horseheads, for there was no other route by which it could go from its initial to its terminal points, that is, from the head of Seneca Lake at Watkins Glen, to Elmira on the Chemung River, nor no other feasible way in which it could be fed by water from the Chemung river, only by constructing a feeder from Horseheads, the summit level between the lake and the river, then by starting from Horseheads and running westward through the town of Big Flats and eastern Painted Post, tapping the Chemung River at or near the Chimney Narrows, two miles below Painted Post. Thus, the citizens of Horseheads were positively assured that the canal would be constructed through their town and be made the center of commerce. At that time, a great discussion was going on in the county of Tioga in relation to the division of the county or the establishment of half-shire towns. The rivalry in the half-shire business was carried on very enthusiastically between Spencer, Owego and Elmira, which finally culminated in a division of Tioga County six years later, and the formation of Chemung county. In the meantime, the canal had been constructed passing through Horseheads as its citizens had foretold it would, the feeder leading from Painted Post down into the very center of the village, from whence it was distributed north to the lake and south to Elmira.

Then came the struggle, Harry, referred to some days ago about the location of the county seat, which I need not again speak of, the result being that Elmira secured the prize and has ever since remained as the county seat of Chemung County for the past forty-nine years. From 1830 to 1840, Horseheads increased rapidly in population and wealth. Hotels, stores, warehouses, schools and churches, grist mills, tanneries, foundries, distilleries were erected and the village assuming the name of Fairport in 1837, and at the same time, a newspaper was established by J. T. Bradt named the Chemung Patriot, which was intended to disseminate far and wide the admirable location of Fairport and the flattering prospects of that energetic little village. It was called Fairport when I left this section in 1841."

"It was changed back, Uncle Jonas, to Horseheads, I think, about the year 1845."

"Well, Harry, I have given you the outline of its history up to 1841, and I want you to continue it up to the present."

"Very well. Uncle Jonas. You state, Uncle Jonas, that Elmira became the country seat, wresting it from Horse-heads. That is true, but she has ever since remained the central point for holding county conventions of all the various political parties. She has also enjoyed the honor of being the point for great social gatherings. It is, therefore, not only the political center, but it has had a fine reputation for its dances and social hops, where the elite of that place and the surrounding country have met to enjoy an evening in that innocent and healthful amusement. You neglected to state, Uncle Jonas, that under the old militia system of the state, that it was at Horseheads, that the regimental training, or "musters" took place for the county fairs were also held there, and at one time the sporting fraternity of Chemung, Steuben and Tompkins met there and had a trial of speed with their fastest and most spirited horses. The "Emancipation," a full-blooded Virginia-bred racehorse, about the year 1855 or 56, contested a nine-mile race, with another blooded animal known as the 'Virginia Mare.' But it is doubtful whether these trials of speed resulted in any permanent benefit or added much to the reputation or character of the village. I merely state this, Uncle Jonas, to show it was a central point. During all these years, up to 1854, Horseheads had been in the town of Elmira. In that year, she became an independent sovereignty, a town by herself. Charles Hulett, Elijah Carpenter, Hiram S. Bentley, and George Bennett were appointed as officers to hold the first election for town officers. The act went into effect on February 14, 1854. In April of the same year, the Horseheads Building Association was formed with Comfort Bennett President; Willis B. Sayre, vice-President; Hiram S. Bentley, Secretary; Charles Hulett, Treasurer. Financially it was a very strong association. It erected a fine three-story brick block during the year 1854, containing a large hall of greater capacity than any in the county. In the year 1855, the boundaries of the corporation were enlarged, and on the 7th of April of the same year, a newspaper was established by Samuel C. Taber, under the wise and euphonious name of *The Philosopher.* In November 1855, the Chemung County Bank was organized by the Hon. William T. Hastings, with a capital of $50,000. In the year 1856, the Chemung County *Republican* was established, and Florus B. Plimpton installed as editor. Thus was Horseheads provided with two newspapers, not to foster her business interests, but to engage in political quarrels. Horseheads was surely on the road to prosperity. A better class of buildings had been erected, capitalists from the surrounding country had sought and made investments, and no village in Chemung county was more prosperous. Boat-building was carried on quite extensively; it had become a center for the purchase and shipment of grain, also for the manufacture of flour and feed, the manufacture of stoves, besides the trade from the surrounding country done by its merchants with the farmers and others. The Chemung Canal was at the height of its usefulness. Millions of feet of sawed lumber and millions of feet of square timber, besides large quantities of coal and agricultural productions, were passing through the village, every boatload of which must stop, while the captain of the boat or fleet would have his shipping bill examined and the toll adjusted and paid. This enabled the grocery and provision merchants, in fact, merchants of all kinds, to make a profitable trade with the boatmen and timbermen.

Comfort Bennett and three of his sons, from Big Flats, representing hundreds of thousands of dollars; Charles Hulett, from Veteran; the Moshers, from Millport; the Marshalls, from Newtown Creek; the Tabers, from Cortland, all representing capital and energy, had located in Horseheads, when on the 12th day of August, 1862, a fire broke out, which destroyed the entire business portion of the village before it could be checked or extinguished. And thus were the accumulations of years swept away in a day. With commendable pluck and courage, the sufferers went to work again to repair their loss by erecting still more expensive and durable structures. Although outwardly, they acted brave and were inclined to make light of the calamity, still there were many who felt for a long series of years the results of that terrible fire. It had a tendency to check their progress.

"The Chemung Railroad was constructed in 1849 (now the Northern Central) having a station at Horseheads. In 1875 the Utica, Ithaca & Elmira Railroad was constructed, passing through Horseheads and having a station at that place, and about five years ago a street railway was built connecting Horseheads and Elmira. A Masonic lodge was instituted in Horseheads in the year 1855. Dispensation granted to James A, Christie, James Barlow, Darius Bentley, Waterman Davis, second, Richard Hetfield. Hiram S. Bentley, George O'Hanlon, John Bachman, O. D. Canfield, Rowland Parker, Vincent Conkling, Mordecai Rickey, Adam L. Staring, John A. Beers, Charles M. Conkling. This has become a very prosperous lodge. In 1871 a Royal Arch Chapter was instituted. Among the charter members were R. B. Bush, M. E. H. P.; Calvin Eddy, E. K.; S. A. Palmer, E. S. Evergreen Chapter, number eighteen, O. E. S., was established July 25, 1870, with Calvin Eddy, Worthy Patron, Sophia V. Humphrey, Worthy Matron, Ruby A. Brown, Worthy Associate Matron, Lydia J. Carpenter, Secretary, Jennie S. Kies, Treasurer."

"A lodge of the Sons of Temperance was organized about the year 1848, and a lodge of Good Templars in January 1869. A farmers' Grange was instituted in February 1873."

"The Horseheads Steamer & Hose company was organized in August 1873, which finally resulted in the incorporation of the Horseheads Fire Department, June 2, 1876.

"The Horseheads Union School was organized on October 11, 1865, and an academic department was added in 1877.

"The Horseheads mills were built in 1837 by Captain Vincent Conkling.

"The Horseheads brickyard was founded in 1840, from which the outgrowth has been the present extensive yard of Benjamin Westlake."

"Harry, I want to hear something about the old citizens of Horseheads."

"Well, Uncle Jonas, there are, but very few of them live. George Bennett, whom you knew as a farmer, has resided in the village for a number of years. He became interested in a business way with the Hon. William T. Hastings, who started a bank in 1855. Mr. Hastings becoming involved, Mr. Bennett, in order to secure himself against loss, was obliged to take possession of the bank and other property, and removed into the village. He is now engaged in banking. Vincent Conkling, whom you knew, is living at an advanced age, still the very courteous and affable gentleman as of yore. Colonel Jacob Westlake, Captain Wood, Charles Hulett, Homer Ryant, Isaac Wintermute, Peter Wintermute, Elijah Carpenter, Joseph McConnell, Mordecai Rickey, Comfort Bennett, Morris Bennett, Richard Hetfield, John Jackson, Albert A. Beckwith, John E. Westlake, Samuel Westlake, Joseph Marshall, William Estes, William Hastings, Sr., William Rockwell, David McConnell, Ebenezer Mather, Orrin Eddy, Hugh Colwell, Jacob G. Widrig, David Shappee, Abner Shappee, Joseph Livesay, Cornelius Tenbrook, Angevine Lockwood, John Hathorn, Judge Darius Bentley, Legrand Barlow, David A. Degraff, William Reynolds, and John Breese are dead. John Bennett, of Big Flats, has two sons living in Horseheads, Josiah Bennett and Miles C. Bennett, and there are three sons of Comfort Bennett living there also, George, Daniel and Andrew J. Bennett. Cyrus Barlow lives there. Perhaps you are acquainted with him. Uncle Jonas."

"Yes, I had a speaking acquaintance with him."

"Well, Cyrus Barlow lives there and is practicing law. I think you must have been acquainted with Jacob Weller, of Veteran."

"Yes, Harry. He has a son Theodore V. Weller, who resides there. "

"You must have known Walter Daily, of Millport."

"Yes. Well, he has a son Walter who resides there and is one of the prominent lawyers of the county. Hugh Colwell has three sons living there, Robert, John, and William."

"I must say, Harry, upon the whole, that Horseheads is a pleasant place. It seems to be well provided with schools, churches, lodges, and railroad facilities and surrounded by one of the best agricultural districts in the country that ought to thrive and prosper.

"Within the township. Uncle Jonas, there is another very thriving and prosperous village. I refer to Breesport."

"Where is Breesport, Harry?"

"It is situated near the eastern line of the town of Horseheads on Newtown Creek about six miles from Horseheads. The Elmira, Cortland & Northern Railroad runs through the village. When the railroad was first built, you recollect I told you that it was called the Utica, Ithaca & Elmira Railroad; but the new management has changed the name. Under the first management, the car and repair shops of the road were located at Breesport. But I understand that the new managers have removed them from Cortland. But, Uncle Jonas, I will not undertake to tell you more about the place until we can have an opportunity of visiting it.

"Harry, we must visit Tioga County, PA, tomorrow. I want to go up there and visit the coal regions while the weather is pleasant and reserve these short trips for more boisterous weather. I want to take a ride over your Tioga, Elmira & State Line Railroad. I want to see Lawrenceville, Tioga, Mansfield, Canoe Camp, Covington, Blossburg, Morris Run, Fall Brook, Arnot, Landrus and Hoytville, The train leaves tomorrow morning at 9AM, does it? All right! I'll be on hand."

THE TIOGA VALLEY.
A TRIP BY RAIL — PERSONAL MENTION —
OLD AND MODERN TIMES.

"We are in good time, Uncle Jonas — ten minutes to spare. I will buy the tickets, and the train will soon back up to the station. Here it comes. We will go into the cars and select a good seat, where we can make observations, and in the meantime, I will tell you about the men who run this train. The engineer is Sanford Gaylord, a veteran in his profession. He is a native of Mansfield, Tioga County, PA, and for the past twenty-seven years has been employed in the various capacities by the railroads of Tioga County, serving as brakeman, fireman, and engineer. He has served in the capacity of engineer for the past twenty-three years, chiefly employed by the Tioga Railroad Company. He is called a safe and careful man, but fearless in the management of his engine, not hesitating to run his engine at the rate of sixty-miles per hour, if necessary. He is annually given a vacation, which he spends in the mountains of Tioga and Potter counties, hunting and fishing, thus strengthening his nerves for the laborious duties of the engineer. He is a genial and companionable gentleman, and I will introduce you to him before we return. His fireman is William Delancy, a trusty man, who has served several years in that capacity and is now really competent to take charge of an engine. The gentleman, Mr. Skidmore, who has charge of the express car, has been in the employment of the express company for the past thirty-five years. He has grown gray in the service, and has ever discharged the trust reposed in him with fidelity. Millions of dollars during his term of service have been in his charge, and every dollar reached its destination. Judson Hadley, the baggage master is an old railroad man. He has been in the employ of the company for the past fourteen years serving in various capacities. He sometimes relieves the conductor, Mr. Shattuck, when that gentleman by sickness or otherwise is compelled temporarily to vacate his position. Mr. Hadley is a trusted official. Isaac Bowen, chief brakeman, is a son of ex-Sheriff Stephen Bowen, of Tioga County, and has been in the employment of the company for quite a term of years. He is kind, obliging and gentlemanly. William Grossbeck, an assistant brakeman, has been but a short time upon the road, but has the appearance of a worthy employee. Charles L. Shattuck, the conductor, is a railroad man of long experience, having been connected with the Tioga Railroad and Tioga & Elmira Railroad for the past eighteen years. He is a gentleman with whom. Uncle Jonas, you would be pleased to make an acquaintance. He is careful and obliging and conscientious in the performance of every duty assigned him. He resides in Elmira and is prominently connected with the Railway Young Men's Christian Association and has done much to advance order, sobriety, and Christian principles among railroad men generally. The association to which he belongs you recollect. Uncle Jonas, owns that cozy brick chapel and reading room on Railroad Avenue and Church Dtreet, in this city. He did his share towards erecting and maintaining that association. The gentleman who has charge of the United States mail car is John C. Whittaker, Jr., formerly of Elkland, Tioga County. PA., but now a resident of this city. He has served twelve years in the capacity of railway postal clerk, first from Corning to Elkland, on the Corning, Cowanesque & Antrim Railroad, and was transferred several years ago to this road, where he has systematized the work in an admirable manner, and assisted the postmasters at Lawrenceville, Tioga, Mansfield, and Blossburg materially in their labors, by his process of 'pouching' the mails that are delivered at these several offices, to be distributed to other points. Mr. Whittaker is a model official and will be likely to be retained in the service. He is a pleasant and agreeable gentleman.

"All aboard."

"Now we are off, Uncle Jonas, for Seeley Creek, the mountains and valley of the Tioga. You can now have a view of the Chemung River and the bridges that span it. The agent here at Southport is Mr. Swan, an old gentleman of good business habits and highly regarded by the company. Now, Uncle Jonas, you can have a better view of the LaFrance steam fire engine company's works and also of the shops and roundhouses of the Northern Central Rrailroad. Uncle Jonas, take a look away off yonder on the point of that mountain opposite of Wellsburg. Can you see that monument there?"

"Oh, yes, Harry."

"Well, that, Uncle Jonas, is a monument erected by the citizens of southern New York and northern Pennsylvania in the year 1879 to commemorate the battle which occurred in the year 1779 between General Sullivan's army and the British Tories and Indians. Many distinguished citizens were present from various sections of the country at its dedication, August 26, 1879. The governors of several states were present. When we visit Wellsburg, I will tell you more about it. This station here is called Wells. The agent here E. J. Bailey, who does double duty, that of agent and telegraph operator. I was busy talking when we passed the junction between this road and the Northern Central.The operator at that place is H. P. Kniffin. We can look across the creek from here and see Pine City, where we visited a few days ago. Wells is quite an important station. There is a large tannery here, which affords considerable freight to the road— lumber, bark, hides, and leather; besides, it is the point where the Pine City people receive their freight and where they take cars for Elmira or westward into the Tioga Valley. From here, Uncle Jonas, we will soon commence ascending quite rapidly. Elmira is 908 feet above tide, and Wells is eighty-seven feet higher, or 995 feet above tide. This is Seeley Creek station. It is 1,041 feet above tide. The station agent and telegraph operator is E. D. Goff. Quite a considerable business is done here. Up, up we go. The next station, Uncle Jonas, is

Millerton, PA. It is in the town of Jackson, Tioga County, PA, and is situated 1,246 feet above tide. R. A. Mitchell is a station agent and operator. Millerton is quite a brisk little village, containing a good school, several churches, a newspaper entitled the Millerton *Advocate*, edited with ability by Harry Graves, a brave soldier, and a good printer and newspaperman; a lawyer's office, (for they must have justice done them, Uncle Jonas, in these Pennsylvania villages), which is presided over by Samuel E. Kirkendall, a good temperance man, a fine scholar, and a sturdy democrat. The temperance and the democracy. Uncle Jonas, I suppose, don't usually accompany each other.

"Well, there are exceptions to every rule. The population of Millerton is about three hundred; I should judge. Still, we are going up. Look, Uncle Jonas. See the trestling we are passing, fully seventy-five feet above the highway."

"I declare, Harry, this is quite a chasm."

"This, Uncle Jonas, is a flag station called Trowbridge in honor of one of the old citizens of Jackson. We have now arrived at an elevation 1,440 feet above the tide. The next station is the Summit, 1,594 feet above tide, and nearly 900 feet above Elmira, to be precise, 685 feet above that city. This is quite a little hamlet. The agent here is H. J. Tobey. He also is telegraph operator. When the road was constructed in 1876 this was a forest here, not a house in sight. We shall now commence to descend to the valley of the Tioga at the rate of about one hundred feet to the mile, or we shall descend 592 feet to Tioga Junction. But before we commence the descent, Uncle Jonas, just step to the rear car door, and look back to the eastward into the valley of the Chemung."

"I declare, Harry, that is a beautiful landscape, to mark those lines of mountains as they appear in regular gradations, one above other. The only fault I find, Harry, in the western landscape is then monotony, so to speak. There is nothing for the eye to rest on — one broad expanse of territory spread out on a plain. That is why I like the scenery of New York and Pennsylvania, the grandeur of their mountain and valley scenery. How cool and bracing the air is — no malaria in this, Harry."

"Now, Uncle Jonas, let us sit down, and as we round this next curve, you can look out of the car window and catch a view of the valley of the Tioga and the mountains, rising higher and higher until their summits are lost in the clouds away to the southwest on Pine Creek, and the Potter County line. This station is about abandoned. It was called Thompson's. Lumbering for several   years was carried on here, a large mill was in operation, sawing hemlock lumber and lath and shipping the same by rail. About a year ago, the mill was consumed by fire, and as the timber in this vicinity was about exhausted, it was not rebuilt. You related your experience with the fire between Horseheads and Elmira, but if you had seen the forest fire that swept over this section a year ago last May, destroying bridges, mills, barns, dwellings, standing timber and sawed lumber, I think you would have been ready to acknowledge that your fallow fires of sixty-five years ago could not compare with it.

"This, Uncle Jonas, is Tioga Junction. We are now 1021 feet above tide. The agent here is J. S. Weeks. From here to Lawrenceville the engine will back the cars down to connect with the trains on the Corning, Cowanesque & Antrim Railroad and will return here again. We might get off here and look around and get a fine cup of coffee or tea from Mrs. Chamberlain, the wife of the gentleman who has charge of this section. Or do you prefer to go on to Lawrenceville?" I prefer to go on — I want to see how that village looks."

"Just as you think best, Uncle Jonas."

"This, Harry, is a fine valley! What railroad is that over west yonder?"

"That, Uncle Jonas, is the Corning, Cowanesque & Antrim Railroad. We shall soon be at Lawrenceville station, and I will explain then so that you will understand it, or perhaps I had better do it now. The old Blossburg & Corning Railroad ran from Corning to Blossburg, and that portion in New York was owned by New Yorkers, and that portion in Pennsylvania by Philadelphians chiefly. About thirty years ago, the Hon, Judge Magee, of Bath, purchased the New York state portion and re-laid the track which had formerly been flat rails or snake headrails, with iron. He induced the Pennsylvania owners to do the same thing with their road. Mr. Magee was then interested in the coal mines at Blossburg and subsequently at Fall Brook, which I will more fully explain to you by and by. In 1872 Magee opened up miles south of Wellsboro, PA, and built a road from Lawrenceville to them, and also leased a road which was built from Lawrence to Elkland on the Cowanesque. He, therefore, consolidated these roads in name, terming them the Corning, Cowanesque & Antrim Railroads. And recently, the Cowanesque branch has been extended up into Harrison Valley in Potter County, and a connection has been made at Stokesdale with the Jersey Shore & Pine Creek Railroad, thence connecting with the Reading railroad at Williamsport. The cars you saw were a coal train on that road. Here we are at Lawrenceville station. We are now 982 feet above tide. The agent here for this road is Cornelius B. Mather, a gentleman of fine business qualifications. The telegraph operator is W. R. Crocker. The train on the Corning, Cowanesque & Antrim road is half an hour late. That, Uncle Jonas, will compel us to wait here thirty minutes."

"Very well, that will give us a chance to look over Lawrenceville some, or rather to talk over old events and speak of some of the old settlers with whom I was acquainted. Years ago, Harry, Lawrenceville was a busy town, and why she has not grown to be a city, I can't see. Well, that doesn't matter; I was acquainted with the Hon. James Ford, Dr. Lewis Darling,

Hiram Beebe, Daniel Seeley, Micajah Seeley, William Seeley, William Repusse, Job Gere, Clark Slawson, Moses Baldwin, Ira Kilbourn, the Ryans, Smith Stevens, Edward Stevens, Captain William Lindsley, (who lived on the Pennsylvania line in Lindsley, NY), Bradley Lindsley, Eleazer Lindsley, Alexander Lindsley, Joseph Lindsley, Phineas Lindsley, Walter Lindsley, Eleazer Mulford, Jeremiah Mulford, Del. Backus, Joseph Miller, and in Lawrenceville, Pardon Damon, Curtis Parkhurst, Simeon Powers, Clarendon Rathbone, Charles Ford, the Walkers — in fact, Harry, I knew almost all the citizens of the place. Oh, years; I came near forgetting Deacon Wells, John Barnes, Robert Stewart. Stewart then was an active young man, a millwright. In those days, Harry, we thought nothing of mounting a horse in Elmira and taking a ride up the river, or over the mountains to Lawrenceville. I really believe that people were more social and friendly then than now, perhaps not, yet it seems to me that such was the case. That generation, Harry, has passed away, and I suppose if I should take the Daggett house omnibus and ride over town, I would not find any of the persons whom I have named, living."

"Very few, Uncle Jonas. Your young friend, Robert Stewart, is living, D. C. Ford, son of Charles Ford, is living on the old homestead of his father — J. F. Rusling owns and resides in the James Ford mansion and is an active business man, a portion of the Lindsley family reside there, and the Walkers you mention occupy their splendid farm of the Cowanesque, the widow of Moses Baldwin I think is alive and resides upon the farm on the west bank of the Tioga River but most all of the persons living there in 1841, are dead or gone away and their places taken by citizens who have since made their homes there. The village has several times been visited by disastrous fires, destroying the business portion of the town, which has been very discouraging. The village now contains about four hundred inhabitants, a good hotel known as the Daggett House, several churches, a graded school, a newspaper office, the Lawrenceville *Herald*, a drug store, a machine shop, several grocery stores, a number of general stores, and is withal notwithstanding its misfortunes, a center of considerable trade. There is one thing that Lawrenceville has ever maintained, that is her fame for hospitality and good cheer. Her people are cordial, frank, open-hearted, and charitable.

"The train is coming, Uncle Jonas, and we will be moving southward in a few moments. We are in the state of New York, now. Here is the state line which was located in the year 1786 by commissioners from New York and Pennsylvania. We are now ninety miles west of the Delaware River. The ninetieth milestone stands over on the west bank of the Tioga River."

"I think, Harry, after going up to Blossburg and the mines, that we must return by the highway. There are so many things I want to see and talk about."

"We are off again. The farmers in this section for a number of years have been quite extensively engaged in the cultivation of tobacco, which has, upon the whole, proved very profitable. Some years the price is low for tobacco and the farmers become somewhat discouraged, forgetting that the price of tobacco is as likely to fluctuate as the price of butter, potatoes, corn, wheat, oats, hay or horses and cattle. Nobody ever heard of a farmer refusing to raise potatoes, because he could only get twenty- five cents per bushel, when perhaps the next year he could readily command seventy-five cents per bushel. Here we are at Mitchells. This station is 1,022 feet above tide. The station agent here is Mrs. Mitchell."

"Harry, I was acquainted with the older Mitchells. They were prominent men in this valley years ago."

"One of their descendants, Uncle Jonas, the Hon. John I. Mitchell, is now one of the United States senators from Pennsylvania. He resides in Wellsboro, but was born here about forty-six years ago, and was raised upon the farm and received his education principally in this locality, although he attended the Louisburg Seminary in Union County, PA, for a few terms. He represented this county several terms in the state legislature, and this district two terms in Congress, and was four years ago elected to the United States Senate for the full term of six years. In politics Mr. Mitchell is a republican. The next station is Tioga. The agent there is H. S. Alford, son of one of the early citizens, of that place. He also performs the duties of the telegraph operator."

"Willardsburg or Tioga, Harry, I recollect well, and its citizens. I came here about fifty years ago on a business trip. The rivalry between Willardsburg and Wellsboro was great. The Tioga people had just established a newspaper, purchasing the material and fixtures of one that had suspended in Wellsboro, thus leaving the county seat without a paper. Doctor William Willard was then alive and a very active and energetic man. I remember many of the inhabitants at that time. Among them were A. C. Bush, William Willard, William Willard, Jr., Allen D. Calkins, Thomas J. Berry, Ambrose Millard, Elijah Depue, J. S. Bush, James Goodrich, Uriah Spencer, Harris Hotchkiss, Vine Depue, Thomas Depue, Benjamin Depue, Mrs. Rachael Berry, Lyman Adams, John Gordon, Gershom Wynkoop, Chauncey Ferry, Ebenezer Ferry, Hobart Graves, Levi Guernsey, Joseph Guernsey, Jacob Schiefflein, Sr., H. H. Potter, the Rev. Samuel McCullough, William Garretson, besides many more whose names do not occur to me at present."

"I believe it will be a good plan to return by the road by private conveyance, as we do not more than get fairly talking about the people of the town before we are hurried away. Tioga station is 1,042 feet above tide. Here, Uncle Jonas, is a siding or short track which leads over the coke works in the southwestern portion of Tioga village. Mill Creek is a flog station, and yet there is considerable shipping done here. Lambs Creek is the next station. B. Lamb is the agent. Although there is nothing but that small shanty of a depot, still the freight and passenger traffic is considerable. The elevation above tide here at Lambs Creek is 1,111 feet. Mansfield is the next station and one of the most important on the line. Its elevation above tide is 1, 140 feet. I am particular, Uncle Jonas, to tell you these elevations so that you may jot them down in your memory, and also show you at what a rate we are ascending. The agent here at Mansfield is W. H. Kinney. He has an assistant. This is Smythe Park, a charming place, where fairs are annually held. We will visit it on our return. The next station is Canoe Camp Creek. The station agent here for many years was Thomas Jeliff, he was killed by a flash of lightning while standing on the depot platform in the month of August last. His widow, Mrs. Jeliff, attends to the duties of the station since the death of Mr. Jeliff. The elevation of this station is 1163 feet above tide. The next station is Covington. The elevation at Covington is 1,208 feet above tide. The agent and operator at Covington is W. H. Lamkin. It is now, Uncle Jonas, only five miles to Blossburg, where we will arrive in a few minutes. There is a fine hotel there, the Seymour House, where we will take dinner and make our general headquarters while we remain in this locality. The elevation of Blossburg above tide is 1,848. The agent is B. J. Guernsey, who has been many years in the service of the company. He is assisted by Charles Rockwell, Kenyon Kilburn and Jacob Griffith. Blossburg is the most important station on the line of the road. The telegraph operator is Charles D. Utley, a gentleman in every way competent to discharge the duties devolved upon him. Here we are at Blossburg. "Sant" has made up the lost time at Lawrenceville. I thought we were whirling through the valley and over the road at a rapid rate. Uncle Jonas, this is E. L. Updike, proprietor of the Seymour House. Mr. Updike, this is Uncle Jonas Lawrence, come to visit this section of the country for a few days."

"You are welcome, Uncle Jonas."

BLOSSBURG AND ITS ENVIRONS.
HOW THE RAILROADS AND THE MINES HAVE
DEVELOPED THE COUNTRY.

"The day is so pleasant, Uncle Jonas, suppose we take chairs and go on the veranda and sit for an hour or more, where we can look over the borough. An incorporated village in this state, Uncle Jonas is named a borough instead of a village. Blossburg is an incorporated borough and contains about three thousand inhabitants. Is it too cool for you, Uncle Jonas?

"Oh no, Harry."

"Well, Uncle Jonas, I will give you a brief history of this hotel. After the railroad was completed here from Corning, in 1840, capitalists came in here from Philadelphia, in fact they had arrived as early as 1835. As I was relating, after the railroad was completed, and the mines of coal and iron were opened up, John G. Boyd, of Philadelphia, who was directly and indirectly interested in the railroad and mining operations, conceived the idea of erecting a large and commodious hotel, one that would accommodate the traveling public, and one at which he could entertain his friends from Philadelphia and elsewhere. He, therefore, gave an outline of his ideas to an architect and he drew up plans and specifications, which were approved by Mr. Boyd. The contract was then made with Phineas P. Cleaver in the year 1841, and he commenced the erection of this building. For those days, it bore the same relation to Blossburg as the Palmer House to Chicago. The banisters, rails and newel posts were of solid mahogany, were turned and made in Philadelphia and brought here and are still in use. The house was finished ready for occupancy in 1842, and Edward Andrews installed as landlord. The house was subsequently in charge of Philemon Doud and Phineas P. Cleaver. It was abandoned as a hotel some years thereafter and the various rooms rented as offices. When the Morris Run railroad was constructed in 1852-53, the office of the chief engineer. Colonel Jarrett was here. The Tioga Railway Company for a number of years were the losses, and in the year 1873 purchased it and renovated and made some alterations in the interior, occupying three of the rooms on the north side on the first floor as a ticket office, telegraph office and an office for the superintendent of the road, and the remainder used as a hotel, with Albert Ward and George W. Morgan as landlords. They have had several successors, among whom is the present one, E. L. Updyke. Since its renovation in 1873, it has been kept in first-class order.

"That building across the street is the car repair and machine shops of the Tioga & Elmira State Line railroad. The foreman in charge is Daniel H. Stratton, who has been years serving in that capacity. Stephen Holland is an assistant foreman in the machine shop. James Kirkwood, Luke Fudge, Albert Fudge, Myron Stratton, Harry Boyle, and Thomas Brown are machinists. In the blacksmith shop connected with the car and machine shop are Robert Davie, James Rose, Samuel Landon, Jerry Healey, Rose, and David Smith. In the car shop, Edward Guernsey is bookkeeper and clerk, and the foreman of repairs is Thomas Evans. The shopmen are George Richter, Sr., patternmaker; James Husted, George Morganstein, Stephen Randall are also employed there. The force is light at present. Usually, there are many more employed. The watchmen about the car shops, roundhouses, depot, freight depot, are Edward Gavigan, Edward Bamberry, George Delounge, George Bamberry. The stationery engine is in charge of Evan J. Evans. All the coal, timber, bark, lumber that you see. Uncle Jonas, passing through here, is weighed at two offices. One located on the Arnot branch of the railroad, with Mart G. Lewis as weighmaster, and the other on the Morris Run branch of the Tioga Railroad, and the Fall Brook Railroad is weighed by Henry Holland and Frank Stratton.

"Blossburg, until quite recently, was headquarters of the super-intendent of the road, but Robert B. Cable, at the Elmira office, is now superintendent, and Walter V. Calkins, who for many years was chief dis-patcher and telegraph operator, has been transferred to Elmira. While we are upon this subject I will give you the names of the engineers, firemen, brakemen, conductors and other employees upon the several trains. The Elmira Express, which leaves Blossburg for Elmira at 7:30AM, is manned by William Green, engineer, who is one of the oldest engineers in point of service upon the road, has charge of the engine, Lloyd Higgins is his fire-man. The conductor is Frank Higgins, who has served many years in that capacity and is one of the most obliging and accommodating gentlemen in the service of the company. George Richter, Jr., is baggage-master, also a first-class man, and Lewis Reifeldeifer is brakeman. This train arrives in El-mira about 10 o'clock in the forenoon, and leaves there for Blossburg about 5, arriving here at 8:15PM. The way freight train is manned by Michael Clauhessey conductor, M. J. Delaney freight agent, and Thomas Kerwin, Nichols Nicholas, Charles Ferris and David Bauman, brakemen. The men on the train are distinguished for their attention to duty and the careful manner in which they receive and discharge the freight at the various sta-tions on the line. That train leaves Elmira at about 6 o'clock in the morning, arriving here at about 5 o'clock. The coal trains are manned, one by James W. Maher, conductor, John Loughridge, Michael Kerwin and Samuel Howard, brakemen. Another coal train is manned by J. M. Horton, con-ductor, Samuel Caldwell, John Sutton, Lone. Boehm and William Weaver, brakemen. The train running from Blossburg to Morris Run is engineered by James Green, one of the oldest engineers on the road. His fireman is Claude Green. The conductor is William M. Butler, who for more than twenty years has served in that capacity, trusty, careful and gentlemanly. The brakemen are Albert Welty, John Booth, Jr., and Henry Hanwell, all careful and painstaking men. The train running from Blossburg to Arnot is manned by Warren Aldrich, conductor, and Warner Aldrich, Frederic Bosworth, Enoch Jones and Michael McCarthy, brakemen. The engineer is George Lewis, who has handled the throttle for twenty years or more and is one of the most trusted employes of the company. His fireman is Drow Gillett. The Hoytville accommodation, which runs from Blossburg to Hoytville, is manned by William Kerwin, conductor; L. Secrist, baggage-master, and Thomas McCarthy and Michael Maloney, brakemen. The engineer is James Bonney, son of master mechanic P. Bonney, one of the best machinists in Pennsylvania. The fireman is William Mould. The extra engineers who are both assigned to regular and special duty are Letson Lounsberry, Richard Hughes, Thomas Tremble, Frank Hebe, and John Evans, Jr., all proficient in their profession and all respected citizens of Blossburg and occupying pleasant homes. I have thus been particular, Uncle Jonas, to give you the names and occupations which these railroad and shop employees discharge, and should be pleased to have you make their acquaintance. You would find them an intelligent, courteous, honest and good class of citizens. They could relate many an interesting incident connected with their service, what distinguished men they had met, whom they had safely conducted to their destination, then hair-breadth escapes from perilous situations and give you many valuable ideas in relation to the construction of engines and the manner of operating them, give you points upon the most approved coal, passenger and freight cars, and many other lessons of value, and which every person should understand."

"That is all very true, Harry. I have made it a rule of my life to become acquainted with as many different classes of laborers and mechanics as possible, and as far as that is concerned I have endeavored to become acquainted with every class in society who are engaged in any honorable pursuit or calling, and I have listened with attention to what you have been relating. I will now speak of my first and second visits to Blossburg. The third visit you are here with me. My first visit to Blossburg was in the year 1824, sixty-two years ago. My father had business relations with Judge John H. Knapp, and he sent me up here with that gentleman. Judge Knapp was from Elmira, or Newtown we then called it, and was a brother-in-law of the late Hon. Levi J. Cooley. Judge Knapp had located here as early as 1823, and had erected a furnace and was having a mill built about 100 rods southeast from the furnace. We left Elmira in the afternoon and drove up as far as Painted Post, and remained there overnight at Erwin's. In the morning, we forded the Conhocton River and followed the Williamson road, cut out in 1792, fording the Canisteo River five miles above Painted Post, NY, and fording the Tioga River three miles from there, arriving at Robert Patterson's at Lindley for dinner. Robert Patterson was one of the men who conducted General Charles Williamson, in 1792, from Northumberland, PA., to Bath, NY, and he and his brother Benjamin discovered coal here in that year. After dinner we pushed on to Lawrenceville and reached Asa Mann's, at Mansfield, at night. We were quite heavily loaded. The next day we reached Blossburg a little afternoon. Then there were not more than half a dozen dwellings in Blossburg. Judge Knapp had opened a small store, to accommodate the citizens and his workmen. Aaron Bloss had opened a hotel on the banks of the Tioga River, near the furnace of Judge Knapp, and on the Williamson road. He had lived there since 1806 — hunting, trapping and fishing, making but a small clearing. His woodshed was stored with bear traps, wolf traps, fox and mink traps, while in his bar room were guns and fishing tackle. The forest of stately pines, hemlocks and maple came down to his door. The Tioga River was literally full of the finest speckled trout, which could be caught at any time. The first night I remained here, the wolves kept up such a howling and yelping over yonder on that island (where you now see those three pine trees, the last of the

Mohicans) that I could not sleep, I remained three days with Judge Knapp, getting acquainted in the meantime with Curtis Stratton, the millwright, Absalom Kingsbury, Samuel Weeks, Isaac Walker, Royal Walker, and Asahel Walker and several others whose names now escape my memory. A vein of coal had been opened up near the furnace, also a bed of iron ore, from which Judge Knapp was intending to make pig iron. The lime used was hauled from the head of Seneca lake or from Williamsport, over the Laurel Ridge mountains. There was something about the place, notwithstanding the howling of the wolves, that was very attractive. The mountain and forest scenery was grand, the fragrance of the fresh blown thorn tree, the clear mountain stream inhabited by myriads of fish, made a lasting impression upon me. I returned home on horseback over the same route that the judge and I had taken, making, however, a much quicker trip. When the railroad was completed I again visited the place in 1840, and came near selling out in Elmira and making Blossburg my permanent home. In the fourteen years that had elapsed since my first visit, quite a change had taken place. Several hotels had been erected, one by Mr. D. P. Freeman, a large and commodious house, as nearly as large as this, a number of stores had been opened, too many I thought for the business. The coal had been opened up on the Clemmons' property, and the Arbon Coal Company had been formed. The Hon. Horatio Seymour, then a young man with his associates, the Hon. Amos P. Granger, and Hon. Thomas Davis, of New York, the Hon. James Ford, Clarendon Rathbone, and Curtis Parkhurst, of Lawrenceville, had made extensive purchases and were selling village lots. There was no land to be bought only in small parcels of one- quarter or half an acre. The Arbon Coal Company had purchased several thousand acres, embracing, with the exception of the Seymour and Granger purchase, all the desirable land or lands of any kind within a radius of several miles of the village. It was this state of affairs which prevented me from locating here at that time. I remained here nearly two weeks but saw no opening which I deemed advantageous, I then made the acquaintance of Dr. Lewis Saynisch, president of the Arbon Coal Company, a very pleasant and agreeable German, James H. Gulick, who was their superintendent, Franklin R. Smith, Brown Whitney, Philemon Doud, Joseph Yonkin, Francis Welch, Alexander H. Gaylord, John L. Evans, David Chatfield, Dr. Joseph P. Morris, Thomas Turner, Benjamin Hall, John James, James R. Wilson, John G. Boyd, Clarendon Rathbone, and a few others. A great rivalry existed between the villages of Covington and Blossburg. The village of Blossburg was situated in the township of Covington, and the question of dividing the township was being agitated very strongly. There was no rivalry from any place to the southward or eastward. The Block House, now Liberty, was a mere hamlet and ten miles distant, and there were no settlements to the eastward until you reached McNetts, twelve miles distant, then on the road leading from Elmira to Williamsport. I returned home via Corning. Corning then was not as large as Blossburg; only a few buildings were erected among the pine stumps. It was, however, quite a stirring business place, as the old Erie railroad was then in the course of construction upon the pile system, which failed, and which was ten years later built upon a different plan and successfully operated up to the present."

"Well, Uncle Jonas, you speak of the rivalry between Covington and Blossburg and the threatened division of the township. The subject of division was agitated until it was accomplished in June, 1841, and separate township officers elected. The township and village continued to increase in population, churches and schoolhouses were erected, the mines developed, and shipments of coal increased. The old furnace had been erected by Judge Knapp and by him abandoned, was repaired and put in operation, and in 1847 a manufactory was established by William Dezang, of Geneva, for the making of window glass and other improvements were instituted. The Arbon coal company had failed and the mines had passed into the hands of William M. Mallory & Co., of Corning. They in turn had failed and their lease about thirty years ago became the property of the Hon. John Magee, who for several years operated then with Duncan S. Magee, superintendent. About the time I spoke of this morning of the change of the old strap rail to a T rail, new mines were opened at Morris Run, four miles eastward, by rail from here, and a railroad constructed to them by a company entitled the Tioga Improvement company, of which I will tell you more in the future. In 1859 a company was formed entitled the Fall Brook Coal Company, consisting of the Hon. John Magee, Duncan S. Magee and James H, Gulick, who opened up mines at Fall Brook and constructed a railroad from Blossburg to that point, a distance of about seven miles. That was a sad blow to Blossburg, for mining ceased here, and the miners and their families removed to Fall Brook, reducing the population of Blossburg from sixteen hundred down to less than eight hundred. In 1862, however, the village began to revive. The Tioga Railroad company removed their shops from Corning to Blossburg and that revived the business prospects of the village materially. April 11, 1866, the Blossburg coal company was organized, consisting of Constant Cook, John Arnot, Charles Cook, Henry Sherwood, Franklin N. Drake, Ferral C. Dininy, Henry H. Cook and Lorenzo Webber, who constructed a railroad from Blossburg four miles southwest to their mines. A mining town was built up known as Arnot, of which I will tell you more about when we visit it. This enterprise materially strengthened Blossburg. Thus, you perceive, Uncle Jonas, that there are three railroads centering here at Blossburg from the mines. But to resume — Blossburg continued to increase in population. There were three villages in the township, viz.: Morris Run, Arnot and Blossburg, with a total population of about six thousand inhabitants, with only one place to hold elections, Blossburg. Accordingly, in August, 1871, the borough of

Blossburg was incorporated. That left the villages of Arnot and Morris Run eight miles apart, with only one polling place, and the space between these villages, to quite a large extent, occupied by the borough of Blossburg. In the year 1872 the township of Hamilton was formed from Bloss township, and so arranged that it included the village of Morris Run, where all the population was centered excepting two or three families. By that arrangement the village of Arnot was made a polling place, where all the people of the remaining township of Bloss were located, with the exception of a few families on Maple Hill. Had Blossburg been able to have held the population in her territory, she might have been incorporated as a city with three wards, for the population now within a radius of five miles is over 10,000 people."

"When the Tioga Railroad shops were removed here from Corning in 1862, Mr. Levi H, Shattuck was the superintendent of the railroad. He also made it his residence, and continued to reside here for twenty-two consecutive years, looking after every interest connected with the road. He had been ten years superintendent of the road before his removal here, making an aggregate of thirty-two years that he had watched over its interests, making himself personally familiar with all of its workings. Three years ago a company was formed entitled the Arnot & Pine Creek Railroad Co., and Mr. Shattuck was elected president. This was a virtual extension of the Tioga Railroad. In addition to the other duties devolved upon him, he gave the construction of this new road or extension a general supervision. These increased responsibilities and the years of continued watchfulness told upon his system, and a few months ago he resigned his position as superintendent, but still acting as president of the Arnot & Pine Creek railroad. He was given a valuable testimonial upon his resignation, and is now enjoying a beautiful home situated upon the west shore of the Tioga River near Mansfield, surrounded by all the comforts which a long life of usefulness entitles him to enjoy."

"Blossburg was visited by a severe conflagration March 6, 1873, which destroyed the entire business portion of the borough. All the way, Uncle Jonas, from where that elegant bank building of Pomeroy brothers and F. E. Smith is now located, south to the Odd Fellows' block was one mass of rums. But scarcely had the smoking ruins been extinguished before temporary buildings were erected. The citizens' committee evinced commendable enterprise and fortitude. Several brick blocks were erected, where before wooden structures had stood. Among the sufferers from the fire were Messrs. Harry T. and Fred L. Graves, editors and proprietors of the Blossburg *Register*, a weekly newspaper which had been established a few years previous. They also caught the spirit of the moment, and although their office was entirely destroyed, yet in a few weeks their *Register* was again issued. A fire department was soon thereafter organized and without going into a detailed history of the trials and struggles with inefficient machinery, suffice it to say that Blossburg today has one; of the most efficient fire departments in northern Pennsylvania, a fine steamer, and two hose companies that cannot be excelled for promptness, activity and good work. This object has been attained largely through the efforts of Mart G. Lewis, who has for many years been chief of the department, and seconded by our efficient burgess, Major George W. Morgan, and our worthy councilmen. You will observe by casting your eye about, Uncle Jonas, that Blossburg is centrally located for manufacturing and shipping. The capacity of the glass factory yonder is about 36,000 boxes of window glass annually, the capacity of the sawmills are about 10,000,000 feet annually, the tannery about 500 sides of sole leather per day; besides, the work turned out by planing mill, foundry and machine shops add much to the interest of the borough. One great draw-back at Blossburg has been that there has been too much coal in the mountains surrounding it, or in this Blossburg region."

"This, Uncle Jonas, may appear to you as strange logic. Well, let me explain. In the first place these coal companies are non-residents. Their local interests are in Elmira, Corning and Watkins Glen. The coal has been so plenty that instead of these companies seeking to establish a home market near their mines, by fostering the establishment of foundries, machine shops, edge tool manufactories that would consume their coal near where it was mined, and create a freight traffic equal to their tonnage now of coal, they have been seeking a foreign market for it. You would naturally think that these several coal companies furnish the people of Blossburg with coal, but such is not the case. They furnish the glass factory and their own shops and one or two other places. While individuals who own mines near here furnish eight hundred families in Blossburg and vicinity with all the coal they use. These companies have so much coal that they are in busy times shipping right through Blossburg from four to six thousand tons per day, which finds a market as far west as Colorado, south to New Orleans, north into Canada, and east to Boston and the New England states. Half of that amount should be consumed in the valley of Tioga, and it would be if the companies had been as industrious in fostering manufactories in the valley as they have been in extending their lines of railroads. As soon as the coal begins to become scarce here, these companies will either abandon their mines by selling out to individuals or companies with less capital and fewer railroad connections, who will take hold and develop a permanent home trade, by offering inducements for industrial establishments to locate in this valley."

"There were originally about fifty million tons of coal in the Blossburg region. About sixteen million have been mined in Tioga county and shipped out of the county, a large portion of it at a price scarcely above the cost of production. The owners of the mines have been governed by a mistaken policy, to hurry this coal upon the market regardless of price, when they should have let it remain in the mountains as a reserve, or endeavored to have had it consumed by manufactories, which would have given the railroads additional freight, increased the population and thereby increased the passenger traffic. The owners of pine timber did the same thing. There was originally about one billion five hundred million feet of white pine timber in this county, and the owners hurried it off to a southern market, realizing in the gross not more than ten million dollars, which, had it been properly managed, would have brought forty million dollars. If a change in policy is adopted, and the coal reserved, other interests will then be developed. The mineral springs, the iron ore, the glass sand rock and fire clay will then receive attention. Here, surrounding Blossburg, are some of the very best mineral springs in America. As soon as the mania for shipping away coal ceases, these springs will be developed and great sanitariums will be erected that will vie with the celebrated Baden-Baden of the old world. Their medicinal qualities have been analyzed by the best and most reliable chemists in the land, and pronounced 'one of the most remarkable mineral waters in existence.' I expect to see in a few years thousands of persons from all sections of the country to regain their health. I expect to see firebrick yards established, and glass manufactories in great numbers, for the sand rock is here, the fire clay is here, the coal, coke and wood are here. I also expect to see edge tool manufactories established here, for the finest of steel can be tempered with the run of mines of the Blossburg vein, or if coke is preferable that is also at hand. Although Blossburg may now not present the most pleasing appearance, she will yet be a city. There are today, owned by individuals, who cannot ship their coal, at least one million five hundred thousand tons, in these hills here within the limits of the corporation which will yet be used for manufacturing purposes, generating steam for driving machinery. Things may look a little discouraging for Blossburg now, but I believe she possesses the location and the elements of a great industrial and health-restoring center. Had there been less coal here she would now occupy that position. The principle is taking root, and I have done all that I could to inculcate it into the minds of manufacturers that the place to manufacture cheaply and advantageously was where the raw material was found; that a manufacturer, for instance, did not nor could not afford to pay $2 or $3 freight per ton on a ton of coal and iron ore that was worth only $1.50 per ton at the mines, when for the same money he could ship a ton of manufactured iron or steel, which was worth from $22 to $500 a thousand miles. The place to manufacture cheaply, Uncle Jonas, is in the section where the raw material is cheap, where the rents and lands are cheap, and the place to sell is in the cities. To illustrate, yonder is an island containing eight or ten acres. It probably could be bought for $2,000. There is sufficient room to establish a large glass or edged-tool establishment. The same amount of land in a city would cost from one hundred to two hundred thousand dollars. The difference in the interest on the investment of that one item alone would be from five to ten thousand dollars annually. Suppose that the establishment used fifty tons of coal per day, which here would cost from $50 to $70, while in a city remote from the mines it would cost $3 per ton; that would be a saving in favor of the country locality of $50 or $75 per day, a saving of at least $400 per week, or from $15,000 to $25,000 per annum. Here, then, are two items, cost of site and fuel, which favor the country, or such a place as this, by an aggregate of nearly $40,000 per annum. Forty thousand dollars saved in these two items would help materially in oiling up the machinery of the establishment, or in paying dividends to the company who had invested their money in the enterprise. I could go on at length and enter into details which would convince any reasonable man of this proposition: Manufacture where the raw material is produced, and sell in great commercial centers. Have your shop in the country and your salesroom in the city."

"Perhaps I have been a little tedious, Uncle Jonas, but I wanted to speak of those things. Suppose we go in and look over the Elmira *Advertiser* and other city papers and make arrangements for going to Arnot and Hoytville tomorrow. "

"Are you through with the *Advertiser*, Uncle Jonas?"

"Yes, Harry."

"Well, I think we had better retire for the night. I believe in the old Franklin maxim —

> *"Early to bed, and early to rise,*
> *Makes one healthy, wealthy, and wise."*

"What a fine room, Harry; I did not expect to see anything like this here. High walls, good ventilation, a delightful fire in the grate; this is as cozy as a sitting room at home. I noticed, Harry, before we left the veranda, that there was a fine brick and stone building over yonder on the hillside, what public building is that?"

"That, Uncle Jonas, is the Blossburg graded schoolhouse. The principal is Mr. G. R. Smith, the preceptress Miss Lizzie Gavigan, assisted by Misses Dora James, Bell Horton, Miss Dunsmore, Miss Hyde and Mina Doud. It was erected about ten years ago at a cost of about thirteen thousand dollars. There is also another schoolhouse in the southern portion of the borough, employing two teachers. Miss Anna Dunsmore and Miss Anna Clement. The citizens of Blossburg deserve much credit for their intelligence and public spirit in providing ample school facilities and the employment of competent teachers."

"I noticed several churches."

"Yes, Uncle Jonas, there are six church edifices in the borough. The one standing nearly in front of us on the corner of Williamson and Carpenter Streets is the Baptist church, and the minister is the Rev. Frederick K. Fowler, a man highly respected in the community by all denominations. He served gallantly in the army during the late rebellion as a private soldier, and at the close of the war studied for and was admitted into the ministry. He is an able pulpit orator and a worthy Christian gentleman. He has been engaged here for the past eight years. The church across the river is the Methodist. The minister in charge is the Rev. Robert Brewster, who is an able preacher and much respected by the congregation and those who have had the pleasure to make his acquaintance. But the trouble is with the Methodists, they shift their ministers around so much that just as they get comfortably located and acquainted with their congregations and doing a good work they are transferred to another field to go through the same program, thus wearing out their ministers in removing from one section to another and in getting acquainted with their members. The Episcopalians have a fine church, but no rector at present. The church is nicely located a few rods north of the Methodist church. On this side of the river, the Welsh Congregationalists have a snug little church and a very able minister in the person of the Rev. J. M. Evans, who is a young man of more than ordinary abilities, a fine scholar and an elegant preacher. Services are held in Welsh and English. The Irish Catholics have a neat church and parsonage. The Rev. Patrick J. Murphy has charge of it. He is a gentleman of fine scholastic acquirements, a good disciplinarian and is much respected by the community. He has quite an extensive field of labor. He ministers at Morris Run Arnot, Fall Brook and Union, besides his home charge, and is an indefatigable and earnest worker. During his ministrations three new churches have been erected. In the southern portion of the borough the Catholic Polanders have a neat church and a parochial school. In the latter the Polish and English languages are taught. The congregation is composed of Poles from Blossburg, Morris Run and Arnot. The minister in charge is the Rev.

Father (an unpronounceable name). Uncle Jonas, but who is an energetic priest, enforcing order and good morals among his parishioners to a great extent. The Hon. Horatio Seymour, having been a property holder here, has contributed largely towards the erection of all these churches. This hotel is named in his honor. There are lodges of Odd Fellows, Free Masons, Catholic Temperance society, Knights of Honor, with a large membership, which expend quite a considerable amount of money for charitable and benevolent purposes."

"Harry, what music is that?"

"That, Uncle Jonas, is the Blossburg Cornet Band practicing in their rooms near here. That band has a fine reputation for their excellent music. It has been organized ten years or more: was at one time the regimental band of the Twelfth Regiment of Pennsylvania State National Guard, and held that position when the regiment was consolidated by order of the adjutant-general of the state. It was called the Twelfth Regiment Band. It has gained a fine reputation in Pennsylvania and New York, and by many it is conceded to be the best in northern Pennsylvania and southern New York. For a number of years, it was led by Dr. Nelson Ingram, a fine musician, but when he removed to Norfolk, Virginia, the leadership was assumed by Charles Ely, a skillful musician, who is now occupying that position. The band is composed of some of the best citizens of Blossburg, gentlemen who are distinguished for their musical talent and gentlemanly qualities. They are finely uniformed, and their major is chief burgess, George W. Morgan, a great lover of music and a man of fine and dignified presence. During the spring and summer months the band give concerts from the veranda of this hotel every Saturday evening, the citizens turning out in great numbers to listen to their exquisite music. The citizens of Blossburg and Tioga county take a just pride in that organization. Perhaps, Uncle Jonas, before we leave this section, may we have an opportunity of hearing it play."

103

"Is there an opera house here, Harry?"

"Not at present, Uncle Jonas. There was a fine hall here fifty by eighty-five feet, with a fine stage and curtains, but unfortunately it was destroyed by fire a few months ago and has not been rebuilt. There is a very neat small hall here in that stone block you saw this afternoon over on Main or Williamson street. Any small gathering can be accommodated there. But large assemblies meet in the skating rink. "

"What have they a skating rink in this place?"

"Yes, Uncle Jonas, and a very large one for a borough of this size. Do you object to them, Uncle Jonas?"

"Well, not exactly, but I think dancing is preferable to those requiring amusements of that kind, yet in the abstract, I can't see anything very criminal in roller skating. But, like any other amusement, it can be carried to excess. I declare, Harry, it is getting late. Between this cheerful fire and your conversation, the time has passed rapidly. It is understood then, Harry, that we go to Arnot and Hoytville tomorrow."

"Yes, Uncle Jonas, we will take the Hoytville accommodation, with 'Billy' Kerwin conductor. Goodnight!"

"Did you rest well last night. Uncle Jonas?"

"Yes, indeed."

"Well we have plenty of time to get breakfast before the train leaves for Hoytville. The porter will soon have a fire for you to get up by and dress."

"Oh, never mind that, Harry, the room is warm enough."

"I want to introduce you before we leave for J. D. Shultz, the supervisor of the Tioga branch. His office is in this building, formerly occupied by the superintendent, L. H. Shattuck. Mr. Shultz is a practicing civil engineer and has had a large experience in the construction of railroads, giving them his personal attention in all of the details, and consequently is eminently fitted for the responsible position he occupies. Among the many railroads upon which he has hitherto been engaged was the West Shore, between Syracuse and Buffalo. His supervision now extends from Hoytville to Elmira, with headquarters at Blossburg. It is seldom that supervisors of tracks are practical engineers, and his employment in that capacity is a step in the right direction. And his mode of inspection of the track is different from that usually in practice. Instead of boarding a train running at the rate of thirty miles per hour, and seated in the rear seat of a passenger car, he has a velocipede which he places upon the track and propels himself slowly over the road, examining every joint, chair, culvert, bridge, frog and siding. He is, therefore, in possession of the knowledge of the actual condition of the road and can give the section foremen instructions on what to do from personal knowledge. We will go down to breakfast now. Uncle Jonas."

"We had better leave our baggage here. Uncle Jonas, as we shall return this evening."

"All aboard for Hoytville."

"Take this seat, Uncle Jonas. Here, Uncle Jonas, is where the railroads branch, one track leading to Morris Run, the middle track to Fall Brook and the right-hand track upon which we are switching to Hoytville. Yonder to the left is the site of the furnace erected by Judge Knapp in 1825, now occupied by T. J. Mooers as a foundry and machine shop. Here is the Tioga River, rather small stream to be called a river, but in times of high water it is a rapid and turbulent stream. This mill here on the left-hand side of the track is owned by the Blossburg coal company and is a portion of the franchise of the Tioga branch of the Erie. The mill is usually in operation about eight months in the year, cutting out about 500,000 feet of lumber per month or 4,000,000 in eight months. It is provided with a powerful engine and all the necessary appliances for good work. The foreman is James H. Mold, an industrious and careful manager, who has just completed the erection of that fine cottage you see over yonder on the Williamson road. Mr. Mold has held the position of foreman for a number of years. The head sawyer is Andrew Parker, the setter is Willard Leisering, the lumber measurer and shipper is N. B. Preston, and the engineer is Thomas Cowley, all trusty and tried workmen in their several vocations. The number of men employed is sixteen. The large buildings with that tall brick chimney or stack is the Monroeville tannery, owned by Messrs. William Hoyt, Oliver Hoyt and Mark Hoyt, under the firm name of Hoyt Bros., No. 72 Gold street, New York City. The tannery, I said, is known as the Monroeville Tannery, although situated in Blossburg. About seventy-five men are employed here in the manufacture of sole leather exclusively. The superintendent is T. C. Peck, who has been in the employment of the firm for the past twenty years — a gentleman well calculated to fill so responsible a charge. The bookkeeper, cashier and bark measurer is A. E. Botchford, who also is an employee, having served thirteen years with the firm, an evidence of the confidence and trust that is placed in him by the firm. George Ludwig also holds a responsible position. This tannery consumes from ten to twelve thousand cords of hemlock bark annually, and turns out from one hundred and fifty to one hundred and seventy-five thousand sides annually. In other words, it would take a drove of seventy-five or eighty thousand of your Illinois four year old steers to supply this tannery one year in hides — and the bark from nine to twelve million feet of hemlock to keep it supplied with bark. You recollect that I told you about the skating rink last night, Uncle Jonas, well here on the left enclosed by that high fence is Brooks' bicycle and foot racing track. So, you perceive that these people, notwithstanding they have to work hard, are provided with means of amusements and sports. The track is owned by J. Brooks, father of the celebrated John Brooks, the bicyclist. That is his residence here on the right. There in that shady retreat are the trout ponds of Messrs. Andrews & Morgan. There are seven ponds intended for the hatching and propagation of trout. It is a pleasant place now, but I am told that many improvements are in contemplation. By the way Uncle Jonas, there is more profit in raising trout, than there is in raising beef and pork. With clear mountain spring water, and with less capital than is required by a moderate farmer, trout can be raised and marketed with three times more profit than cattle and swine. The highway leads to Liberty or the Blockhouse, Uncle Jonas."

"I recollect that road, Harry, as far back as when the Bellmans kept a wayside inn on that road a few hundred rods above here."

"This land upon either side here belongs to the Fall Brook coal company and containing large deposits of coal, which in time will be opened up and developed. They have been holding these fields in reserve. There are almost four thousand five hundred acres in the tract.

HOYTVILLE AND ARNOT.
SOCIAL FEATURES, MERCANTILE, MINING, AND
MANUFACTURING ENTERPRISES.

"This stream is known as Johnson's Creek. Do you observe that fine quality of moulding sand, Uncle Jonas, there in that cut? It is found here in inexhaustible quantities, beside the same rock, suitable for the manufacture of glass. We are now approaching Arnot. The smoke you see rising is from the coke ovens. There are two hundred of them making the very best quality of coke manufactured in America. While perhaps there may be some that equal it, none surpass it in its adaptability for furnace and other purposes for which coke is generally used. For domestic use it cannot be excelled. There is no smoke, no gas, nothing disagreeable in the smell when used in the cooking range, but a clear, steady heat, and there is no good reason why coke should not in America, as well as England, be used exclusively for locomotive use on locomotives drawing passenger trains. In England a passenger can ride five hundred miles without soiling his clothes in the least, but here in America the passenger is annoyed by smoke and coal-dust cinders, and his clothes are destroyed in riding fifty miles. It is an insult to American machinists to say that they cannot construct a locomotive that will burn coke and make as good time and speed in America as they can in Great Britain. These ovens were constructed. Uncle Jonas, under the direction of Simon B. Elliott, for the Blossburg Coal Company in the years 1879-80. That high building on the right of the track is a coal washer and crusher. All the coal used in the manufacture of coke is first crushed fine and its impurities cleansed by water, and also all the smithing coal undergoes the same process, thereby putting upon the market a coal unsurpassed. The capacity of the crusher and washer is about 2,700 tons per day and is the largest establishment of the kind in Pennsylvania or "elsewhere in the United States. The product of these ovens, as well as the coal mines, are controlled by the Erie company. I have referred in a former conversation, Uncle Jonas, but I will give you a brief history of it now."

ARNOT.

"The Blossburg Coal Company was incorporated by an act of the legislature of Pennsylvania approved April 11, 1866. The incorporators were Constant Cook, John Arnot, Charles Cook, Henry Sherwood, Franklin N. Drake, Ferral C. Dininny, Henry H. Cook, and Lorenzo Webber. Constant Cook was a prominent banker and businessman of Bath, NY; John Arnot was a banker and one of the foremost citizens of Elmira; Charles Cook was a banker and distinguished citizen of Havana, NY; Henry Sherwood was a prominent lawyer of Corning, NY; Franklin N. Drake was a prominent businessman and lumberman of the upper waters of the Conhocton River; Ferral C. Dininny was a lawyer of distinction from Addison, NY; Henry H: Cook was a prominent citizen of Bath, NY, and Lorenzo Webber was a successful businessman of Watkins Glen, NY, later of Elmira. No stronger or more reliable company was ever formed in northern Pennsylvania. It represented all the elements of success in capital and business experience. The company purchased several thousand acres of valuable coal and timberland. It was by the charter permitted to construct a sufficient number of miles of railroad to enable them to transport their coal to a connecting line. In the summer of 1866, they constructed a railroad from Blossburg to this place, a distance of about four miles, in the meantime erecting a sawmill for cutting out lumber to erect the necessary dwellings, shops, schools, stores, and offices.

The site of the village was covered with a heavy growth of hemlock, beech, maple, and other timber. This had to be removed to make way for the contemplated buildings. For several months Messrs. Webber and Drake gave the work their personal attention. Mr. Drake removing from Steuben County to Blossburg, the better to oversee the preliminary developments. About the year 1867, the company purchased the railroad from Blossburg to the state line at Lawrenceville, twenty-five miles, and from Blossburg to Morris Run, four miles, aggregating about thirty-four miles with what they already owned. Ferral C. Dininny, one of their corporators, was selected as superintendent, which position he occupied very satisfactorily until he severed his connection with the company by selling out and engaging in the anthracite coal trade. By the way, Uncle Jonas, when we get back to Elmira, we must call on Mr. Dininny. He has built a large and very costly residence on the Colonel Foster farm. But to proceed. The company proceeded to erect buildings as fast as possible and to open up the mines and to increase their domain by adding several thousand acres more of valuable timbered land. Like all new enterprises, it had some drawbacks, but as early as 1873, they mined and shipped to market three hundred and twenty-one thousand, two hundred and seven tons of merchantable coal, besides quite a large amount of timber and lumber. Thus, did the company continue to prosper until about ten years ago, when some of the members withdrew, and Franklin N. Drake became the president and held that position until the company sold out their interest to the Erie railroad company about two years since. During the presidency of Mr. Drake, new openings were made, the coke ovens constructed, and many valuable improvements made. The sale of coal increased, and the reputation of the coal and coke was established upon a firm basis. There are now about 400 dwellings, several churches, and schoolhouses, besides the necessary shops, mills, and stores, schutes and weigh offices required. The population is variously estimated from 2,800 to 3,000 persons. During the construction of the Arnot and Pine Creek railroad from Arnot to Hoytville, Arnot probably contained

4,000 people. The past year has been a severe one for the miners, the coal trade being dull and the mines not working more than one-half time, and some months less than half time. The miners are of different nationalities. English, Irish, Scotch, Welsh, Swede, Polish, and German. As a class, they are very social and companionable, fond of music, lodges, churches, and associations. A mutual and aid society entitled the "Friendly Society" has, at times, been very strong here. There are a large number of Odd Fellows, quite a few Freemasons, besides Knights of Honor, Knights of Pythias and other societies. Many of the miners are great readers and are well informed. A public reading room was maintained here for several years. They are also very fond of music, both vocal and instrumental, have fine choirs, glee clubs, orchestras, and brass bands."

"The superintendent in charge is H. J. Landrus, a gentleman who has served many years in that capacity and is familiar with every portion of the work. He is a native of the township of Bloss and was employed several years before the war as weigh-master at Morris Run. He resigned his position in that place to enlist in the service of his country. At the close of the war he came home and was employed as bookkeeper for the Blossburg Coal Company and finally promoted to the position of superintendent, served in that capacity several years when he resigned and was elected sheriff of Tioga county. He is a staunch republican. Before he had completed his term of sheriff he was prevailed upon to again accept the position as superintendent, which he did, appointing a deputy to perform his official duties. He is a gentleman of fine physique and a person of great practical knowledge in business affairs and the management of mining operation. Civil engineer and surveyor R. A. Wentworth, is a young man of fine acquirements who has recently been engaged. In the paymaster's office, Frederic Wingrave, an old employee, is the cashier, assisted by William M. Dunsmore, with F. H. Dartt and F. H. Hyde clerks. The overseer at the mines is John

Dunsmore, a practical miner of long experience, who is assisted by John Hill, Schute boss, William B. Gilmore. The weighmaster is James N. Patterson. The coke ovens are in charge of Alexander Logan, who has competent workmen and assistants. In the store J. L. Higgins is manager. Mr. Higgins has filled this responsible position for many years, is a trusted employee and a fine merchant. The clerks are Richard Smith, John Burke, William R. Logan, George C. Lee and Matthew Blair, gentlemen who have been long employed and thoroughly competent and reliable. There are three schools maintained in the village; Andrew B. Dunsmore is the principle of number one, assisted by Miss Kate VanNess; number two; Miss Kate Neil and Ella McInroy; number three, Miss Aggie Logan, Mamie Smettem, Laura Brown and Mina Hall."

"The company is owners of a first-class steam fire engine, and the Dunsmore Hose company constitutes their fire department. It is a very efficient one, too. They have about 1,500 feet of hose and other necessary appliances. Frank H. Dartt is foreman of the company."

"There are four church edifices: Catholic, Presbyterian, Welsh Baptist and Swedish. The Methodists hold service in the schoolhouse. The resident physicians are D. C. Waters and Charles S. Logan. Dr. Waters has been many years located here, and is highly esteemed by the citizens: Dr. Logan is a young physician who bids fair to win an enviable fame. The Arnot cornet band consists of sixteen members, with Thomas Heron as leader. Mr. Heron is a fine musician, and the band is distinguished for its excellent music. The sawmill is in charge of Nicholas Shultz, an old employee of the company. About 4,000,000 feet of lumber is annually manufactured. The feed mill is in charge of Charles Hahn, a very competent miller. Frank Keagle is the foreman in the blacksmith shop and Nathan Edwards in the carpenter shop. The employees in L. H. Drake's store are Andrew Bowers, William Bowers, Sr., William Bowers, 2nd, John Bowers, and Charles Warner. The postmaster is H. J. Landrus. The station agent is H. A. Mitchell, who also is telegraph operator. Mr. Mitchell has been employed several years in that capacity and is an efficient employee."

"The township officers are School director, John Hill, president; Fred Wingrave, secretary; "John Dunsmore, treasurer; and members, Alexander Logan, Albert S. Johnson, Silas E. Shepard. Justices of the peace, Samuel Heron, Jonathan Hutchinson; constable, George Allen; supervisors, Robert Esgar, James Morehess; town clerk, William M. Dunsmore; treasurer, Richard Grant; assessor, Frank H. Dartt; collector, Fred Wingrave."

"You say, Harry, that this village, consisting of over four hundred dwellings and all of its shops, stores, schutes, coke yards, mines, mills, etc., belong to the Erie railroad company?"

"Yes, Uncle Jonas, together with over twenty thousand acres of land. The railroad boys have about finished switching out the cars, and we shall soon move on towards Landrus."

"Observe, Uncle Jonas, that pagoda or bandstand up yonder on the hill, by the schoolhouse? The Arnot Band often meet there, and from their elevated position, every citizen of Arnot is enabled to sit in their own doors and listen to the fine music rendered by that admirable organization. The melody is softened, borne on the evening breeze, and wafted up and along the hills and valleys and enjoyed by those wearied by the day's toil, and their spirits enlivened and quickened by the melody that floats in the air. When there is plenty of remunerating work, no happier community exists than this. For the distance of five or six miles now, Uncle Jonas, we will pass through the lands of the company. On either side you perceive that the timber has been cut and removed. A year ago, last May, a terrible fire raged through this region, consuming much valuable property and destroying a number of dwellings at Arnot."

113

"The settlement with this mammoth sawmill is Landrus. This also belongs to the Erie Railroad Company. The sawmill, if run to its full capacity, would manufacture from eighteen to twenty million feet of lumber annually. This lumbering village is in charge of Robert F. Cummings, a gentleman who has had a large experience in work of this kind. He was many years connected with the Fall Brook coal company's works at Fall Brook, and about three years since he took charge of this place, commencing with the mill from its foundation and directing its construction. The company is fortunate in securing his services."

"The village is named Landrus in honor of H. J. Landrus, the superintendent at Arnot. A post office has been established here with R. F. Cummings as postmaster. The station agent here is William B. Jones, a young man of excellent morals and good business habits. He is also telegraph operator. We have passed the Summit, Uncle Jonas, and we will descend grade to Hoytville. There are one or two flag stations between here and there."

"Hoytville, Uncle Jonas, is situated in the township of Morris on Babb's creek."

"Oh, I remember Samson Babb well. He was one of the pioneers in northern Pennsylvania. He came here about the year 1800, so he told me. He occasionally came to Elmira. He and his sons had quite a fine farm here forty years ago or more."

"We will talk over, Uncle Jonas, the early history of this place at a future time. I want you to see the largest tannery in the world, and we have but a little time to look it over and return to Blossburg on the train."

"Very well, Harry, give me its modern history."

"About four years ago, to be brief. Uncle Jonas, the Hoyt brothers, of New York, purchased the Babb property and some twenty thousand acres of hemlock lands surrounding it and commenced the erection of this mammoth tannery. They must have expended around millions of dollars in

114

lands and plants. This vast expenditure of money attracted persons in here from all parts of the country. Stores, shops, dwellings, mills and hotels, were soon erected by persons not connected with the company. The company, however, in addition to their tannery, erected about fifty dwellings or more for their employees. Contemporaneous with the erection of the tannery, a company was formed, consisting principally of those who were interested in the Tioga Railroad Company, known as the Arnot & Pine Creek Railroad Company, who constructed a railroad from Arnot here so that by the time that the tannery was in readiness to commence the manufacture and shipment of leather, the railroad was finished. The tannery is known as the Brunswick tannery. The superintendent is Samuel S. Van Etten. The overseer in charge of inside work is Michael Lawler, gentlemen competent to fill their responsible positions. The bookkeeper and paymaster is A. E. Spicer, assisted by Eugene Clark. Several clerks are employed in the store. The capacity of the tannery is about one thousand sides per day or three hundred and thirteen thousand annually. It would take, Uncle Jonas, a drove of five hundred of your best western steers per day to furnish the rawhides for this tannery or one hundred and fifty-seven thousand annually. And here let me remark, Uncle Jonas, that the sixteen tanneries in Tioga County now in operation would require one million four year old western steers to furnish the hides —your state of Illinois is not equal to the task, so the proprietors of these tanneries are obliged to purchase South American hides. This is indeed a remarkable village, Harry, surrounded by wilderness in this valley of Babb's creek. Yes, Uncle Jonas, and here are all the marks of civilization. Yonder is a schoolhouse, down there is a church, and up yonder is another, here is a fine depot, across the way is a bakery, there a hotel, yonder a sawmill, and across the track is a handle manufactory, while stores, millinery shops, drug stores, dry goods stores, meat markets, and other establishments go to make up a bustling and thriving village of 1,000 inhabitants. It was commendable foresight which induced the Erie managers to purchase this Tioga branch, which from here to Elmira runs through so many thriving villages and towns and penetrating these centers of industry — thus furnishing passengers and freight to their great trunk line and affording the tourist so many pleasing and romantic views. The station agent at Hoytville is John J. Gavigan, a young man who has from boyhood been a trusted employee of the company. Now we are off to Blossburg again."

"I declare, Harry, this has been a very pleasant trip today. I have seen many things new to me and upon which I shall reflect in the future. The immense tanneries, the coke yards and ovens,   the   mines   of semi-bituminous coal, the mountains, and forests, the busy hum of industry, in the great mills here made a deep impression upon me, which I shall not soon forget."

"Here we are in Blossburg again. We will get a room and prepare for supper at once, for this mountain air has given me a sharp appetite. "

"Tomorrow, Harry, you say we are to go to Morris Run and Fall Brook."

"Yes, Uncle Jonas, that is the intention. I had intended to give you an idea of the township south of us — Union and Liberty — tonight, but as you seem fatigued I will put it off to a more convenient season. Perhaps, too, we may find time to take a trip to the Blockhouse, and thence east into Union to Ogdensburg, and thence to Blossburg before we leave this vicinity. If we do not, I will describe them to you."

MORRIS RUN AND FALL BROOK.
INTERESTING STATISTICS AND PLEASANT PERSONALITIES.

"All aboard for Morris Run."

"That is meant for us, Uncle Jonas. Yonder is the train, in charge of that veteran conductor, William M. Butler, who for more than twenty years, in sunshine and in storm, has made his regular trips. The engineer is also a veteran of thirty years or more service in railroading. I allude to James Green, heretofore spoken of. Uncle Jonas, this is William M. Butler, the conductor."

"Are you a son of William Butler, a former citizen of this place?"

"Yes, sir."

"I am very glad to meet you, Mr. Butler; your father and I met years ago at Elmira in a masonic lodge. There was another gentleman also who usually accompanied him, the Hon. Clarendon Rathbone."

"Yes, Mr. Lawrence, they were both Freemasons and frequently went to Elmira to attend masonic meetings before any were instituted in this county. You will have to excuse me, Mr. Lawrence, for the present. I will see you again."

"This, Uncle Jonas, is the weigh office, where the coal is weighed from Morris Run and Fall Brook. I mentioned this before. Henry Hollands and Frank Stratton are the weighmasters and shippers."

"What cemetery is that, Harry,"

"That, Uncle Jonas, belongs to Arbon Lodge of Odd Fellows. They are beautiful grounds. Here on the west side of the track is the union cemetery. Many of the old pioneers of Blossburg and surrounding country are laid to rest there. Adjoining that is the cemetery owned by the Catholics. It is well kept. Right opposite the Union cemetery on the banks of the Tioga

River is where Judge Knapp erected a sawmill sixty years ago. No trace of it is seen now."

"Look, Harry! We must be ascending a very steep grade. Only a few minutes ago we were on a level or nearly with the river, but now we are at least eighty feet above it."

"The grade is nearly 100 feet to the mile, Uncle Jonas. Blossburg, you recollect I told you, was 1,348 above tide, and the mines at Morris Run are 1,678, a little over three miles distant, making the elevation of the mines at Morris Run 330 higher than Blossburg.

"Here we are at Morris Run. Now, Uncle Jonas, suppose we walk up to the Morris Run Hotel, kept by Matthew Waddel, and where we can look over the village and rest ourselves. I can from this porch point out the various places of interest, and at the same time give you a brief history of this interesting and busy mining village. This creek that we are crossing over is Morris Run. It is named in honor of the late Hon. Samuel W. Morris, of Wellsboro, who was prominently connected with the construction of the Corning and Blossburg railroad, nearly fifty years ago. I was acquainted with Judge Morris, Harry; He represented this district in Congress in the years 1836-7."

"Oh, yes, Harry, I have met him. But we will speak of him again. Go on with your history."

"Well to continue, over thirty years ago, a company named the Tioga Improvement Company opened up the mines here and constructed a railroad from Blossburg here. The mining superintendent in charge was John Young, who resided in that log house you see here to the left of us. The Tioga Improvement Company operated the mines until the year 1862, and then leased them to the salt company of Onondaga, who soon made preparations to carry on mining on a more extensive scale. They erected a sawmill, store, and a number of dwellings, built new schutes and made many improvements. In 1861 the salt company sold out their lease to the Morris Run Coal Company, who continued to enlarge the capital of the mining operations. About nine years ago the Morris Run Coal Company surrendered its charter and the Morris Run Coal & Mining Company was incorporated, which has operated the mines up to the present, a controlling interest being held by the trustees of the estate of the late Hon. John Magee. Mr. Waddell, this is Uncle Jonas Lawrence, who has come to make this village a visit."

"Glad to meet you, gentlemen, walk-in."

"No, thank you, Mr. Waddell, we will sit here a few minutes on the porch and take a look at the town. Mr. Waddell, Uncle Jonas, is one of the pioneer miners in this village. He has been a resident here for many years, is a Scotchman by birth. He has been prominently connected with the establishment of an Odd Fellows' lodge in this place, and also at Blossburg — holding all the responsible positions in the lodge and discharging the duties with marked ability and fidelity. That large store across the track, Uncle Jonas, belongs to the company and is in charge of Major T. B. Anderson, formerly of Syracuse, NY. The major came here in the year 1863 and took charge of the mercantile business for the salt company previously referred to, and when it sold out to the Morris Run Coal Company he was retained by the incoming company, and has continued to occupy most faithfully and honestly that position up to the present, with the prospect of remaining many years to come. No man in northern Pennsylvania has done more than the major to put into practice the principles of friendship, love, and truth. He is a prominent Odd Fellow and Free Mason. His heart is overflowing with charity, benevolence, and goodwill towards his neighbors, the sick, and the afflicted. He is truly a noble grand. He is assisted in the store by Albert C. Frost, H. A. Monroe, William Glenright, Edward Kilbourn, William Hayes, clerks, and Miss Aggie Gilmour, bookkeeper. Do you observe that octagon roofed building with a store vault attached to the rear, over yonder on the hillside? "

"Yes."

"That, Uncle Jonas, is the office of the Morris Run Coal & Mining company. The officers of the company are General George J. Magee, president; Daniel Beach, treasurer; W. S. Nearing, general superintendent; Lewis Nearing, assistant superintendent. The occupants of the office are P. F. O'Donnell, paymaster; J. Norman Anderson, bookkeeper, and Thomas V. Keefe, accountant, and telegraph operator. Mr. O'Donnell is a gentleman who has, for the past twenty years, been connected with the office and during that time has received and paid out millions of dollars, disbursing this large sum with honesty and fidelity. He has taken no forced trips to Canada. His accounts have always been accurate to a cent. He is a man of pleasing address, courteous and gentlemanly. His associate, J. Norman Anderson, is a son of Major T. B. Anderson and has, for many years, occupied the responsible position of bookkeeper and assistant paymaster. He inherits the many good traits of his father and is distinguished for his urbanity, his prominence in the order of Odd Fellows and Knights of Honor and for the faithful performance of the work assigned him. Thomas V. Keefe is also a gentleman of merit, who has for many years faithfully and industriously attended to the duties devolved upon him. He is a fine musician and leader of the Morris Run Cornet Band. The general superintendent, William S. Nearing, has had charge of the work for the past twenty-one years and is one of the most skilled civil and mining engineers in the state of Pennsylvania. He has introduced into the workings of the mines the most approved appliances and the best system of mining and ventilation in the state. This is conceded by all who have examined the mines and are competent to judge. His son, Lewis Nearing, is a young man of rare accomplishments as an engineer, and assists him in the management of the mines, and for nearly two

120

years has had a personal supervision over them. William K. Gilmour is a mining foreman. He is one of the oldest residents of Morris Run, having been employed here in various capacities for the past thirty years or more. Mr. Gilmour is a distinguished Odd Fellow, a good miner and every way competent to discharge the work assigned him. At the Jones' mines, Michael Driscoll is the foreman. He has been employed for many years by the company, and is a faithful and competent man. The weighmaster at the Jones' mines is Samuel Woodhouse, a gentleman who was for many years a justice of the peace, and now metes out justice by giving fair and just weight between the miner and the company. The dispatcher or boss mule driver is Thomas Tuckey. That position, Uncle Jonas, is a very responsible one. He dispatches the different drivers, as a division dispatcher on one of the trunk railroads do trains. You will observe one characteristic, Uncle Jonas, about these men, that most of them have long been employed by the company. That I take is a compliment to the men and shows the sagacity of the company in continuing the old hands. At the new mine, Campbell Haddow is foreman and the weigh-master is William Tipton, and the boss mule driver or dispatcher, Edward Kelley, schute boss, Thomas E. Emms, all trusted men in their vocations. At the east mine, William R. Gilmour, heretofore alluded to, exercises general supervision. The weigh-master is O. T. Smith. The blacksmiths at the Jones mines are Michael Brown, James Brown and Michael Whalen. At the new mine the blacksmiths are James Woodhouse and Samuel Woodhouse, Jr. At the east mine the blacksmiths are John Stephenson and Thomas McMahon. Besides doing general blacksmithing work incident to the mining operations, one of the specialties is the sharpening and pointing of drills and miners' picks. The picks used by the miners are pointed with steel and drawn out to a point as small as a fork tine. When the pick becomes blunt it must be re-pointed. This is done by the blacksmith in a common blacksmith forge with a fire made from raw coal as it comes from the mines. If there was any sulfur in the coal this could not be done, as the sulfur would make the steel brittle and the pick point would break upon its first trial in the mines. This shows the superiority of the semi-bituminous coal of the Blossburg region, and this is the reason why it is sought after so extensively for smithing purposes. You notice steam issuing from that building down yonder on the creek?"

"Yes, I see it."

"That is the sawmill of the company. The outside foreman of the lumber department is Frank Church, who has a supervision overall outside work. Mr. Church has been employed for many years and is a faithful and competent man. This community, you perceive, Uncle Jonas has not neglected their educational or religious duties, for there are two schoolhouses and four church edifices. The churches have been erected by Primitive Methodists, the Welsh Congregationalists, Welsh Baptist and Catholic. The Rev. Thomas K. Beecher about five years ago came here from Elmira and preached in that church to a large and interested congregation. The teachers at present in the schoolhouse yonder to the south, in what is termed the Tioga district, are A. M. Johnson and wife. The teachers in the new school house are Mr. Hitchcock and Miss Cass. Besides the schools and churches there is one of the strongest and most influential lodges of Odd Fellows in this section, and a lodge of the Knights of Pythias and a Welsh secret benevolent society called the "Ivorites," besides quite a membership of Free Masons and Knights of Honor. There is a splendidly equipped and uniformed brass band here of twenty-two pieces under the leadership of Thomas V. Keefe. The people here are very fond of music, and some excellent and meritorious glee clubs have been formed here, as well as choirs and instrumental bands. There is also a baseball club here of considerable merit composed of the young men who work in the mines. This building opposite of us is a drug store owned and conducted by the resident physicians, William and H. E. Caldwell. Dr. William Caldwell is an old resident here, having located here about twenty years ago. His nephew, Dr. H. E. Caldwell, has resided here for about five years. That building down by the railroad track is used as a tin shop. William Halliday has charge of that and is a young man well skilled in his trade. The building farther down the track is the post office, ticket office and market. The market is owned and conducted by Ross & Williams of Mansfield, PA."

"The air compressor, one of the most useful inventions of the age, is located where you see that steam and smoke issuing from the pipe and stack between those schutes. James Middaugh is master of machinery. The air compressor is used in hauling coal by means of an endless rope from the mines, and also for working "iron men" or coal diggers by machinery. I will give you a full description of it at some future time. The engineers in charge are J. E. King in the day time, and E. N. King in the night time. The village of Morris Run contains about two thousand inhabitants, all directly or indirectly employed by the company. All the buildings are owned by the company. There is mined annually about three hundred and fifty thousand tons of semi-bituminous coal, which finds a market as far west as Colorado and east into Boston and the New England states. The vein of coal is about four feet thick, and lies nearly horizontal, between a top of slate and sand rock and a bed of hard, fine clay. The mines are laid out in squares, like any well-planned city. The streets are narrow and are gangways. In mining, every alternate square is left at first, until the ground has all been gone over. Then the mining is commenced at the rear end or side, and the pillars mined out towards the opening or mouth of the drift or mine. In going over the territory first, when the coal is mined out, props are set upright to prevent the chambers from being filled or broken down. The coal mines in northern Pennsylvania are all mined upon the same principle, and when we get to Fall Brook, Uncle Jonas, perhaps we will go into the mines and you can see how the mining is performed. It is a mile and a half from here. Uncle Jonas, over to Fall Brook. Shall we get a conveyance to take us over, or shall we walk?"

"I would prefer to walk, Harry. I can then go along carefully and examine the rocks and coal strata and many things that I would lose sight of were we to ride. Besides, the air of the elevation (about 1700 feet above tide), is rather too chilly at this time of the year for an old man like me to ride."

After spending a few minutes with Mr. Waddell, conversing on general topics, they leave for Fall Brook.

"There are one or two things, Uncle Jonas, that I neglected to point out to you, the Odd Fellows' Hall, that large building which you see down yonder on that high ground, and the public hall in   the valley below. That little locomotive you see over there is used in hauling the coal from the mouth of this drift here by the schutes. It performs the work of many mules. We will take it slowly until we get past that airshafts where you see the smoke coming out. The road there is nearly level for some distance. There is a large furnace at the bottom of that shaft, where a very hot fire is constantly kept burning for the purpose of heating or rarefying the air in the mines. It is the surest way of causing a current of air to pass through the mines. It is as certain as the law of gravitation, and based upon a principle that heated air forms a vacuum, and cooler air rushes forth to equalize the temperature. The bottom of that shaft where the furnace is, is connected with all the various chambers or working places in the mines, and by heating the air here at the mouth of the mine, all impurities and bad air are drawn to this point and escape into the open air by means of that shaft or flue. We have now reached the summit, about two thousand feet above tide. Now, Uncle Jonas, turn around and look to the south and westward."

"Oh!, Harry, these mountain landscapes are grand! To those who are penned up in the walls of a city what a relief it would be for them to stand here, breathe this pure mountain air and feast their eyes upon this landscape of mountain and valley scenery."

"This, Harry, is about the right altitude. The peaks of the White Mountains in the east and the Rocky Mountains in the west are too high for comfort and too rare for health. This is a happy medium. To the south and west here we can trace the outline of the mountain ranges as they extend towards the valley of the west branch of the Susquehanna, or northward to the valley of the Chemung. To the eastward we can see the ranges lessen in altitude until we approach the valley of the Wyoming, the summits and sides covered with a forest rich in all the colors which the artist nature has painted in their foliage. The dark green of the hemlock, the variegated colors of the maple, the beech, the oak, chestnut and birch as they are dressed in their autumnal suits, the outlines of farms, farmhouses, fields with their herds of sheep and cattle, present a picture unsurpassed in loveliness and grandeur. It brings one who feasts upon its splendor nearer to that great Architect who created all these things for the pleasure and enjoyment of the creatures of His handiwork. Then, again, as winter comes on, to see this region wrapped in a mantle so white and spotless, the thousand little rivulets locked in the embrace of the icy king, with icicles and pendants sparkling, refusing to melt beneath the feeble rays of the sun; and then again in springtime, when the sun has mounted high in the heavens, the thousand rills are released from their icy fetters and go dancing and singing on to the great ocean; when wildflowers are shedding their balmy odor broadcast upon the air, and the forests put on their brightest spring suits, the myriads of birds warbling their sweetest and most cheerful notes calls forth from man his adoration of that beneficent Creator, and inspires him with grand and noble thoughts and a love for the beautiful in nature. It makes his pulse beat warmer and quicker. It softens his heart. It always animosities and leads him to take a broader and more charitable view of mankind, and a greater reverence for God, and higher regard for His goodness and love for all."

"Here we are at the Fall Brook hotel, kept by John F. Dwyre, one of the best landlords in northern Pennsylvania. Mr. Dwyre, this is Uncle Jonas Lawrence. We have come to take dinner and spend the afternoon with you."

"Walk in, gentlemen; I am pleased to meet you."

"I declare, Harry, I did not expect to find so fine a hotel up here in the coal regions."

"Well, Uncle Jonas, while we are resting, I will give you a brief history of the hotel. It was erected during the year 1864, twenty- one years ago, and occupied by Warren Goff, of Howard, Steuben County, in the spring of 1865. It is a durable structure, a strong and lasting frame. Wages and material were high at the time of its erection, and the cost of the hotel with furniture was about $13,000. It was built by order of the late Hon. John Magee, upon a plan made by the late Humphries Brewer, manager for the Fall Brook coal company. The mechanic who had charge of the work was David Cooper, of Steuben county, N. Y. It was first opened by Warren Golf, as I have stated, and kept by him for about one year, who retired, and Libbius Phillips, of Addison, NY, kept it for five years or more, and was succeeded by C. B. Whitehead, John Van Order and others, and by the present accommodating host. Since its erection, among the many distinguished gentlemen who have been guests here I recall the names of the Hon. Horatio Seymour, Hon. Daniel E. Howell, Hon. Mr. Pillsbury, of Maine, Hon. E. K. Apgar, Hon. Richard Haldeman, Hon. John Arnot, Hon. C. L. Ward, Hon. B. F. Bruce, Hon. John Magee, Hon. Reuben E. Fenton, Col. John F. Means, Hon. Henry Sherwood, Hon. Stephen F. Wilson, Rt. Rev. Bishop

O'Hara, of Scranton, Bishop Stevens, of Philadelphia, Bishop De Wolfe, of Reading, PA, Hon, Stephen Pierce, Hon. Theodore Wright, Hon. Jerome B. Niles, and many other distinguished citizens of the country, who came here for business or pleasure. The hotel has an elevation of about 1,800 feet above the tide, and it is one of the pleasant retreats in summer for those seeking rest and quiet and pure air. Dinner is ready, Uncle Jonas."

They go to dinner, and after dinner, they go up to "Magee's room," from which they command a view of the borough of Fall Brook.

"Now, Uncle Jonas, take that easy chair by the cheerful fire in the grate, and I will give you a brief history of Fall Brook. When I think of the founding of Fall Brook, Uncle Jonas, by the Magees, I cannot help to remark how small things sometimes take men out of the channel which they had marked out to sail in, and how a trifling circumstance may change their whole course of action. To be more definite, Uncle Jonas, the Hon. John Magee was a banker at Bath, NY, and was largely interested in the Conhocton Valley railroad, now a branch of the Erie. In his business relations with the bank of Corning, NY, its officers became indebted to Mr. Magee. The officers of the Corning Bank held leases of the mines at Blossburg, and Mr. Magee, in order to secure his claim against the bank and its officers, was obliged to seize upon their lease of the mines, also upon the fifteen miles of railroad from Corning to the state line at Lawrenceville. I was at that time directly interested in the prosperity of the Corning Bank, whose officers were Hiram W. Bostwick, William, and Laurin Mallory, and was familiar with the transaction. After Mr. Magee had secured the lease and the dilapidated fifteen miles of railroad, there was an informal meeting of the stockholders of the bank at Corning, at which Mr. Magee, the Hon. John McBurney, Jonathan Brown, Benjamin Patterson, John L. Sexton, Robert Patterson, Nathan Reynolds, David H. Bonham, William Wambaugh, Frederick K. Holcott and Eli Lyon were among the persons present. Mr.

127

Magee desired that the men should purchase the road and lease of the mines from him, offering to make liberal deductions from his claims. The amount of Mr. Magee's claim was about $25,000, and he offered to take the notes of the above-named gentlemen for $18,000, 'for,' said Mr. Magee, 'I have an elephant on my hands, and I want to get rid of him.' The parties did not see fit to accept of Mr. Magee's proposition, and the meeting disbanded. Before, Uncle Jonas, that Mr. Magee left Corning I had a conversation with him, told him I was acquainted with the Blossburg region, the coal, the lumber along on the line, and that I believed it would pay him to send Duncan S. Magee, his son, up to Blossburg, continue the mining of the coal, and if needs be to construct a new road up the Tioga Valley— that it was rich in coal and timber. The old gentleman and I parted, Mr. Magee, still claiming that he had all the business he could attend without going into the mining and shipping of coal. Mr. Magee, as the sequel proves, reconsidered, sent his son Duncan S. Magee to Blossburg, and commenced mining coal under the lease. This business he carried on for two or three years, and then organized a corps of explorers, consisting of Humphries Brewer and G. A. Beckus, civil engineers and geologists, Thomas Farrar, John James, William Griffiths, Thomas Morgan, George Cook, John Evans, and Stephen Bowen, and explored this region, and finally prevailed upon his father to purchase about 6,000 acres surrounding this place. When it was once demonstrated that there were fine fields of coal here, the old gentleman, the Hon. John Magee took hold of the matter with great energy. The explorations commenced in 1856. The Fall Brook Company was incorporated in April 1859, consisting of John Magee, Duncan S. Magee, and James P. Gulick. The railroad was constructed from Blossburg here in the summer and fall of 1859. The first officers of the company were the Hon. John Magee, president; John Lang, treasurer; D. S. Magee, superintendent; H. Brewer, a civil engineer. The first shipment of coal from here was in the month of December 1859. In the spring of 1860, the coal trade opened quite briskly. The company secured valuable- franchises at Watkins, NY, at the head of Seneca Lake, and opened up an office there, erected schutes, trestles, and shipping docks. An office was also opened at Corning, with Andrew Beers agent. At Fall Brook, a sawmill was erected on the falls, and the work of cutting down the forest, erecting dwellings, stores, and shops were prosecuted with great vigor. A supply store was opened here upon the site of this hotel, and James Heron installed as a storekeeper, with Alfred T. James and Thomas J. Hall clerks. Old number one drift. Uncle Jonas passed a few feet north of where you sit, and the schutes and weigh offices were where that sawmill now stands. The coal soon gained a good reputation, and for years all that could be mined was readily sold at a fair price. The little store which stood upon the site of this hotel was found to be inadequate in size, and a larger one was erected up yonder a few rods north of here. In about four years, a wing was attached. Mr. Heron was the store agent, paymaster, etc., for several years, when the business of the office demanded his whole time and attention, besides the assistance of two clerks, O. Pattison and C. L. Pattison, brothers, which had to be increased from time to time. The store was placed in charge of Frank Lewis, with several clerks to assist him. Mr. Lewis was transferred to Bath, and Charles E. Halsey, of Hammondsport, NY, installed in his stead, who occupied that very responsible position for more than ten years. Among the old clerks that I recall, who served in the office and the store, were Charles Ford, Daniel Wheeler, Frederic Barrows, John L. Sexton, Jr., James Mills, John Forrest, Jr., William Forrest, A. J. Pollock, T. J. Hall, William E. Butts, Sam Sexton, J. W. Personius, I. S. Marshall, Roland Hall, and R. F. Cummings. The company opened up the mines in several places. For many years Alexander Pollock was foreman of drifts numbers one and two. William Griffiths foreman of drifts number three, number two A and number two B.

The first weighmaster and shipper of coal was John Morse, succeeded by Peter Cameron, Jr., and he by John L. Sexton, Jr., and William D. Lynahan. Thomas Reese was for many years weighmaster at drifts numbers one, two, and three. Duncan S. Magee continued superintendent for several years, giving the work his personal attention, becoming acquainted with all the employees, and with the very details of the business. As the work developed and the coal trade increased, he had his headquarters at Watkins Glen, and Humphries Brewer was manager until his death, December 25, 1867. Mr. Brewer was a geologist and civil engineer and was eminent in his profession. Contemporaneous with the building up of the town came the erection of schoolhouses and churches and the establishment of lodges and friendly societies. There are two schools in the borough, sufficient to accommodate 300 scholars. After the death of Mr. Brewer, in 1867, James Heron, the cashier, was promoted to that position, and C. L. Pattison to that of the cashier. In the year 1872, Mr. Heron died and was succeeded by D, W. Knight, who had previously taken place in the office held by C. L. Pattison. John Hinman was for many years a valued assistant in the office but was transferred in the year 1871 to the company's new mines at Antrim, PA, where for several years, he held the responsible position of paymaster at that place and resigned to enter into business in Raleigh, North Carolina. John Forrest, Jr., was for many years in the office and was transferred to Clermont, McKean County, to take charge of the office at that place. In the year 1804, Fall Brook was incorporated as a borough — taken from the township of Ward. L. C. Shepard was the first burgess and held the position for ten successive years when he refused to accept the position longer, and John L. Sexton, Jr., was elected, but soon after resigned to accept a position in the office of the secretary of internal affairs at Harrisburg, PA. The office has since been filled by James Pollock, R. F. Cummings, and others. Mr. Shepard is the present burgess. He has been for many years a resident of Fall Brook. The Presbyterian Church was organized in the year 1860, upon the petition of Alexander Pollock, James Heron, Alexander Pollock, Jr., James Pollock, Peter Cameron, Jr., Robert Logan, John Dunsmore, George Snedden, William Watchman, E. J. Evans, David Pryde. The petition was granted and the church organized with twenty-two members, and the Rev. George Blair secured as its first minister. Its first officers were the Hon. John Magee, Duncan S. Magee, Alexander Pollock, Sr., trustees; H. Brewer, treasurer; James Heron, secretary; Alexander Pollock, Sr., Robert Logan, David Pryde, Samuel Heron, William Watchman and Reese Thomas committee of management.

"Episcopal services were held in 1864 by the Rev. E. D. Loveridge, of Hammondsport, NY. In 1866 Bishop Lee, of Delaware, visited Fall Brook and confirmed Mary Frazee and Mary Brewer. C. E. Halsey and John Hinman about that time organized a Sunday school, which grew into a very large and numerously attended school. July 30, 1867, application was made to the court of common pleas of Tioga County by Charles E. Halsey, John Hinman, Lewis Clark, John B. Christie, J. W. Personius, John L. Sexton, Jr., John Alderson, and Thomas Gaffney to be incorporated under the title of the Rector, churchwarden, and vestrymen of St. Thomas church. Fall Brook, which application was granted December 5, 1867, and ordered on file in the notary's office. Its first officers were Charles E. Halsey and John Hinman, wardens; John L. Sexton, Jr., Lewis Clark, John B. Christie, M. D., Joel W. Personius, and John Alderson, vestrymen."

"The cornerstone of the Catholic church was laid with appropriate ceremonies on August 31, 1873, by the Rt. Rev. Bishop O'Hara, of Scranton, PA, assisted by the Revs. Gerald McMurray, John A. Wynne and John McDermott. It was first used for religious services April 26, 1874, the Rev. Father Garvey, of Williamsport, assisted by the pastors, the Rev John A. Wynne and John McDermott, performing the opening ceremonies."

"One schoolhouse was erected in the year 1860, and it was proving insufficient another was erected in 1864-65 and in the summer of 1873 both were enlarged and refitted. As the population increased it was found advisable to secure the services of a competent physician to reside in the town. Dr. Davidson was the first regular resident physician and he was soon succeeded by Dr. Henry Kilbourn, and he by Drs. John B. Christie and Robert Christie, and the two latter by Dr. A. R. Barton, who remained for several years."

"There are many incidents, Uncle Jonas, which I would be glad to relate to you concerning the early development of Fall Brook, which our limited visit will not permit. You can see that notwithstanding this was a new town erected in the wilderness, it was not wanting in those requisites necessary to civilized societies. They instituted schools, churches, lodges, friendly societies and library associations. The Fall Brook Lodge, Kd. 765, I. O. O. F., was instituted June 15, 1873,— the Fall Brook Friendly Society May 15, 1873. The population consisted of Americans, English, Irish, Scotch, Welsh, Swedes and Germans. It was very seldom that the supposed natural national prejudices existing between these people culminated in any breach of the peace or disorderly conduct. Instead of any manifestation of that kind showing itself the other and more fraternal feeling existed among the citizens of all nationalities. They became acquainted with each other, they mingled in churches and lodges, at their work in the mines, in the mills, in the store, and in the forest, and learned to respect each other, and their rights and privileges. They assisted each other in sickness and in death. No person ever became a town or county charge. Although, Uncle Jonas, the history of Fall Brook only dates back about thirty years from its first exploration, still it has not been slow in interesting events. We will walk around after a little and make the acquaintance of A. J. Owen, the store manager, a gentleman who has for many years been in the employ of the company, having been their agent at Corning for a number of years, and about fourteen years ago he came here. We will find Mr. Owen in the office. In the office we will find A. N. Williams, bookkeeper, and D. S. Krull, order clerk. Mr. Williams is a gentleman who for the past twenty years has been in the employ of the company, and is a very courteous and pleasant official. Mr. Krull has recently been employed, but comes well recommended, and no doubt will meet the expectations of his friends. In the store we will find Fred G. Elliott, son of the Hon. N A. Elliott, of Mansfield, and the only brother of the Hon. Mortimer F. Elliott, the distinguished lawyer of Wellsboro, PA. Fred G. Elliott is a gentleman with whom it is a pleasure to meet, gentlemanly, courteous and social. His assistants m the store are M. S. Murray, Frank Kennedy and D. L. Laraby, gentlemen well suited to the Work at hand, competent and trusty. We must go up to the mines and call on Fred H. Wells and his assistant, Robert Russell. Messrs. Wells and Russell are practical miners. Mr. Wells is also a civil engineer, and has been employed in various capacities by the company for the past twenty-five years or more. Mr. Russell has not served quite so long, but about twenty years. They are competent men. We also want to make the acquaintance of John Shepard, the boss mule driver, and see with what dexterity he dispatches the drivers to their various places in the mines. Mr. Shepard has been many years employed by the company. And, while we are in that locality we must call on the venerable Anson Wells, the blacksmith who for a quarter of a century or more has sharpened and pointed the picks and drills for the mines. There we will also find another old veteran, John McCann, who has been employed for the past quarter of a century by the Fall Brook company. We will meet Sanford Dewey, another old and faithful employee. We must also call on D. S. Dewey, weighmaster, and see with what accuracy and dispatch he weighs the coal as it comes from the mines. We must also call on John G. Jones, the telegraph operator and shipper. He has served the company for several years and holds a very responsible position. We must not omit, Uncle Jonas, to call at the school and see with what care Miss Anna Gilmore and Miss Clements instruct the rising generation. We will on our return call on J. W. Taylor, outside foreman, having in charge the lumber department. His position is a very responsible one, and calls into action a great degree of knowledge and experience. In the same office we will find L. C. Shepard, the worthy chief burgess, who for the past quarter of a century has been employed by the company in various responsible capacities. We then want to cross over into the mule barns and interview John Junk and James Chambers, who have charge of a large number of mules and horses, and perform other labors. They are both worthy citizens and have long been residents of Fall Brook. We then should go and call on William F. O'Donnell, an old and valuable employee of the company, who now has charge of the market. In that same building we will find the town hall, and the elegant lodge rooms of the Odd Fellows and the Knights of Honor. Passing up the track we must look into the sawmill of the company, now in charge of Hugh Crawford, and see what admirable work he does in sawing lumber for the mines and for market. We will then pass along by the store and office to the northward. In the fallow as it is termed. We will pass the Presbyterian church and the shipping yards of A. Van Sickels & Co., Edward Sullivan, contractor. The lumber and bark comes from the estate of the late Hon. C. L. Ward and hauled there for shipment. About 3,000,000 feet of hemlock lumber and 1,000,000 of hardwood lumber and 3,000 tons of bark are annually shipped there and go over the Fall Brook railroad. Beyond the shipping yard, we will find the Fallow schoolhouse, capable of seating comfortably 150 scholars, divided into two rooms, both on the ground floor, and so arranged by sliding doors that it can be used as one room. There we will find Miss Kate Purcell laboring to instruct the children. And should we have time we will visit the cemetery on the hillside, where we would find the graves of Humphries Brewer, Gustavus A. Beckus, James Heron and many others who once held prominent positions with the company or were pioneers in the work. Should we still have time at our disposal we might go out to Holmesville, a lumbering town, just over the fine of the borough, and in doing so pass the shaft recently put down by the Fall Brook coal company and from which they are hoisting coal to the surface. At the shaft we would find several old employees, Nelson A. Welles, who has charge of the engine in the daytime, and O. L. Fields, who has charge of it at night. In the blacksmith shop we would find Malachi Kane, who for twenty years has continuously been employed by the company. At Holmesville, PA, we would find a lumbering village of twenty buildings, a sawmill owned by Edward Holmes, a good businessman, and a gentleman."

"Returning we could call on G. W. Ingham, the homeopathic physician, and Dr. D. W. Brown, the regular or allopathic, both genial and companionable gentlemen and proficient in their profession. And then, Uncle Jonas, we could sit here in the evening by this genial fire and talk over the history and development of this mining town away up here in the mountains of Northern Pennsylvania, and show how it was indirectly the cause of stimulating the opening up of other mines in this county, the building of railroads and establishments of tanneries, glass manufactories and the increase and population of the county — to speak of its influence in developing the agricultural interest of the surrounding country and its future."

"I am surprised, Harry, at the intelligence and public spirit of these mining communities. I had been led to believe that they were pretty generally uncivilized districts."

"There, Uncle Jonas, you are mistaken. The company employs the very best business talent in the country. When they get a good man, he is retained for years. The father of this landlord, Patrick Dwyre, has been over thirty consecutive years in the employ of the company, and there are many instances I could cite you where men have been employed continuously for ten, fifteen, twenty, and twenty-five years, proving faithful to their trust. By this course, the men become interested in the work, interested in schools, churches, lodges, and whatever conduces to the best interest of the community. A large number of newspapers are taken and read by these people. You can go to the post office here and find London, Glasgow, Dublin, Glamorganshire, Berlin, Stockholm, as well as New York, Elmira, Philadelphia, Harrisburg, and local county papers. There is less litigation in the mining districts of Tioga county than in any other section. There is no petty thieving, no pilfering, and plundering going on here. They may be rather uncultivated in their manners, bat they possess the true elements of politeness and civility. Let us go out among them.

TIOGA COUNTY CONTINUED.
PIONEER DAYS AND MODERN TIMES COMPARED.

"How do you feel this morning, Uncle Jonas?"

"Very well, Harry, I am gaining strength every day."

"After breakfast, Uncle Jonas, we will take a walk down to the falls and see the waters dashing and tumbling over the rocks on its way to the Tioga River, thence to the Chesapeake Bay. The descent of Fall Brook is about eighty feet in a few rods as it goes over the falls, forming one of the most attractive views in the country. No doubt, the red man frequently sat and gazed upon the scene with delight and prized it as one of his most valuable and cherished resorts."

"The Fall Brook coal company formerly utilized the water by erecting a sawmill upon the rocks, which manufactured the first lumber used herein the erection of dwellings, stores, schutes, and other necessary buildings. They, however, removed the mill and erected a large one driven by steam."

Uncle Jonas and Harry visit the falls and then take the cars for Blossburg. On their way down, they observe the well-planned device for ascending and descending the mountains by means of back switches, the railroad having for the first mile and a half the form of the letter Z. After reaching O'Neill's switch, the course of the railroad is upon a regular grade of about eighty feet to the mile, down the ravine or narrow valley of Fall Brook to its intersection with the upper waters of the Tioga River. In their descent, they observe the openings in the mountain on the west, made by the Morris Run Coal & Mining Company, which extends through the mountain to Morris Run. As they arrive at the Tioga river, they soon come to Somerville, a little hamlet, where for years, the coal shipped to market by the Fall Brook Coal Company was weighed and properly consigned.

137

William D. Lynaham now of Corning, NY, for many years resided there and manipulated the weights. A few rods below Somerville, the river and the railroad escape through a narrow pass in the mountains, and from that point, the valley widens and grows broader and more fertile until you reach the state line at Lawrenceville, some thirty miles to the northward. From Somerville to Corning, one engine will haul one hundred and twenty-five coal cars, it being downgraded most of the way. In a few minutes. Uncle Jonas and Harry reach Blossburg and are kindly received at the Seymour house. They secure a carriage from the livery with Sammy Sage as driver and proceed down the valley of the Tioga upon the old Williamson road.

"We are now approaching. Uncle Jonas, the Township line between the borough of Blossburg and the township of Covington. Does this look natural to you?"

"No, Harry, I think the highway has been changed some in its course since I came this way many years ago. We must be now, Harry, upon the Captain David Clemmons estate."

"Yes, we are, Uncle Jonas" — "I recollect Captain David Clemmons well, Harry. He was a native of Hampshire County, Massachusetts, and had been a resident of Essex and Clinton Counties in New York before he came here. While he resided in Clinton county he was commissioned by Governor John Jay May 3, 1798, a lieutenant in the uniformed companies of that county, and while residing at Jay, Essex County, he was commissioned by Governor George Clinton March 10, 1803, a captain, and discharged the duties of that office until he removed to Covington in 1806. He purchased in the township of Covington several hundred acres of land, a portion of which was located in the present borough of Blossburg. He opened up a vein of bituminous coal, which subsequently was mined quite extensively, for those days, by the Arbon Coal Company, and their successors, William M. Mallory & Co., Duncan S. Magee, and is now owned and operated by Mr. Jacob Jones, of Blossburg. The coal, therefore, with justice, should be called the Clemmons coal instead of the Bloss coal, as it was upon the lands which the captain owned, that the greater portion of the coal that was shipped was mined. When he came here into Covington township he was a widower with three children, Camilla, Colborn and Hanson. He was afterwards married to Ruth Reynolds, and their children were William, Cuyler, Susan, Roxanna and James, and many of the captain's descendants are living in this locality, and a portion of the Clemmons' estate is still owned by them."

"Some people on this day, Harry, claim that the old settlers were prone to tell large and extravagant fishing and hunting stories which cannot be substantiated by facts. Right across the river, Harry, is an indisputable evidence that this section was once the very center of fishing operations, where they were generated by the million. Away back in the geological history of the world, before man was created, there existed in the Silurian age, untold numbers of fishes, for behold, at the foot of that mountain there is a deposit now to be seen of fishes, while the summit of the mountain is a thousand feet higher. It would seem that in order to dispose of the immense multitude of fishes that abounded in this region, the rocks of the Devonian age, the deposits of the Carboniferous or Coal age, the reptilian, mammalian and the age of man, six great periods embracing countless million years, were piled upon this age of fishes to hide and exterminate them. Yet in this nineteenth century the rivers and streams were literally overflowing with fish, so tenacious are they of life and so prolific in propagation. The strata of fish extends beneath that mountain and have remained there for countless centuries, while above it are deposits of sand rock, lime, slate, iron, fire-clay, coal and immense deposits of rock and earth. That is a fish story which has defied the hand of time to obliterate its outlines, or modern storytellers to invent a larger or truer one. Where that orchard of old trees is, where

Captain Clemmons once lived and hereto the left is what is termed his homestead. This, Harry, is where I stopped with Judge Knapp in 1826. A little farther on is the homestead of Richard Videan, Esq., or Uncle 'Dick,' as he was familiarly called. He was an Englishman by birth and settled on that farm about the year 1831. He was one of the most industrious, genial and companionable men on the road. He accumulated a fine property and cleared a fine farm in an unbroken wilderness. He died April 6, 1873, aged seventy-four years six months and twelve days.

The present owner of the beautiful farm and homestead is A. J. Watkins, who is the owner of about 400 acres of land, the largest portion of which is under a high state of cultivation. Another old settler on this road was Tilley Marvin, who settled here in the year 1817, cleared up a large farm, and was one of the most industrious men in this locality. He was four times married and was the father of twenty-four children."

"Sammy, drive over on the east side of the river. This, Uncle Jonas, is the residence of Charles F. King, who owns this grist mill and a large farm surrounding it. This is the late residence of John Wilson, son of one of the early pioneers, Sumner Wilson. Here, Uncle Jonas, is the old Covington graveyard, where Aaron Bloss and many other of the old citizens who have passed away are buried. The glass manufactory on the right here belongs to Hirsch, Ely & Co., the same firm that operates the factory at Blossburg. It is a co-operate company each one being assigned a particular duty. It is about sixteen years since they organized with ten members at Blossburg. They have been eminently successful. At the two factories they make about sixty thousand boxes of window glass, which is shipped to all points east, west, north and south. John B. Hirsch is the superintendent of the Covington factory, and Benjamin McCoy of the Blossburg factory. Michael Ely has charge of the store here at Covington. Altogether, Uncle Jonas, it is a firm which gives employment to about one hundred men in both factories for ten months a year, and is the means of giving employment indirectly to a number of laboring men besides."

"Covington, Uncle Jonas, is one of the oldest villages in Tioga County, and for many years was the most prominent business town in the county. The township was formed in the year 1815, taken from Tioga. Since its formation there has been taken from Covington the town of Sullivan, in February, 1816, a portion of the town of Liberty in 1823. Richmond in the year 1824, a portion of Rutland, which was formed in February, 1828, was in the original limits of Covington. Union was taken from Sullivan in 1830, Bloss in 1841, Ward in 1852, Hamilton in December 1872, and the boroughs of Covington in 1831, Mansfield in 1857, Mainesburg in 1859, Fall Brook in 1864, Roseville in 1876 and Blossburg in August 1871, have all been formed from the original territory of Covington. The townships of Liberty and Union lie south of Blossburg upon the highlands and join the Lycoming County line. These townships are quite thickly settled, with the villages of Ogdensburg, Roaring Branch and Gleason, in Union township, and the villages of Liberty, Barfelden and Nauvoo in Liberty township. To the southeast is the township of Ward, which joins the Bradford county line on the east, also the townships of Sullivan to the east and northeast Rutland, aggregating in population nearly twenty thousand people in the original boundaries of Covington. The coal and iron mines at Blossburg, the mines at Morris Run, Fall Brook and Arnot were within the territory of Covington. So, you perceive. Uncle Jonas, that Covington has been generous with her daughters, the various towns and boroughs which have set up business for themselves. For many years "Covington Four Corners," as it was then called, was a great distributing point.

The Williamson Road was cut out in the year 1792, and extended from Williamsport, on the west branch of the Susquehanna, up the Lycoming Creek or river to Trout Run, thence over Laurel Mountain to the Block House or Liberty in Tioga county, and thence to Blossburg and down the valley of the Tioga, passing through Covington, Canoe Camp, Mansfield/Tioga, to Lawrenceville, thence to Painted Post and up the Conhocton Valley to Bath. Soon after this Williamson road was cut out and worked a road was made by the state of Pennsylvania which ran north from Luzerne County to Towanda, in Bradford County, thence west to Troy, Sylvania, Sullivan to Covington, and on west to Wellsboro, the county seat of Tioga County, thence westward on to Pine Creek and up that valley until the summit was reached, and thence westward to Coudersport, the county seat of Potter County, which was located upon the headwaters of the Allegheny River, thence westward to Smethport, the county seat of McKean county, and westward again to Warren, the county seat of Warren county.

These northern tier counties, Tioga, Potter, and McKean, were formed in 1804, Bradford county in 1810, although previous to that date, it was known as the county of Ontario. This state road was finished to Covington in the year 1808-9, intersected, and crossed the Williamson road. At that time there was no other road running east and west through Tioga County until you reached Lawrenceville, twenty miles to the northward, and that was confined principally to the path which had been made by the surveyors of New York and Pennsylvania when they located the state line in the year 1786. The transit used was very heavy, weighing not less than eight hundred pounds, and had to be drawn on a sled by a team of oxen. The construction of the state road that connected the county seats of Bradford, Tioga, Potter, McKean, and Warren, was a great enterprise, and Covington township covering an immense territory was the mecca to which many of the early pioneers directed their footsteps. Those who settled in the eastern portion of the township on the highlands east of the valley of Tioga, now in the township of Sullivan and Rutland, were principally from the New

England states. A number of them were from Vermont and had served in the revolutionary war under Generals Stark and Sullivan. In the year 1815, there were in the original territory of Covington the following list of tax-payers: David Austin, Samuel Aldrich, Ebenezer Burley, David Burley, Alpheus Button, Joseph Bunn, Rufus Butler, Aaron Bloss, Gideon Briggs, Abner Cochran, Henry Campbell, John Cochran, Elijah Clark, Seth Clark, David Clemmens, Stillman Cannon, Samuel Campbell, Levi Elliott, Eli Getchell, Aaron Gillet, Charles Gillet, Asahel Graves, Josiah Graves, Levi Gifford, Noah Gifford, Samuel Higley, George Higley, Timothy Higley, Christopher Huntington, Shubb Huntington, John Keltz, Peter Keltz, Henry Knowlton, Absalom Kingsbury, Daniel Lamb, Henry Lamb, Gad Lamb, Minard Lawrence, John Lovegood, Silas Lamphere, Erastus Lillibridge, Jacob Miller, George Matter, Richard Miller, John Marvin, Asa Mann, Samuel Negley, Thomas Overton, Elias Pratt, Rufus Pratt, William Patton, Levi Prentice, Thomas Putman, Elijah Putman, Nathan Rowley, Nehemiah H. Ripley, Ichabod Rowley, Cephas Stratton, Thomas Sampson, Joshua Shaw, Amos Spencer, L. H. Spencer, Ichabod Smith, John Shaffer, Jonathan Sebring, Nathan Whitman, Isaac Walker, Archelius Wilkins, Daniel Wilkins, Tilley Marvin, David Harkness, David Harkness, Jr., Royal Walker, Lorain Lamb, Seneca Stratton, William Merritt. A number of these then lived in that part of Covington, which was formed into the town of Richmond, in the year 1824. The early settlers in that portion of Covington now known as Sullivan were in the year 1817: John Andrews, Isaac Baker, Ananias Baker, Simeon Briggs, Simeon Briggs, Jr., Griffin Bailey, Constant Bailey, Thomas R. Corey, Paul Cudworth, James Cudworth, David Crippen, Jacob Collins, Peleg Doud, Josiah Dewey, Joseph Dewey, John Ellis, David Fellows, James Gray, Timothy Knowlton, John King, Uriah Loper, Allen Lane, Jr., Lemuel Lane, Allen Lane, John Luddington, William Luddington, Benjamin Lawrence, Henry Lawrence, Asa Mann,

Reuben Merritt, Ira Mudge, Eli McNett, John Newell, Jesse Orvis, Joseph Orvis, Timothy Orvis, David Palmer, John Packhart, Jonathan Partridge, Stephen Palmer, H. Pitts, Clement Paine, Samuel Reynolds, Enos Rose, Daniel Rose, Jeremiah Rumsey, Noah Rumsey, Smith Rumsey, Thomas Raxford, Elisha Rush, John Simpkins, Gardner Seaman, Jesse Smith, Jonathan L. Spencer, Lyman Spencer, Benjamin Trout, Nathaniel Welch, Elijah Welch, Nathan Welch, Jr., Roswell Webster, Abial Webster, Zebedee Woodward, Noah Weast, John Watson, Ephraim S. Marsh, Eli Getchell, Joseph Ford, Lyman Rumsey, Abijah Hawley, Samuel Hardin, Robert Potter, Apollos Cudworth, John Benson, Jr., Daniel James, Levi Fox, Isaac Benson, Thomas Bennett, Benjamin Harrison."

"A number of these were residents of that portion which was subsequently organized into the townships of Rutland, Union and Ward. The settlers in Rutland township, Uncle Jonas, in the year 1829, at the time of its formation were, Stewart Austin, John Argetsinger, Isaac Benson, Ephraim Bryant, Bethuel Spencer, Ebenezer Bacon, Daniel Bunker, Halsey Barton, Hiram Benson, Green Bentley, Jacob Benson, Caleb Burrell, Silas Burrell, Sylvester Benson, Hiram Beales, Constant Bailey, Peter Burrell, John Benson, Joseph Beman, Johnson Brewer, John Britton, Peter Backer, Abraham Brown, W. D. Bacon, Sylvenus Benson, William M. Corey, Jabez M. Corey, Asa Crippin, David Crippin, Sydney Clark, Cornelius Clark, Seeley Cook, Hiram Cooley, Edwin Currie, Joseph Clark, Samuel Clark, Lemuel Clark, Harris Corey, John Crippin, Enos Curtis, Samuel PI. Coates, Isaac Clymer, John Drake, James Dann, James Dann, Jr., John B. Dann, Joseph Fletcher, Judah Gilford, Nathan Gifford, Nathan Goodwin, Gardiner Gould, Jonathan Grey, Eli Grey, Justus Garretson. James Goff, Calvin Hathaway, Hazeal Howland, William W. Howland, John R. Howland, James Husted, Nathaniel Howland, Henry Hull, Seth E. Howland, Baldwin Haywell, Isaac Hagar; David Huntley, Calvin W. Hammer, Thomas Johnson, James

Job, Daniel King, Benjamin Lawrence, Nathan Newberry, Sylvester New-
berry, Lucinda Newberry, Elisha Nash, Levi Osgood, Richard Lamberton,
David Prutsman, Erastus Rose, Virgil Rose, William Rose, Levi Rose, Sam-
uel Reynolds, D. B. Reynolds, John Reynolds, Avery Smith, H. Stemmetz,
Jesse Smith, Betsey Sherman, Jacob C. Stout, Harvey Smith, I. S. Smith,
Isaac Smith, Cornelius Sharp, Andrew Sharp, Herman Suher, Jefferson
Sherman, Robert Searles, John Selover, John Snyder, Silas Smith, E. Strong,
John Slingerland, Tunis Slingerland, Albert Slingerland, William Turner,
William Updike, John Updike, Henry Updike, Abram Updike, William
Wolf, Jonathan Wood, Solomon Wood, Ira Weldon, Daniel Wattles, Seth
Ward, William M. Ward, Justus Wood, Lewis H. Weldon, Ezra Wood, Sol-
omon Wood, 2d, James Roselle."

"You will recollect, Uncle Jonas, that it had only been about twen-
ty years, prior to the formation of the township of Rutland, that the first
settler had located there, a very commendable progress. In that portion of
Covington, now known as the township of Union, the early settlers were:
Uria Loper, Joseph Groover, John McNett, Eh McNett, Samuel McNett,
William Taylor, Nelson Rutty, Jewett Spencer, Sr., Jewett Spencer, Jr.,
Charles O. Spencer, Martin Robinson, Labau Landon, Ezra Landon, John
Newell, Charles M. Dibble, John Ogden, Luther Ogden, Joseph Wilbur,
George W. Terry, Alfred Jackson, Nathan Palmer, Martin Middaugh, Mar-
tin R. Harrington, Peter Skelley, Patrick Skelley, Abram Randell, William
Barrows, Joshua Reynolds, Thomas Tebo, Ithiel B. Reynolds, Thomas Stull,
Hiray Gray, Jay Whitehead, William Rathbone, Thomas Decoursey, G. G.
Collins, Peter B. Harrington, Patrick McCormick, Patrick Wynne. The
township of Union, Uncle Jonas, is situated in the southeastern portion of
Tioga County and is touched by the Northern Central railroad at Roar-
ing Branch. The early settlers in that portion of Covington, now known as
the township of Ward, were William Mcintosh, Simon McIntosh, Mathias

Mcintosh, Harry Coovert, James Lyon, Andrew Kniffin, Erastus Kiff, William R. Lyon, Daniel Hagar, Waterman Gates, John Purvis, Simon Conkling, A. J. Teeter, John Kiff. The township was formed in 1852. We have already, Uncle Jonas, been in Blossburg, Morris Run, Fall Brook and you know about that portion of Covington township. The township of Liberty, which was a portion of Covington and on the line of the Williamson road, was early settled at the "Block House." Among the old settlers were, Jonathan Sebring, George Miller, Peter Secrist, Frederic Bower, Jacob Beck, Peter Moyer (Jonathan Sebring kept the hotel for many years), Joseph Opdegralf, Samuel Keagie, Isaiah Thompson, Frederic Harrer, Leonard Harrer, John Harrer, Peter Sheik, George Schambacher, Fred Schambacher, Leonard Schambacher, Joseph Rochenbrode, John Keltz, Phillip Kohler, R. C. Cox, C. F. Veile, George Wheeland, Janus Merrell, Jacob Welty, Henry Costerison, Jacob Reith, Frederic Bower, Daniel Gaup, Henry Schaumeder, John Levegood, Noah Runk, John McCurdie, Mathias Yowdis, Michael Bastian, John Weaver, Rudolph Crist, Jacob Manaval, Jacob Shreiner, George Bastian, John Welty, John Moyer, Samuel Landon, John Lenhart, Michael Linck, George Levegood, Christian Corson, Isaac Werhne, John Ridge, Henry Springer, Daniel Hartsock, Solomon Roup, James Alexander, Daniel Spangler, George Wheeland, Horace Fellows, Isaac Foulkrod, John Shetfer, John C. Beiser, John F. Hart, George Hebe, Henry Zimmerman, Mrs. Lydia Jane Pierson, the authoress. The enumeration of so many names, Uncle Jonas, must be quite annoying to you?"

"Oh, no, Harry, I recollect a number of them. There is Jonathan Sebring, John Sheffer, Isaac Foulkrod, a considerable number of other names you mention in Liberty came to Elmira. Then there were the McNetts, of Union, and the Ogdens, of Union, I had dealings with. Mr. McNett kept a hotel on the line of the stage route between Elmira and Williamsport, in the town of Union, now McNett township. Then there were the McIntoshes of Ward, frequently came to Elmira, as well as the Luddingtons, the Rumseys and Mains, of Sullivan. The Roses, of Rutland, used to go down through Jackson township by way of Daggett Hollow and come into Elmira by the Southport way. Then the Spencers, the Lambs and the Manns, of Richmond (then Covington) made frequent visits to Elmira, or Newtown, as it was then called, while from here were the Putnams, the Dyers, the Wilsons, the Graves, the Walkers, the Strattons, the Marvins, the Gaylords, the Smiths, and many others I was acquainted with. You know, Harry, that Butler B. Smith was from Southport— near Elmira. I knew him well. I also knew Tilley Marvin, Sumner Wilson and his boys, John C. Bennett, his son-in-law, who married Olive Wilson, in fact Harry there are many names you have repeated that are perfectly fresh in my memory. Elijah Putnam, Harry, was a relative of General Israel Putnam, of revolutionary fame. He came here as early as 1809. One of his daughters. Miss Sally, married Peter Keltz, an energetic businessman. His son, General Tom Putnam, I was well acquainted with. In those days, Harry, I believe the people were more social than now. When I left Elmira, there was scarcely a family that I did not know from Elmira to Towanda and Canton, from Tioga Point to Owego, and from Elmira to Painted Post, Bath, Addison, Canisteo, Hornellsville, Lindley, Lawrenceville, Beecher's Island, Elkland, and Knoxville. Silas Billings, from Southport, went and located at Knoxville as early as 1823 and became one of the greatest lumbermen in Tioga County. All along this Tioga Valley I had acquaintances, also from Elmira northward to Geneva, and northeastward to Pony Hollow, Spencer, Newfield, Ithaca and Cortland. I am told that the Rev. Harvey Lamkin resides here now. He was born in Ulysses, Tompkins County, about the year 1812. He is also an associate judge of this county. Harry, have Sammy drive over the bridge across on the west side of the river, I want to see how it looks over there."

"Uncle Jonas, you saw that gentleman go into the smith shop, there? "

"Yes."

"Well, that is George Baker, brother of Richard Baker, of Southport. He has resided here many years. Thomas Putnam lives there on the right in that neat cottage. Above here on the river road is the residence of Victor Gray, one of the oldest locomotive engineers in the country. He ran on the old Corning & Blossburg Railroad forty-five years ago. This side of his house is the gun-shop of Ira Patchin, son-in-law of the late General Thomas Putnam. He has resided in Covington for forty-eight years. He has secured a competency for his old age. His trade was a very important one for many years. People came for twenty-five and fifty miles to get their guns repaired or new ones made. There was a seminary established here in 1841 by Professor Julius Doane, who instructed students in the higher branches. He died quite recently at a very advanced age. Dr. Henry Kilbourne, Sr., settled in Covington in the year 1828. He came in from Vermont. He practiced medicine for fifty-five years and now resides at Blossburg. There are many interesting reminiscences connected with the history of Covington, which I would like to recall, but which I fear we shall not have time to do so. I see. Uncle Jonas, that the borough of Covington now contains four churches, Presbyterian, Baptist, Methodist and Christian, a graded school, an Odd Fellows hall, a glass manufactory, a mineral water bottling establishment, a fruit evaporator and the usual complement of stores, saloons, drug stores, etc. There are a number of neat and cozy dwellings, with fine yards and lawns. Covington has increased materially in population in the past three years and now contains about one thousand inhabitants. It is surrounded by a splendid farming country and is gradually gaining back her old-time character as a business center.

TRIP TO MANSFIELD
UNCLE JONAS FINDS MANY THINGS TO INTEREST
HIS READERS.

"We will drive up to the store of A. M. Bennett, son of John C. Bennett, where will find quite a number of the old residents and sons of old residents. It is about time for the reception of the mail from the north."

They drive up and Uncle Jonas and Harry alight. Uncle Jonas is introduced to J. C. Bennett, Matthew Skelley, Otis G. Gerould, son of Ephraim Gerould, John S. Hoagland, Floyd C. Phelps, Frederic M. Patchen, Jacob Hartman, Doctor Robbins, Stephen F. Richards, G. A. Spring, G. W. Keltz, Captain Daniel Wilson, Sumner Wilson, Charles Rowland, ex-Sheriff Delos H. Walker, Judge L. B, Smith, A. L. Meeker, Henry Fick (an extensive farmer), Thomas Putnam, and it so happened that several were present from the eastern portion of the township, among whom were James T. Frost, Charles Jacques, and Lyman Frost. Uncle Jonas and Harry talked over old times and inquired after many old settlers who had gone to their last resting-place.

A half-hour was thus enjoyably spent when they again took their carriage and were driven off down the road towards Canoe Camp. Uncle Jonas was in the best of health and spirits, and as they passed down the valley, he pointed out to Harry the former residences of the old settlers. Up Elk Run were the early homes of Alonzo Reddington, James Pettis, Asahel Graves, Jonathan Jennings, Isaac Bliss (father of the celebrated P. P. Bliss, the evangelist, who met with such a fearful death at Ashtabula, December 30, 1876), and along the valley he pointed out the old Sumner Wilson homestead, the James Negely place, Robert Searles's and all the points of interest until they arrived at Canoe Camp. There, he explained to Harry the origin of the name "Canoe Camp," It was at that place that in 1792, when Robert and Benjamin Patterson were conducting the German and English emigrants from Northumberland to found Bath upon the Pulteney estate, that canoes were made at the mouth of this creek, in which the emigrants were floated down the river to Painted Post, from where they ascended the Conhocton River. The emigrants were discouraged. They were nearly out of provisions and halted there for rest. Benjamin Patterson ordered the woodsmen connected with the party to cut down pine trees and hew out canoes or "dug outs." At the same time, he would strike across the mountains and unbroken wilderness to Tioga Point, -where there was a trading house, and secure provisions to be poled up the Chemung River in boats. He successfully accomplished his mission, purchased the provisions and hired eight stalwart boatmen to deliver the goods at Painted Post or near there.

When he returned from Tioga Point the boats were completed but the emigrants at first refused to enter the boats, saying that they were being taken into the wilderness to starve or perish. The Patterson brothers were determined men, had both seen service in the border Indian wars of the revolution, and were not to be trifled with. They seized their rifles and tomahawks, and threatened to shoot the first emigrant who refused to enter the boats. The women and children with their baggage were first embarked, followed by the old and the sick, while many of the men were compelled to run along the bank of the river in the old Indian path, hallooing and shouting in German or broken English, imploring and imprecating at each alternate breath. About five o'clock in the afternoon, as they approached Painted Post, they met the boatmen with their cargoes of flour, bacon, pork, sugar, coffee, and tobacco. A landing was effected on an island near the present site of Fox, Weston & Co.'s sawmill, a fire was soon built, and the evening meal was prepared in haste. As the odor of the fragrant coffee was inhaled, the drooping spirits of the emigrants revived.

When they had eaten to their hearts' content, the Pattersons - the modern Moses, who had delivered them, and their chants of praise were as earnest as had their imprecations and anathemas been. From that circumstance, Canoe Camp derived its name.

"There is another circumstance, Harry, connected with its history that I will mention. On January 16, 1836, Governor Joseph Ritner approved the act incorporating the Tioga Navigation Company, which, finally, by supplements become the Tioga Railroad Company or the Corning & Blossburg Railroad Company. The idea had been entertained as early as 1824 to make the Tioga River navigable for boats. In the year 1836 Christian H. Charles and Charles Sikes constructed arks at this point, loaded them with the Blossburg coal and ran them down the river to Corning. There was no way of getting them back, so they were sold, and ex-Sheriff William T. Reeder, then a resident of Big Flats, purchased them and erected a dwelling in the village of Big Flats, a few rods north of the Erie railroad. This place has also been known as Spencer's Mills, in honor of Amos Spencer, who located here in 1806, and erected one of the first grist mills on the Tioga River. The property is still in the hands of his descendants, and the milling business is carried on now quite extensively by A. M. Spencer. That fine residence there on the left is his. The early settlers here were Isaac Lounsberry, Ichabod Rowley, Amos Spencer, and Cephas Stratton. This was formerly in the township of Covington, but now in the township of Richmond. The game upon the hillsides and flats here was very plenty years ago, and one of the finest hunting grounds in the Tioga valley. The hills were low and easy of access, and the river was a great watering place. There was other game besides the deer and elk — bears, panthers, wolves, and wild cats. A panther once came down from the hillside and killed a yearling heifer in the yard near here. A pursuit was made, and the huge monster, after a few hours, was captured on the mountainside south of here, near the Captain David Clemmens farm. The early settlers had many obstacles to contend with. The hewing down of the forest and the letting in of the sunlight to warm and fertilize the earth was only a portion of their strife. In the year 1817, a frost killed all the corn, wheat, and rye in this valley. It was termed the cold season. Corn brought three dollars per bushel and was scarce at that. With heroism and bravery equal to the Spartan band, they maintained their ground and lived to see the hand of plenty distributing her munificent and well-earned fruits. I see, Harry, that the farmers of this valley are quite extensively engaged in growing tobacco. Whose large tobacco shed is that?"

"That shed, Uncle Jonas, belongs to Isaac P. Lounsberry, son of one of the early pioneers here. We are now approaching the Mansfield borough line, which divides the township of Richmond and it— Mansfield was organized as a borough in 1857, and taken from the township of Richmond. Richmond was organized as a township in 1824, taken from Covington. Mansfield was named in honor of Asa Mann, an early settler and an enterprising and public-spirited gentleman. He came into this valley in 1810. He was prominent in the affairs of the county, and in the year 1817 was named as one of the trustees of the Wellsboro Academy, chartered and founded by the state of Pennsylvania. Prominent also among the early settlers of Mansfield and the town of Richmond were: Gad Lamb. Lorain Lamb, Benjamin Corey, David Miller, Cheeney Ames, Lemuel Ames, Elihu Marvin, John Cochrane, Joshua Shaw, Levi Gitchell, Eli Mitchell, Elijah Clark, Ebenezer Burley (a revolutionary soldier), Peter Kelce, Jacob Allen (a revolutionary soldier), Daniel Holden, Hezekiah Gaylord, Stillman Cannon, Marcus Kelley, John Kelley, Dexter Parkhurst, M. D., Christopher Huntingdon (a revolutionary soldier), Isaac Lounsberry (a revolutionary soldier), Almon Allen, Elijah P. Clark, Justus B. Clark, Abner Cochran, the Rev.

Nehemiah Ripley, William C. Ripley, Ebenezer Ripley, Letson Lounsberry, Ira Lounsberry, Elihu Marvin, Isaac Lounsberry, Peter Whittaker, Aaron Gillett, Alvin Gaylord, Porter Gaylord, Daniel Sherwood, Daniel Lee Sherwood, the Rev, Abijah Sherwood, Michael Fralich, the Rev. Asa Donaldson, Loren Butts, Ezra Davis, and prominent among the citizens of Mansfield and Richmond at a later date were Dewitt Clinton Holden, Isaac Holden, John A. Holden, Dr. Joseph P. Morris, Colonel Joseph S. Hoar, George W. King, Mart King, Lyman Beach, L. H. Elliott, the Hon. Charles V. Elliott, Daniel Pitts, the Hon. Simon B. Elliott, Benjamin M. Bailey, Levi Cooper, William Hollands, John Murdaugh, Captain A. M. Pitts, E. L. Sperry, Philip Williams, A. J. Ross, Charles S. Ross, Clark W. Bailey, Thomas H. Bailey, William Adams, John W. Adams, Frank W. Clark, J. M. Clark, Professor Charles H. Verrill, Professor D. C. Thomas, Apollos Pitts, Captain E. R. Backer, Andrew Sherwood, Charles Kingsbury, Dyer J. Butts, Isaac Lounsberry, Jr., Charles Sherman, A. M. Spencer, Thomas Jerald, G. N. Welch, Colonel Nathaniel A. Elliott, Homer Kingsley, Captain Samuel Hunt, James R. Wilson, Charles Knapp, Henry M. Allen, L. H. Shattuck, Oliver Elliott, Edward Doane, Robert Crossley, Colonel Victor A. Elliott, P. M. Clark, Benjamin Wilson, A. J. Webster, R. K. Brundage, George W. Vorhees, T F. Rolason, P. M. Spencer, N. Kingsley, Clarence E. Allen, R. E. Olney, Dr. L. A. Eidgeway, Frank Kohler, Dr. Cole, T. V. Moore, Burt Schrader, Vine R. Pratt, F. M. Allen, and Professor F. A. Allen."

Without detracting anything from the reputation of any other gentleman who has resided in Mansfield since its first settlement, the name of Professor Fordyce A. Allen stands out most prominent. No more successful businessman, no more able teacher of the youth, no more public-spirited or more distinguished citizen ever resided within its limits. He made the state normal school a success; he founded the Soldiers' Orphan School. He made it a success, reflecting honor upon himself and the commonwealth, and conferring a lasting benefit upon the soldiers' orphans of the state. He did more to elevate the profession of teaching than any man in the United States. His voice was heard in teachers' institutes from Maine to California, from the sources of the rivers of the north to their sunny entrances into the great bays and gulfs of the south. Wherever he went he took lessons of common-sense and practical ideas, and impressed them upon his hearers with that clearness and systematic deduction, that made a permanent and lasting impression. While his elocution might not have been faultless, yet his rhetoric was of that pleasing, instructive and insinuating kind, that his voice was like the harmony of blended chords of the sweetest music. His logic was as accurate as the fundamental principles of mathematics. With a heart overflowing with goodwill towards mankind, he controlled his pupils by kindness and his hearers by the gentleness of his manner and the smiles of his countenance. He not only left a monument in his honor in the educational department of the country, but he was for several years a member of the state board of agriculture of Pennsylvania, and by his thorough knowledge of the chemistry of different soil incident to the valleys, plains, plateaus and hills of Pennsylvania, he impressed his coadjutors with his practical theories and by the personal application of his knowledge demonstrated the truth of his position. That beautiful farm you see on the west side of the Tioga river. Uncle Jonas, was owned by the professor in his life-time and is a certificate of his practical and scientific knowledge. He was born in Cummington, Massachusetts, July 10, 1820. In the year 1822 came with his parents to Mansfield, and received his early education in the common school. After many years' absence from Mansfield, he returned in the year 1865 and took charge of the state normal school, putting his whole energy and practical knowledge to the building up of the reputation of that institution. In 1867 he instituted the soldiers orphan school and carried that on successfully. Whatever was calculated to benefit the interests of the school and community at large, that he entered into with a spirit and will, that knew no such word as 'fail.' I was well acquainted with him. Uncle Jonas, and never weary in speaking his praise. He attended a meeting of the State Board of Agriculture at Harrisburg about the 1st day of February, 1880. It so happened. Uncle Jonas, that I was there at that time. The meeting was held in the state library room, and was overheated by steam. The professor was warmly clad going down there from Northern Pennsylvania. His labors were great. In going from the room, he went immediately to the railroad station and took a sleeper for Elmira. He caught a severe cold, which culminated in pneumonia, and on February 11, 1880, he died. I took a very severe cold, and was so sick that I was unable to attend his funeral. It was indeed a sad day for Mansfield."

"This is Smythe Park, Uncle Jonas. A most successful fair is held here annually. Drive into the gate, Sammy, and we will look over the grounds! This association was organized in the year 1879; one of the prime movers in the organization was Professor F. A. Allen. Its present officers are Thomas H. Bailey, president; D. J. Butts, vice-president; Mart King, secretary; Phillip Williams, treasurer; Mart King, T. H. Bailey, D. H. Pitts, V. R. Pratt, J. A. Elliott, J. M. Clark, trustees. The fairs are held under the auspices of the Tioga County Agricultural, Mechanical and Industrial association."

"Well, I declare, Harry, these are beautiful grounds, with all the necessary sheds, stalls, exhibition rooms, tracks, grandstands, pavilions, and dining halls. What a beautiful shade these trees of natural planting make! It reminds me of those trees that years ago grew on Clinton island at Elmira."

"Now, Sammy, drive around by the State Normal school! These splendid buildings and the prosperous schools are the outgrowth of the "Mansfield Seminary," which was organized February 15, 1855, under the patronage of the East Genesee Methodist Episcopal Conference. The first building was opened for school purposes in January, 1857, J. R. Jacques, A. M., first principal. The school had only been in operation three months when the building was burned. The work of reconstruction was commenced immediately, but the trustees were sorely pressed for money to carry out their plans. The building, however, was partially completed and school re-opened November 23, 1859, the Rev. J. Landreth, A. M., principal. The successor of Mr. Landreth was Professor E. Wildeman, the next year the building was completed. In the year 1862, the school was reorganized as a State Normal school, being the third normal school in the state of Pennsylvania, and the Rev. W. D. Taylor succeeded Professor Wildeman. Professor Taylor was succeeded by Professor F. A. Allen, of whom I have already spoken — who served five years most acceptably, placing the institution upon a firm basis, and securing appropriations and aid from the state to enlarge the capacity of the school. Professor J. T. Streit was chosen to succeed Professor Allen, but being in feeble health was unable to enter upon the work, when Professor C. H. Verrill, a successful teacher, was selected. Professor Verrill was succeeded by Professor J. N. Fradenburgh, who acted as principal for some time, when, upon the very urgent requests of the trustees. Professor F. A. Allen again became the principal. I might here remark, Uncle Jonas, that during the early financial history of the institution the Hon. John Magee, of Bath, loaned the institution $6,500, which he subsequently donated to it. After the death of Professor Allen in 1880, Professor D. C. Thomas was chosen principal, and is ably discharging that duty at present. I have, Uncle Jonas, only given you an outline of its history, for it would take hours to relate all the history, its hours of adversity and moments of prosperity. It is a successful institution now, and is annually making improvements, extending its influence wider and wider, and diffusing lasting lessons of science and education. Drive down on to Main or William street, Sammy!"

"That building on the corner is the soldiers' orphan school, founded by the late Professor F. A. Allen, and opened October 1, 1867. In 1872, a farm of 150 acres was purchased by Professor Allen, located on the west side of the river near the school, where boys in attendance at the school were given practical lessons in farming. The girls, in addition to their studies, are taught practically how to be good housekeepers. There are usually about 200 pupils in attendance, about equally divided in regard to sex. I have visited this school frequently, Uncle Jonas, and regard it as one of the model schools of the country. There is more practical common sense exercised in its management and instruction than any school I ever visited, either in Pennsylvania or New York. For many years Professor Vine R. Pratt was the chief assistant of Professor Allen. After the decease of Professor Allen his widow, Mrs. Jane Allen, a lady eminently qualified for the task, who had always been in sympathy and accord with the professor in his plans and designs, assumed charge of the school and continued Mr. Pratt as her assistant and superintendent. If we had a little more time at our disposal. Uncle Jonas, I should insist upon making a visit to the school. That fine brick edifice on the west side of the street below the post office is the Mansfield Business and Commercial College. F. M. Allen, son of Professor F. A. Allen, erected that fine brick on the right of us as a commercial college, and had a very successful commencement; but subsequently concluded to remove to Elmira and opened a commercial and business school in the Advertiser association building. The elegant and costly brick edifice on the west side of the railroad, with its fine yard and playgrounds, is the Mansfield graded school. The cost of the building and its furniture, steam heating apparatus, etc., was about $18,000. It was erected in the year 1881. We will now drive to the Grand Central Hotel, kept by W. S. Earnest, and we will take dinner."

"Mr. Earnest, this is Uncle Jonas Lawrence, who is visiting your beautiful village."

"Glad to meet you, Mr. Lawrence, walk in, dinner will soon be ready."

"Well, Harry, this is cheerful and cozy. These Tioga County landlords have a faculty of making their guests feel comfortable and at home. Mansfield has grown wonderfully since I saw it forty-four years ago. It was a mere hamlet then. The business places are substantial, the dwellings are elegant, and the whole appearance of the place is bright and cheerful."

"Across the river yonder, near where you see the smoke issuing from that stack, a furnace was erected about the year 1855 by a company incorporated for that purpose. The manufacture of pig iron was carried on quite successfully for several years. A large portion of the ore used was obtained from an ore bank a short distance to the west of the furnace. The furnace finally passed into the hands of a firm who resided at Reading, PA. In the year 1880 the company owning it got into difficulty concerning the running of the business and it was finally torn down about a year ago, not because the manufacture of iron was unprofitable, but for the reason the owners could not agree upon the manner in which the business should be conducted. John W. Phelps was for many years its superintendent and manager."

Dinner being over, they dismiss Sammy Sage, the driver, and send him back to Blossburg, well pleased with his service as a teamster. Uncle Jonas and Harry take a walk about town.

"Is there a printing office in the village, Harry?"

"Oh, yes, Uncle Jonas, there is a most excellent newspaper printed here now under the title of the Mansfield *Advertiser*, whose editors and proprietors are F. E. VanKeuren and S. E. Coles. They publish a four-page, eight-column weekly, neutral in politics. It has a large circulation. The office is supplied with a steam power press and all the facilities for doing first-class business in job work. A newspaper was first started in Mansfield in the year 1856 with I. M. Ruckman as editor. The name of the paper was the *Balance,* subsequently christened the Mansfield *Express.* The editors were in the order named: I. M. Ruckman, the Hon. S. B, Elliott, J. S. Hoard. The type and fixtures were finally sold and taken to Kansas. In 1872, Henry C. Mills, of Lawrenceville, removed from that borough a newspaper office and established it at Mansfield under the title of the *Valley Enterprise.* Mr. Mills sold out his interest, and the paper was issued as the Mansfield *Advertiser,* which name it has since borne. The editors have been V. A. Elliott, O. D. Goodenough, D. A. Farnham, Vine R. Pratt, William A. Rowland, and the present editors and proprietors, Messrs. Van Keuren and Coles, who have added largely to its facilities in every respect. This, Uncle Jonas, is a no-license borough. In the year 1870, in view of the many students who were attending the normal and other schools, a law was passed prohibiting the sale of intoxicating liquor within two miles of the state normal school. It is claimed by many that the effect of that law is beneficial to the inhabitants of the borough as well as the students of the school, and it is also claimed by others that its provisions are evaded in many ways, and that liquor is smuggled in from other localities. It is not clear in my mind whether it operates for the benefit of the student or to his injury. The churches of Mansfield are the Baptist, Methodist, Presbyterian, Episcopal, and Universalist. The Baptist church was organized in 1813, the Methodist in 1814, the Episcopal in May 1867, the Presbyterian in April 1870, and the Universalist in 1882. They are all well attended and supported. A church of Christ was instituted as early as July 5, 1832, by the Rev. David Higgins, of Bath, and the Rev. E. D. Wells, of Lawrenceville, who were a committee appointed for that purpose by the presbytery of Bath, N. Y. The members constituting the church were Amariah Robbins, Joel Harkness, Joseph Thompson, John Backer, John W. Donaldson, Timothy Orvis, John Kelley, Mary Cooley,

Hannah Kelley, Thanks Webster, Delia Donaldson, Emily Sexton, Anna Finks, Roxalana Brown and Rachel Orvis.

The missionary in charge was the Rev. Asa Donaldson. The church was known as the First Presbyterian Church of Richmond. It ceased to exist as an organization a number of years ago. The first store erected in Mansfield was built by Daniel Holden in the year 1826. The first brick house was erected by ex-Sheriff Benjamin Gitchell in the year 1841. It stands in the southern portion of the borough, a few rods west of Smythe Park. Several canal boats designed for use upon the Chemung and Erie canals were built at Mansfield in the years 1815, 1816, and 1817 by Edward Faulkner, Amos Bixby, Gurdon Fuller, and John Holden. They were floated down the river to Corning when there was a freshet. The first framed house was built in Mansfield by Peter Keltz in the year 1810. The first post office in the township of Richmond was established at Canoe Camp in the year 1822, with Amos Spencer as postmaster. The first grist mill in the township was erected by Elchee Marvin, in the year 1805. In a year or two thereafter, a grist mill was erected by Amos Spencer at Canoe Camp. Canoe Camp and Mansfield for many years were rival settlements and situated only about two miles apart, the rivalry at sometimes was very exciting, particularly so when Amos Spencer succeeded in getting a post office established at Canoe Camp, his place of residence. In the year 1824 Chandler Mann erected a tannery at Mansfield, and Almon Allen, father of Prof. P. A. Allen, built a woolen factory."

MANSFIELD.
CONTINUATION OF PIONEER REMINISCENCES —
PROMINENT MEN OF TODAY.

Prominent among the many who worked diligently and intelligent-
ly for the success of the State Normal School and the prosperity of
Mansfield was the Hon. Simon B. Elliott, for many years a resident
of Mansfield, but now living in Clearfield County, PA. He is a son of Larman H. Elliott and was born at Sheshequin, Bradford County, PA, in the
year 1830. He came to Mansfield when he was about seventeen years of age,
and by diligence and industry acquired the trade or profession of architect,
civil and mining engineer. He was the architect of the State Normal School
building and deserved great credit for his untiring efforts in its behalf. In the
year 1860, he was elected a member of the state legislature of Pennsylvania
when Tioga County had only one representative in that body. He served
his constituents and the commonwealth honorably and acceptably. He was
elected as a republican. While a resident of Mansfield, he did many things
to advance its prosperity. He was an indefatigable worker — laboring at
his profession, caring for the public welfare, occupying the editorial chair,
and bringing into public notice the educational advantages of Mansfield. In
1871 he became interested in the Tioga Railroad Company and later was
superintendent in charge of the company's coal mines at Arnot. While in
that capacity, he superintended personally the erection of coke ovens and
the building of the largest coal washer and crusher in the state of Pennsylvania. He also superintended the erection of four hundred coke ovens for the
Fall Brook Coal Company at Tioga village and all the necessary appendag-
es and is probably one of the very best experts in the construction of coke
ovens and their attendant appliances in the state. Place and position have
not made him arrogant and unapproachable. He is held in high esteem by

the laboring men, miners, and all classes of persons in Tioga County.

"This. Uncle Jonas is the office of John W. Adams, Esq., lawyer, who is a son of William Adams, Esq., one of the pioneer printers of Tioga County, and that is the office of Henry Allen, a lawyer who has been district attorney of Tioga County. In the same building Mart King, a justice of the peace has an office. He was, for many years, a prominent manufacturer of Mansfield but has met with severe losses from fire. He was one of the prime movers in the Smythe Park Association and for six years was its active and energetic president. He is now the secretary of the association, and a large share of its management devolves upon him. He is a son of the late George W. King, who was a soldier of the war of 1812, and who settled in Mansfield forty-three years ago. Mart King was for six years the popular conductor on the Corning and Blossburg railroad from the year 1852 to 1858 and became widely known for his gentlemanly bearing and his careful attention to duty. For about ten years he was extensively engaged in milling and the purchase and sale of grain, when he established a bedstead manufactory, supplying it with the most approved and costly machinery. In about a year thereafter his manufactory was burned, which he immediately rebuilt and continued to increase and enlarge his business, giving employment to a large number of men, until July 4, 1884, when Mr. King and a large number of citizens from Mansfield were enjoying themselves at a celebration in Blossburg, the manufactory took fire and was entirely consumed, involving a loss of many thousand dollars. Mr. King did not rebuild. He is a pleasant gentleman sixty years of age, genial and companionable. He was born in Washington County, New York, in the year 1825. You would be pleased, Uncle Jonas, to make his acquaintance. He is a staunch Republican."

"This, Uncle Jonas, is the business place of S. J. Shepard, and over across the way is the drug store and office of Dr. Charles V. Elliott, one of the prominent citizens of Mansfield. He is a son of Larman H. Elliott and brother of the Hon. Simon H. Elliott. He is a graduate of the medical college at Geneva, NY, and has been a resident of Mansfield for the past thirty-eight years. He is a republican in politics, was postmaster from 1860 to 1872, and in the year 1876 was elected one of the representatives from Tioga County in the state legislature, serving two terms in that body, and being on some of the most important committees of the house, among them the committee of ways and means and the appropriation committee. He is one of the trustees of the state normal school.

"This is the store of William Holland, one of Mansfield's most honored mechanics. He is a harness-maker by trade and has been a resident of Mansfield for the past thirty-five years. He is an Englishman by birth and is a zealous churchman. He has acted in the capacity of superintendent of Sunday schools for fifty-six years — thirty-three years of that period in Mansfield."

"One of the most substantial business and banking firms of this borough has been that of Ross & Williams. Andrew J. Ross was born in Pike township, Bradford County, PA., February 23, 1827, and died August 18, 1875. Phillip Williams was born in Troy township, Bradford County, PA, in the year 1826 and came to Mansfield in 1837. In the year 1855 he and A. J. Ross entered into co-partnership, and on the 21st day of May 1872, they established Ross & Williams' Bank. Three years later Mr. Ross died and his son, Charles S. Ross, succeeded him in the business. The firm of Ross & Williams is thus continued. Mr. Charles S. Ross is a thorough and energetic man, and Mr. Williams a careful and judicious financier. Both have been conspicuously connected with every enterprise calculated to foster and build up the business interests of Mansfield and surrounding country. Mr. Ross was for several years the very energetic secretary of the Smythe Park Association, and Philip Wilhams the treasurer. Across the way, Uncle Jonas, is the store of the Pitts brothers, Daniel H. and A. M.

Pitts. For many years they have been engaged in the mercantile business and are gentlemen who stand high in the community."

"What about the Holdens, Harry? I was acquainted with Daniel Holden and his sons Daniel Holden, the elder, came to Mansfield in the year 1819 from Albany, NY, and in the year 1820 erected a store in the southern portion of Mansfield and continued in the mercantile business until his death in 1830. Dewitt Clinton Holden, his son, occupied the Holden homestead and increased its domain. He was for many years one of the most enterprising businessmen in the Tioga valley. He was born October 4, 1818, and died in the year 1871. A large portion of the dwellings in the southern portion of Mansfield are located upon his estate. His brothers were Daniel L., Isaac, John A., George R., Horace W. Horace is now a resident of Elmira."

"That building on the left, Uncle Jonas, is used as a cigar manufactory and occupied by Voorhees & Co. The senior member of the firm is G. W. Voorhees, son of your old Southport friend, Henry W. Voorhees. The establishment employs about fifty men and women. Yonder comes Colonel Elliott, Uncle Jonas. I want to make you acquainted with him. Colonel Elliott this is Uncle Jonas Lawrence.   "Glad to meet you, Uncle Jonas, and glad to know that you are visiting your old-time haunts and publishing your very interesting sketches in the Elmira *Advertiser*. I read those sketches with very great interest. My father, Levi Elliott, was one of the early settlers in this valley. He came from the state of Maine in the year 1809 and settled in the township of Covington, which embraced a large township now composed of several townships and boroughs. I was born in Covington in the year 1817 and have always lived in this county."

"Well, Harry, the colonel is a well-preserved and active old gentleman."

"Yes, Uncle Jonas, he is and has been one of the active businessmen of this valley. He represented this county in the state legislature in the year 1848 as a democrat. Has since been a county commissioner for six years, one of the most responsible offices in the county. You will bear in mind. Uncle Jonas, that in Pennsylvania, three county commissioners perform the duties allotted to the supervisors in the state of New York. The commissioners in Pennsylvania equalize the assessments, levy the taxes, take charge of the county buildings, courthouse, jail, poor house, and county bridges and roads, look after the poor and insane, pass upon all accounts presented against the county and collect all claims in its favor, and exercise generally a supervision over county affairs. It is, therefore, of the utmost importance that honest, capable, and thorough businessmen should be selected for that purpose. Colonel N. A. Elliott filled the bill, and the people of the county retained him for six years in that capacity. He is the father of the Hon. Mortimer F. Elliott, the distinguished lawyer of Wellsboro and ex-congressman-at-large for the state of Pennsylvania.

"Harry, there was a family of Gaylords here with whom I was acquainted."

"Yes, Uncle Jonas, Hezekiah Gaylord came to Mansfield from Vermont in the year 1822. His brother Elijah had settled in Sullivan township in the year 1819, and in the year 1820 settled at Covington. Both had large families. Hezekiah Gaylord died in Mansfield in the year 1850, aged eighty-one years. Alvin Gaylord, one of the sons, who reared a large family, died in the year 1876, aged seventy-seven years. He was a very active member of the Methodist church, being one of the charter members, and was the first high constable when Mansfield was formed into a borough twenty-eight years ago. The descendants of the Gaylords are quite numerous in Mansfield today. Uncle Jonas, permit me to make you acquainted with Captain E. R. Backer, one of Mansfield's prominent citizens. Captain

Backer, Uncle Jonas, is a native of Rutland, Tioga county. Pa., and was born January G, 1840. During the late rebellion he raised a company of cavalry, serving with distinction during the term of enlistment. He received an honorable discharge and raised another company and re-entered the service. Captain Backer, Uncle Jonas, is a staunch republican, and a pleasant and agreeable gentleman. Mr. Lawrence, I am really pleased to meet you and your nephew, Harry Sampson, and should be pleased to receive a call from you at my house. I thank you, Captain, but Harry and I are strolling about, looking over old landmarks and conversing upon the people and the changes that have taken place within the last forty years. Captain, I once attended the raising of a barn erected by Clinton Holden about the year 1840. It was at the time that the railroad was being graded and completed. Business called me here from Elmira, and I wanted to see several gentlemen; but upon going to their homes or places of business, I found they were all gone to Clint. Holden's barn raising. Anxious to see them that afternoon, I went to the "raising. There I found about one hundred men and boys from the surrounding country. They were down from Canoe Camp, Covington, Elk Run, from Corey Greek, Lambs Creek, Mill Creek, Mainesburg, Roseville, and West Richmond. The frame was a heavy one, and the work of putting the sills on the foundation had just commenced as I arrived. Older men, soldiers of the revolution and the war of 1812 were there, some in active duty, and some counseling and advising the younger and more stalwart men. Boys were there taking lessons, handling pins, braces, chains, and pike poles, putting them in place ready for use by the men. A number of women and girls were there, too, or rather at the house nearby, cooking venison, mutton, chickens, and otherwise assisting in preparing a great feast for the men after the barn should have been raised. Rude, long tables were made of pine boards supported by benches in the shade of a huge buttonwood tree, while baskets of dishes, knives and forks, table cloths, and napkins were being overhauled and placed by willing and deft hands upon the table. Rapidly the frame takes shape under the combined efforts of the men, while the stentorian word of command was given by a man whose lungs were evidently in the most healthy condition."

"He-o-heave, he-o-heave, away, heave away!" resounded up and down the valley and inspired the men to renewed and concerted action. At length the frame was raised, the purloins and rafters put in place and stay-lathed. It had been a laborious and exciting work. No sooner had the last rafter been put in place, when the supper horn was blowed. But before its summons could be attended to the building must be christened and this must be done by one selected for the purpose, who mounted to the northeast corner of the upright port on the plate, and delivered a speech, thanking the people for their assistance and concluding by pronouncing the name, 'Cornucopia,' the horn of plenty. This being done, the multitude assembled at the tables. The minister of the place was given the seat of honor at the head of the table, flanked by soldiers of the revolution and the war of 1812, while along down the line were farmers, merchants, manufacturers, and laborers. Grace was said with all due reverence, and the feast was commenced. Liquor had been passed at intervals during the afternoon, but to the credit of those pioneers, be it said, none were intoxicated. They had assembled to assist their neighbor and in extending that courtesy then so prevalent among the pioneers forty-five years ago. There was a mutual dependence upon each other that does not exist at the present day and hence the indifference of the present generation to those neighborly acts which were a distinguishing trait in the character of the early and pioneer settler."

"Uncle Jonas, allow me to introduce you to Frank W. Clark, one of Mansfield's prominent lawyers. Mr. Clark is a democrat, but liberal and broad-minded in his views."

"Happy to welcome you, Mr. Lawrence, to our borough; I hope you will enjoy yourself during your visit."

"Thank you, Mr. Clark. I am very much interested in your thriving and prosperous village."

"Mr. Lawrence, let me introduce J. M. Clark, a brother of mine, who is a merchant here. We are sons of Elijah P. Clark."

"Ah, Mr. Clark, I knew your father and grandfather well. Your grandfather was Elijah Clark, a native of Massachusetts, and lived for many years a few miles north of here, near Lamb's Creek, did he not?"

"Yes, sir, and he died January 5, 1864, aged eighty-one. My father, Elijah Pinchen Clark, died a short time since, aged about seventy-eight years. I knew them well, Mr. Clark. It is thus the old landmarks are fading out and passing away."

"Uncle Jonas, we have an hour or more at our disposal, suppose we go out Wellsboro Street to the Tioga River. This burnt district and where this new building is being erected, was the former site of Straight & Kohler's hardware store."

"This cut, Harry, was thought in 1840, when they were constructing the railroad, to be one of the heaviest on the road. It was deemed then a great undertaking. With modern appliances and machinery, it would now be deemed a mere trifle."

"Down yonder, Uncle Jonas, where you see those glass cases, are the market and floral garden of Robert Crossley. You should have seen it two months ago. It would have convinced you that the west is not the only place where vegetables can be raised to advantage. I wished we had time to call on Dr. Joseph P. Morris. He purchased in 1850 what was termed the town plat of Mansfield. He came from Philadelphia to Blossburg in the year 1835, and was interested in the Morris Run lands. He subsequently resided at Wellsboro and married Miss Sarah E., daughter of the Hon. Samuel W.

Morris, one of the most prominent early settlers of that borough. In 1853 he came here to Mansfield, where he has since resided. He was prominently associated with a company who erected the furnace hitherto spoken of in the year 1854. Has been a trustee of the State Normal school, and every enterprise calculated to benefit Mansfield he has done well his part. That new building belongs to Thomas H. Bailey, one of Mansfield's energetic men. Mr. Bailey is president of the Smythe Park Association. Near him is the residence of Burt Schrader, another active businessman. That gentleman you see with a white hat walking across the track, is William H. Kinney, the active station agent at Mansfield, and also the general passenger and freight agent for the Tioga branch of the Erie. Mr. Kinney has been in the employ of the company for nearly ten years here at Mansfield, and is one of the most efficient officials of the road. That gentleman going from the freight depot is Andrew Sherwood, the geologist, a gentleman who has been connected with the second geological survey of Pennsylvania, He has rendered great service to the state by his untiring and intelligent work. He is now engaged in the milling business in the northern portion of the borough. That fine farm you see on the west side of the river yonder in the northwest is called the 'Sherwood farm.' Its former owner was the Hon. Daniel L, Sherwood, a prominent citizen of Mansfield and Tioga County. He was born in Marathon, NY, December 5, 1809, and came to Mansfield in the year 1830. In the years 1842 and 1843 he was elected to the popular branch of the state legislature. In the years 1844, 1845 and 1846 he was elected senator in the district composed of Tioga and Bradford Counties, and in 1846 was chosen speaker of the senate of Pennsylvania. He was an ardent democrat. He removed to Northumberland County, PA, in the year 1869, and served two terms of two years each in the legislature, representing that county in the years 1877 to 1880 inclusive. The farm that you see further to the north, where that wind-mill is in operation, is owned by L. H. Shattuck, the old superintendent of this road. Mr. Shattuck, for thirty-two consecutive years wag the superintendent of this road and voluntarily retired from that position. He is a gentleman highly respected for his impartiality and kindly treatment of those employees who came in contact with him in the management and working of the several departments of labor connected with the road. That gentleman, Uncle Jonas, who passed by here a moment ago, wearing spectacles, was Joseph S. Hoard, Jr., a young man of rare business qualifications. His father. Colonel Joseph S. Hoard, was a former prominent citizen of Mansfield. He came to Mansfield in the year 1844. Ten years later he was prominently connected with the establishment of the State Normal School, and with the erection of a blast furnace. When the rebellion occurred he enlisted and was finally promoted to the several intermediate grades until he reached that of lieutenant-colonel. He died a few years since in Florida. Uncle Jonas, suppose we go around on to Main street again. I want to call on my friend M. L. Clark, who for many years has officiated as the village postmaster with more than ordinary satisfaction to the public."

"Very well, Harry."

"That gentleman going into the bank is Mr. Charles Kingsley, a tanner, one of Mansfield's prominent citizens. This gentleman that we are about to meet is Fenton Allen, son of Almon Allen, one of the pioneers of this place, and brother of the late Professor Fordyce A. Allen."

TIOGA AND ITS ENVIRONS.
ITS PEOPLE AND ITS BUSINESS ADVANTAGES —
THE RETURN TO ELMIRA.

The train, Uncle Jonas, is reported half an hour late. That will enable us to get an early supper before leaving Mansfield, and have ample time to go to the depot. I must again repeat that I am pleased with my visit to Mansfield. There are some old settlers whom we have not called on or talked about. But that will always be the case.

"As we go down the road tonight, we will pass through Kelleytown and Lamb's Creek. Gad Lamb was the first settler at the latter named point. He arrived there July 4, 1797. At this place (Mansfield) he found Benjamin Corey located in his bark cabin. The creek yonder, Corey creek, is named in his honor. We have neglected to call on Lorin Butts, who lives in the southern portion of the borough, and upon the Jeralds, who live on Corey Creek, east of here, and many others whose names, however, I have mentioned. Ten years ago. Uncle Jonas, I called on Lorm Lamb, who then resided in this place, and who was an old man then, but his mind was fresh and active. He gave me an account of his father's coming to Pennsylvania in 1797 and related many incidents connected with the early settlement of this valley and Tioga county. He was born in Springfield, Massachusetts, in the year 1789, and recollected well the trip from that state to Mansfield in 1797. His father, Gad Lamb, was born in Wilbraham, near Springfield, Massachusetts, November 20, 1744, and was married January 7, 1779, to Miss Jerusha Ripley, of Windham, Connecticut. Their children were Daniel, Harry, Sally, Patty, Jerusha, Lorain, Nancy, Clarissa, Maria and Ebenezer. An old settler, Harry, of the name of Ripley, with whom I was acquainted, lived at Lamb's Creek. His name was Ebenezer Ripley. He had been an officer in the revolutionary war— major, I think. He settled at Lamb's creek about the year 1817 and was a brother-in-law of Gad Lamb, Jerusha, wife of Gad Lamb, being his sister. He died April 30, 1849, aged eighty-three years. With his son, William C. Ripley, I was also acquainted. I frequently saw him in Elmira and at his home at Lamb's Creek. The family were from Cooperstown, Otsego County. New York, but formerly of New England origin I am told that William C. Ripley is still living at the advanced age of eighty-eight. The Cochrans were old residents at Lamb's Creek — John and Abner. They were from Bennington, Vermont, and came into this valley in the year 1816. John died in the year 1877, aged ninety-eight years, seven months, and fourteen days. His brother Abner died the same year, aged eighty-eight years. One of their descendants is a celebrated Methodist minister and has been a presiding elder.

"David Corbett was an early settler on Lamb's creek. He settled on Lamb's Creek in the year 1830 and made the first clearing on that stream. In 1831, Michael Fralich, from Marathon, NY, settled at Lamb's Creek, and for many years was a prominent citizen. His death occurred quite recently. His wife was Angelina, daughter of Daniel Lamb. His sons, Daniel and Henry Fralich, are energetic men engaged in farming and lumbering upon an extensive scale."

"Our time is up, Uncle Jonas. Well, Mr. Earnest, you have made our visit pleasant, and in our travels about the country, we may call on you again."

"Thank you, gentlemen; I shall be pleased to entertain you whenever you call this way."

"Uncle Jonas, there is one place that I would have been pleased to see. That is the elegant cemetery situated upon the hillside east of the railroad, a few rods north of here. You can always judge of the character of a community by the manner in which it cares for the city of the dead. There is no better standard. If you visit a cemetery that is overgrown with weeds and briars, the fence and walks neglected, the grave-stones or monuments moss-covered and out of place, you can safely conclude that the community is a shiftless, careless, thoughtless and irreverent people. The people of Mansfield take great care of their cemetery. It is not a gloomy, cheerless spot, and robs death, the grim monster, of much of his terrors by the loving care and watchfulness exercised by the men and women of the borough."

"Harry, I have thought that we might as well spend the week in this valley. This is only Friday night. Suppose we go to Tioga tonight, look over the village tomorrow, and take the afternoon train."

"Suit yourself, Uncle Jonas."

"Buy tickets, then, for Tioga, Harry. Yonder comes the train."

"Good evening, Mr. Shattuck! We are going only to Tioga tonight and will go down to Elmira tomorrow afternoon on the freight. I want to cross over the mountain and descend into the valley of the Chemung by daylight."

"I know that the freight train is a slow train, but then it gives me time to look about me and observe the country."

"That is true, gentlemen. I suppose, Mr. Lawrence, that you and your nephew, Mr. Sampson, have had a good time this week."

"We are passing now the residence of the late James R. Wilson, for many years president of the Corning & Blossburg Railroad. He was a native of New Jersey; born in the year 1807, and a graduate of Princeton College. He studied law and was admitted to practice, but being interested in the mines at Blossburg and in the Corning & Blossburg Railroad, he came into the valley about the year 1838, and assisted in the construction of the railroad and became its president. He was also prominently connected with the enterprise of relaying the track with T iron in the year 1852. He was polished in manners, refined in his taste, considerate of the rights of those with whom he had intercourse, warm-hearted, benevolent and kind,

173

a friend to the poor, an efficient officer and an obliging neighbor. He was familiarly known as 'President Wilson.' The last time I saw him, Uncle Jonas, was at the funeral of the Hon. John Magee, which occurred April 7, 1868. President Wilson attended the funeral which was held at Watkins Glen, NY. A strong tie of friendship existed between President Wilson and Mr. Magee, and Mr. Wilson was nearly overcome with grief. He wept like a child, thus manifesting that kind sympathy, which was one of the distinguishing traits in his character. President Wilson died December 24, 1871, aged sixty-five years. He and his wife, Margaret Smith Wilson, were among the founders of St. James Episcopal Church at Mansfield, Mr. Wilson being its first senior warden."

"Where, Harry, did the Rev. Asa Donaldson reside?"

"We have passed his old homestead. It was situated on the west side of the Tioga River, near the farm of Levi H. Shattuck. I remember Mr. Donaldson well. He was one of the pioneer ministers of this valley. I was acquainted with him before he came to Pennsylvania. He was born in Massachusetts, September 4, 1788, and subsequently settled in Otsego County, NY, about the year 1805 and studied for the ministry, and was licensed to preach in the year 1811. He was for several years stationed at Guilford, Chenango County, New York, and while residing there several times visited Elmira. He was a Presbyterian. Over a half-century ago, he came to Tioga County. PA, locating temporarily at Lawrenceville and Tioga. In the Rev, Asa Donaldson, the pioneer of this valley found a friend. One that did by his amiable character and example lead them to high and noble aspirations. He guided with a steady hand their actions to a great extent, and taught them scriptural truths, the amenities and civilities of a Christian community. He was aided largely by his accomplished and amiable wife. He raised a large and respectable family, who have honored his memory by becoming useful and influential men and women. His death

174

occurred in the centennial year, in the state of Iowa, and his remains were buried in my adopted state, Illinois, at Malden, beside his deceased wife."

"Here we are at Tioga. We will take the Park Hotel omnibus, Uncle Jonas, and go and call upon Mr. Cole, the hospitable landlord. This, Mr. Cole, is Uncle Jonas Lawrence, come to spend the night in your well-kept hotel."

"Good evening, Uncle Jonas, glad to receive you as a guest."

A pleasant room is assigned to them, warm, comfortable, cozy, and well-furnished. Here they spend the night, and after breakfast the next morning, Uncle Jonas and Harry take a walk around in that beautiful village, discussing old times, old settlers and the present inhabitants. Among the many citizens whom they meet is that genial, warm-hearted, and companionable gentleman, the Hon. Thomas L. Baldwin, who for two terms represented Tioga County in the assembly of the state, and who for many years was the leading merchant in this village. Time has dealt kindly with him, and, although Mr. Baldwin has met with many reverses by fires and financial misfortunes, yet he is the same courteous gentleman as of yore. There is no acidity in his manner or conversation but meets his present customers and old friends with affability and politeness. A child or an old and infirm person receives the same kind attention in his store as those who are in the health and vigor of ripe manhood, or in affluent circumstances. He never lost a friend by any act of his but has gained thousands by his uniform courtesy. His ancestry in America dates back to its early settlement. They meet and converse with the Hon. Frederic E. Smith, a distinguished lawyer, and prominent citizen, with Dr. R. B. Smith, Jacob Schieflein, S. M. Geer, W. T. Urell, Colonel Gabriel T. narrower, Dr. Barden, Frank Adams, Jabin Bush, E. P. H. McAllister, T. L. Baldwin, Philo Tuller, O. B. Lowell, T. A. Wickham, E. A. Smead, C. B. Farr, H. E. Smith, Paul Kraiss and many others conversed regarding the Jesse Losev family, the Roberts family and the families and pioneers, the Mitchells, the Ives, the Adams, Kiphart, Berry, Jennings, Spencer, Niles, Willard, Millard, Bush, Elliott, Prutsman, Guernsey, Bentley, Inscho, Hotchkiss, Baldwin, Depui, Daily, Lawrence, Goodrich, Caulking, Vail, Allen, Westbrook, Welsh, Garretson, Mayord, Bigelow, Wickham, Farr, Seymour, Tuttle, Warren, Schiefflein, Hathaway, Duvey, Daggett, Bishop, and many others, spending one of the most pleasant and agreeable forenoons in many days. They admired the streets, the neat and costly dwellings, the fine churches, the substantial business places, visited Bush's Park, the coke ovens, of which we shall refer to visit Tioga via the Fall Brook Railroad again."

Uncle Jonas became intensely interested in recalling the old families named and speaking of their many distinguished traits of character, their social relations, their pioneer hardships, their sports of the field and forest, and concluded by saying:

"Harry, l am more surprised at the change witnessed here by viewing this beautiful village than I would have been had a great and populous city been found here. Here is a beautiful village, with wide and shady streets, elegant homes, neat churches and schools, provided with waterworks, with ample railroad facilities, one railroad traversing the eastern boundary and another her western, leading south to Philadelphia, and north and eastward to New York and westward to Buffalo and Chicago, with a soil as fertile as a garden, with landscape and mountain scenery, grand in the extreme. Surely, Harry, it is a great surprise to me that Tioga, with all these natural and acquired facilities, has not been seized by the hand of industry and made the center of a large population engaged in manufacturing and varied industrial pursuits. She yet will be spied out, and the hum of machinery will be heard in this rural borough now so serenely sitting on the banks of the Tioga crooked creek and the Elkhorn in the shade of these mountains, now covered so magnificently with the autumn foliage of the forest trees."

176

"One lucky capitalist and manufacturer will yet locate at this point and will be followed by others in quick succession. Fortunate indeed is he who is the pioneer in this industrial enterprise. Northern Pennsylvania and southern New York, within a radius of seventy-five miles, will, in the next half-century, become one great workshop. The position holds geographically, and her juxtaposition it bears to the forests of timber, coal, iron, and glass material will accomplish it. The child is living today who will witness it. Already is the foundation laid for such an achievement, and year by year will labor, capital and enterprise, rear the super-structure. I saw Chicago, Harry, forty years ago, the germs of a great city, and plead with and implored my eastern friends to go thither and invest. Some went, but many lost the golden opportunity. One million souls now inhabit the spot, where forty years ago there were not then sixty thousand people, and perhaps today in this little borough, far-seeing individuals, without capital, are pleading with their friends to come hither and invest, who will turn a deaf ear to their solicitations, but who five or ten years hence, will be mourning over lost opportunities and golden chances and sighing over "what might have been."

It was dinner hour when Uncle Jonas had finished his remarks, and he and Harry entered the Park Hotel and passed into the elegant dining room of Mr. Coles.

Dinner being over, Uncle Jonas and Harry leisurely prepare for the train that would take them to Elmira. On their way from the hotel to the depot, they had an opportunity of viewing the hillside park so admirably and elegantly fitted up by the late Hon. A. C. Bush, and during his lifetime kept in such a tasty and attractive condition, provided with so many conveniences and amusing appliances, where people by the thousand could assemble, promenade its shady groves, recline in its easy chairs, enjoy music and dancing in its halls, lunches and sumptuous dinners in its spacious dining rooms, siestas in its arbors, refreshing draughts of clear spring water, without charge or fee. Where patriot anniversaries were held, where Sunday school picnics, family gatherings, church parties, temperance meetings, religious or other services were held, reflecting upon the generous mind that conceived, and the benevolent hand that furnished all these things for the amusement, gratification, and convenience of all who chose to enter its limits and conduct themselves with decency and propriety. When Harry had described to Uncle Jonas the beauty of the park, the commanding view it gave of the valley of the Tioga, to those who chose to enter its domain and cast their eyes over the landscape spread out before them. It made a great impression upon the mind of the old gentleman and recalled the sturdy pioneer and active businessman, who more than fifty years ago left the banks of the Chenango and made a home on the banks of the Tioga, another branch of that grand old river, the Susquehanna, of his struggles in the vocation of lumberman, merchant, and farmer, and his ripe old age, blessed with wealth and affluence, and a heart overflowing with kindness towards his fellow man, made the name of Asa C. Bush doubly dear to him. For a few moments, they walked in silence. At length, Uncle Jonas said: "Harry, I do not believe in prodigality or spending one's substance in riotous living or erecting costly dwellings for the gratification of a desire to do something to excel neighbor or overshadow his less expensive edifice; but I do believe that my old friend, A. C. Bush, set an example which it would be well for men of wealth to imitate. When fortune has smiled upon them when they have secured a competency for themselves and those in their care, that it is their duty to provide as far as it is within their power facilities for their less favored friends and the public generally, some way whereby they can be amused, their reasonable desires gratified, their spirits enlivened, their courage renewed, or the sorrows, griefs, and disappointments allayed by retiring to a spot like Bush's Park or in some central hall, library, museum, drive or walk, enlivened by music, while away a few hours, leaving behind them their burdens and gathering strength for the future battles of life. I do not believe that well-directed charity lessens the independence of manhood, but on the contrary, strengthens mankind and stimulates them to greater exertions. Very many men, Harry, I have seen in a great financial strait when it only took a few encouraging words and a little substantial aid to tide them over the threatened rock of disaster, and they sailed on thereafter with greater prudence and renewed effort, coming out of the difficulty victorious and acquiring a position which enabled them, to not only take care of themselves but assist their neighbor who was on the point of being stranded! Yonder comes the train, Harry. Buy the tickets, and we will board it when it arrives."

"All aboard!"

When the conductor, Michael Clauhesey, comes to gather the tickets, Harry introduces Uncle Jonas to him and makes an arrangement to telegraph to R. B. Cable, the superintendent of the road, to get permission to ride on the engine from Tioga Junction to the Summit, in order that they may improve the time while the train is running from Tioga Junction to Lawrenceville, in looking around, and perhaps walking down to the next station east of the summit in order to catch a view of the valley of the Chemung. Permission being granted, Uncle Jonas is introduced to John Keating, who has charge of the train from Tioga Junction, and to William Wallace, the engineer of the "pusher," two old and experienced railroad men. Being comfortably seated in the cab of the engine, the signal was given and the ascent began. The first exhaust showed the giant power of that iron horse. Up, up they go, the tireless engine exerting itself to its utmost capacity until the summit is reached. Having left their baggage in the car at the foot of the mountain, Uncle Jonas and Harry determined to walk about half a mile from the summit, and go out into the fields to the south of the railroad track, whence they would have a better view of the distant valley to the east. Arriving at the desired point, they stood and gazed upon the delightful landscape before them. Uncle Jonas, after a few minutes, turned to Harry and said: "Each sovereign state, whether in the eastern or western hemisphere, claims 'the right of eminent domain.' All titles to land must originally come from them, reserving in their grants, in many instances the ownership of all precious minerals. They also reserve the right for all time to come to exercise jurisdiction over all territories or lands sold and conveyed. In time a multitude of persons inhabit these concessions or grants. Communities are the outgrowth, families are reared, children are born and grow to manhood and womanhood. However rude the dwelling in which these children are born and reared, and however rugged the country in which they are surrounded, that dwelling, that country, and its hills, mountains, rocks, rivers, lakes, and streams, becomes theirs not by purchase, but by association. Seventy-five years ago I was born in the valley of the Chemung. It was there I was reared and educated. It was there I spent my boyhood, youth, and early manhood. I became acquainted with its rivulets, cascades, rivers, plains, hills and mountains. They were impressed upon my mind, and became a portion of myself and my possessions. The valleys, hills and mountains have been stripped of their forests to a great extent, but their outlines remain. The state exercises a jurisdiction over them, the farmer cultivates the soil, the merchant has erected warehouses, the citizen has built costly dwellings, the hand of industry has founded workshops, commerce has dug canals, constructed railroads, science and art have combined to make it beautiful, religion and education have built churches, schools and colleges, and although in law there is not a foot of land in that whole region I can hold, yet originally all that territory was mine, is mine now, because it was my heritage, and remains not only my heritage but the property of thousands of others like me, who were born there and reared there the same as I, and whose claim does not interfere with mine, nor mine with theirs.

Children for generations to come will claim it as I claim it. With such a state of claims existing what becomes of the principles of eminent domain. It is such claims as those I make which create the love of home and country, begets patriotism and incites the soldier to defend with his life not only his fireside and family but his country. Often, Harry, I have sat in the union depot in Chicago and seen the tide of emigration flow in from Germany, Italy, France, England, Ireland, Scotland, Switzerland and the countries beyond the great ocean, and saw them hurried further onward towards the setting sun, have I pictured in my mind the naive homes of those foreigners as they passed me, and wondered whether they carried with them as I did the memories of my childhood home? And I instinctively answered the question for them in the affirmative. Then it was that I could tell why the images of the landscapes upon the Rhine, the sunny climes of France and Italy, the merry farms of England, the emerald shades of Erin, the rugged hills of Scotland and Switzerland were boldly outlined in their faces, and mirrored their nationality in every action. Each one, no doubt, held the memory of their native home in sacred remembrance, and however loyal they may be to the land of their adoption, yet close to their heart is their native land. So, did I carry to my western adopted home the memories of the valley of the Chemung. And as I stand here upon this summit, overlooking that lovely valley, I cannot resist the impulse to revert to these things and give voice to my thoughts."

"The train will be due herein half an hour at the summit, Uncle Jonas, and we had better return to the depot." They return, take the cars and in due season are landed at the Erie depot at Elmira, and in a few minutes are at their homes on West Water Street, pleased and delighted with their trip over the Tioga branch of the Erie into the valley of the Tioga and the Blossburg coal region.

Next week they will go to Big Flats and Corning, and thence over the roads owned or leased by the Fall Brook Coal Company.

THE ERIE RAILWAY.
HISTORY OF THE GREAT ROAD —
MEN CONNECTED WITH IT.

U ncle Jonas and his faithful companion decided to rest for a short time in Elmira before resuming their pleasant wanderings. Among the many exciting topics considered by them during their breathing spell was the construction of the Erie Railroad, now known as the New York, Lake Erie & Western, was discussed, and Harry gave Uncle Jonas a general history and description of this great trunk line, which for the past thirty-five years has been the pride of the inhabitants of the southern tier of New York. In doing that, Harry said:

The New York & Erie Railroad was chartered April 24, 1832, the proposed initial point being Piermont, on the Hudson, and the terminal point, Dunkirk, on Lake Erie. The road was opened from Piermont to Goshen in September 1841; to Middletown in June 1813; to Port Jervis in January 1818; to Binghamton December 1848; to Elmira October 1849; to Corning January 1850, and completed to Dunkirk May 14, 1851, a little over nineteen years from the time it received its charter. The recitals of its trials and tribulations, its years of misfortunes and bankruptcies, its days of prosperity and adversity, would fill a volume. It was originally designed as a great trunk line from New York through the southern tier of counties, adjacent to the almost inexhaustible forests of timber, coal, and iron of northern and northeastern Pennsylvania and the rich and productive agricultural districts of Broome, Tioga, Chemung, Steuben, Allegany, Cattaraugus and Chautauqua counties in New York. No sooner had it been completed than lateral branches were surveyed, located and constructed either by the company or by other compa-

nies who desired to avail themselves of the facilities it afforded of rapid, safe, and cheap transportation to New York in the east or Lake Erie in the west. Year by year have these branch roads been constructed until now they extend north into central and northwestern New York, to Rochester and Buffalo and Newburgh on the Hudson, and southward into the anthracite and semi-bituminous coal fields of Pennsylvania, and the rich and productive oil fields of that state, thus making tributary to their trunk line railroads which bring to the mainline millions of tons of coal and iron, millions of barrels of oil, immense quantities of lumber and bark, almost a countless number of passengers, and a freight traffic in agricultural and manufactured articles, which employ thousands of locomotives and many thousands of freight cars in moving this immense volume of commodities which are seeking a market over their lines. This road has from time to time made connections with railroads reaching from its western terminus in New York which traverse the great states of Ohio, Indiana, Illinois, Michigan, Wisconsin, Minnesota, Missouri, and the south and west that delivers to it the grain, cattle, and other commodities of the west, and in return transports the goods and merchandise of the east to these remote and intermediate points in the west. Its freight traffic is not its only source of revenue. The passenger business is simply enormous. Nor is that line of business confined chiefly to those thousands of emigrants from the old countries, who fill its long trains, but the merchant, the mechanic, the citizen, the businessman, the tourist and those who desire to spend a vacation in gazing at the many beautiful landscapes, the cities, and towns that are located along its line. Before the Erie had completed to Dunkirk, it made arrangements whereby it ran into New Jersey to Jersey City, keeping open, however, its original line from Suffern to Piermont. For years, therefore, the passenger going west departed from Twenty-third Street, New York

City, crossed the ferry into Jersey City, and at the latter point has taken a Pullman sleeper or elegantly upholstered passenger car, and the rate of forty miles per hour has been whirled through New Jersey up into the Catskill ranges of mountains, a portion of the eastern spurs of the Alleghenies, which divides the waters of the Hudson, Delaware and Susquehanna rivers, passing through the great manufacturing city of Paterson, with its busy population of sixty thousand, and with tireless energy the locomotive has drawn him up into one of the grandest scenic localities of the middle states. He sees away up in the mountains the waters of the Delaware River, which flows southward until it reaches the populous city of Philadelphia with its millions of inhabitants. He sees the lofty mountains in all their grandeur, the rippling stream, the dashing river, and the rocks, which for untold ages have held their place, unshaken and unmoved by the hand of time — the rugged forests, the plains and plateau, the land of milk and golden butter, and finally arrives at Binghamton, upon the Susquehanna, after having been crowded into Pennsylvania by the mountains of New York. At Binghamton, a new and varied landscape is presented to him. The wild and picturesque scenery of Delaware is exchanged for a country rich in agricultural products, elegant farmhouses, and pleasing landscapes. Binghamton is a city, the offspring of the Erie, which reflects credit upon its foster parent, with its 25,000 inhabitants, its schools and churches, its asylums, its manufactories, its grand hotels, its costly dwellings, its spirited and intelligent press, its enterprising merchants and its refined and cultured people. Leaving Binghamton the traveler glides smoothly down along the bank of the eastern branch of the Susquehanna, a valley made historic by the sturdy pioneers, who, nearly a hundred years ago, took possession by purchase of its then primeval forest and made their homes in the wilderness upon soil held dear by the red man of the six nations, passing through

Owego, the county seat of Tioga County, with its 7,000 inhabitants, elegantly located upon the north shore of the beautiful east branch, with its many points of local and historical interest made memorable by its historian and orator, Judge Avery, and the classical scholar and poet N. P. Wills, the home of Colonel David Pixley, who distinguished himself at the siege of Quebec in 1775, under General Montgomery, and who was the pioneer settler in 1790, and thence onward, rolling swiftly through many varied and pleasant views, reaching Waverly near the great Indian gateway, which for a century was guarded and vigilantly watched by the red men, lest some pale-faced intruder from the south should ascend the north branch of the Susquehanna and trespass upon their hunting grounds along the valley of the Big Horn (Chemung). Leaving the east branch of the Susquehanna to unite its waters with those of the Chemung and thus form the north branch of the Susquehanna, the traveler is propelled northward up the valley of the Chemung, which at every revolution of the driving wheel continues to open up into a wider and more fertile region, passing under the shadow of the Chemung monument, a memorial erected by the patriotic citizens of the Chemung and Wyoming valleys in the year 1879, to commemorate the victory won by General John Sullivan over the British, Tories and Indians, during the revolutionary war in August 1779, a hundred years before; speeding away through rich and alluvial regions, over historic grounds to Elmira (Newtown Point), the scene of Indian treaties (Kanaweola) with the chiefs and warriors of the six nations, and now the site of the Queen City of the Southern Tier; thence northward along the beautiful valley, following nearly the old Indian pathway to Seneca Lake for a distance of four or five miles from Elmira; then by a short curve wheeling westward through a broad and fertile valley to Big Flats, and thence westward to Corning in a valley unsurpassed in loveliness

185

and rich in agricultural products. At Corning the passenger can diverge if he chooses from the main line and ascend the Conhocton to Bath, a town founded in 1793 by General Charles Williamson, agent for the Pultney estate of England, and in doing so will pass through one of the finest valleys of the upper waters of the Susquehanna and enter a section of country distinguished for its fertility, its neat villages, refined inhabitants, its fields of waving grain, its flocks and herds, its vine- yards and orchards of delicious fruit, reaching Rochester, on the Genesee, with its one hundred thousand inhabitants, surrounded by a country rich in nurseries, flowers, fruits, and cereals, and view the Genesee River as it tumbles over rocks and precipices until it reaches Lake Ontario, a few miles distant; or he can continue on the main line from Painted Post, a town whose annals are famous in Indian history, which modestly reclines upon the east bank of the Conhocton River, and thence up the valley to the westward to Addison on the Canisteo River, a tributary of the Chemung, and thence westward along the historic valley of the Canisteo to Hornellsville, the terminus of the Susquehanna division. At Hornellsville the traveler will find a large and populous incorporated village, teeming with industrial and commercial pursuits, and he can either take the Buffalo division route up to Canaseraga, Dalton, Warsaw, Attica to Buffalo, or continue on the Western division to Wellsville, Cuba, Clean, Salamanca to Dunkirk, passing through the counties of Allegany, Cattaraugus, and Chautauqua, and crossing the Genesee River, and touching the Allegheny River at Olean, which rises in the highlands of Potter county, Pennsylvania, and flowing northward into New York, thence westward and southward until it unites with the Monongahela at Pittsburgh, PA, to form Ohio. He will be delighted with the passage by the varied and pleasing scenery. Here a busy and thriving village supported by an agricultural district, there a town en-

gaged in manufacturing, again another stimulated by the production of petroleum, huge tanks of oil in great numbers will be seen. He will also have an opportunity of seeing the red man upon his reservation in his semi-civilized state. He will also see hills, mountains, and meadows, orchards, fields of waving grain in their season, elegant farmhouses, capacious barns, and manufacturing establishments of every conceivable kind. He will also see miniature railroads, ascending a grade of 150 feet to the mile, with a three-foot gauge, winding around the face of the hills, crossing ravines, and scaling heights not attainable by the standard gauge locomotives. He will also see pumping stations for forcing petroleum through pipelines to near and distant places, and a thousand and one things, Uncle Jonas, which I will not task your patience to relate. It takes an army of men to conduct the affairs of this grand old Erie and all of its branches. I will only attempt to name its principal officials today, but before you leave for the west Ave will take a trip over the Susquehanna division from Susquehanna to Hornellsville, and talk over matters of interest, and become personally acquainted with many of its subordinate officials and visit the principal cities and towns along its line. John King is president of the Erie company; S. M. Felton, Jr., vice-president; Charles Paine, second vice-president; James A. Buchanan, attorney; A. R. MacDonough, secretary; Edward White, treasurer; B. Thomas, general superintendent; F. M. Wilder, superintendent of motive power; H. D. Blunden, engineer maintenance of way; W. G. Fuller, purchasing agent; Stephen Little, controller; A. J. McDowell, auditor; John N. Abbott, general ticket and passenger agent; John Hammond, general freight agent; J. M. Drill, division freight agent, Jersey City; William C. Buck, division freight agent, Elmira, NY; J. M. Horton, division freight agent, Rochester, N.Y.; J. Deuell, division freight agent, Buffalo, N.Y.; E. G. Hill, superintendent eastern division, Jersey City; E. Van Etten, su-

perintendent Delaware division. Port Jervis; R. B. Cable, superintendent Susquehanna division and Tioga branch, Elmira, NY; W. J. Murphy, superintendent Buffalo division Buffalo, NY, also superintendent Rochester division; W. B. Coffin, superintendent Western division, Hornellsville, NY; C, A. Brunn, superintendent Buffalo and Southwestern division, Buffalo, NY; D. H. Blackham, superintendent transportation.

"No, one, Uncle Jonas, can adequately estimate the benefits which the construction of the Erie Railroad has conferred upon the people of the city of New York, the southern tier counties of the state, and the northern tier of Pennsylvania, and the great west. Cities and towns have sprung up along its line, industrial establishments have been constructed, mines have been opened, wells of petroleum have been sunk, agriculture promoted and the country developed, waste places made fertile and fruitful, schools, colleges, churches, asylums, established directly and indirectly by its developing influence. It has been a great promoter of punctuality in the business affairs of life. Until the Erie was constructed we had no standard time in southern New York which we were compelled to observe. Under the old stagecoach regime, a great allowance was made for the variation of time, a half-hour is considered of no consequence. When Erie put forth its first timetable or schedule of arrival and departure of trains, the businessman, traveler, and laboring man entered upon a new era. It taught lessons of punctuality in business, in the hours of labor, and generally impressed the people of the necessity of being on time. Before this there was a general go-as-you-please program. Each businessman or manufacturer had a different schedule of time by which they regulated the business hours or hours of labor, while some had no fixed hours and adopted the rule of working from daylight till dark, regardless of whether the sun shone eight or fifteen hours per day. All these things were in time remedied. The tardy traveler, male or female, was left in the depot to ponder over their lack of punctuality, the incorrectness of their chronometers, or to use the King's English in an ungrammatical style, for being only five minutes behind schedule time. Uniform time has thus. Uncle Jonas taught the people lessons of punctuality, unknown before the era of railroads.

"Tomorrow, Uncle Jonas, we will take a short ride over the Erie to Big Flats and Corning, when you can have an opportunity of riding on this grand old pioneer railroad, the first to enter the valley of the Chemung."

IN CHEMUNG COUNTY.
A VISIT TO BIG FLATS— THE FARMING AND
BUSINESS COMMUNITY.

"Good morning, Uncle Jonas. I hope my long talk about the Erie and its branches did not fatigue you?"

"Oh, no, Harry, I am never better pleased than when I am listening to the recital of the history connected with the construction of a great thoroughfare like the Erie."

"I have arranged it, Uncle Jonas, that we take a train this afternoon on the Erie at 1:10PM and go up to Big Flats and remain there overnight. It will give you an opportunity of meeting some of the descendants of your old friends in that town and village."

"Very well, Harry, I will be ready in time. Your remarks upon time, yesterday, impressed me very much. I never thought before of giving the railroads of the country credit for the uniformity of time, and lessons of punctuality which they enforce upon the businessman, laboring man, traveler, and the community in general. Upon reflection, your remarks are reasonable and remind me of the miscellaneous way in which time was observed before the era of railroads."

"This is our train, Uncle Jonas. Here is your ticket, uncle. Now for Big Flats. What a comfortable seat; and smoothly and swiftly we glide along. Here we are at West Junction; we will soon be in the town of Big Flats. Perhaps I have told you when the town of Big Flats was organized; if not, I will now. It was organized by an act of the legislature April 16, 1822, session forty- five, as will be seen by Chapter 121 of that year, taken from Elmira. I recollect well when it was organized and what was said about it in Elmira. The legislature convened that year on January 1 and adjourned on April 17, the next day after the bill was passed for its organization. The Hon. Jared Patchen represented Tioga County in the assembly and the Hon. Gamaliel H. Barstow in the senate. Chemung had not then been formed. But, Harry, I do not wish to recall or revive the memory of old feuds, and will therefore desist from further explanation. Here we are at the town line. The early settlers in this vicinity were Nathan Saunders, Roswell Goff, Jr., son of the Rev. Roswell Goff, Comfort Bennett and his sons George, Horace, Daniel, Morris and Andrew J., Peter Mead, Benjamin Whitney, Calvin Hawkins, Isaac Manning, Abram Scofield, John C. Scofield, Daniel Scofield, John F. Delaney, Jonathan Kent, George Shilver, Joseph Rowley, Noah Hawley, John Bennett, Ebenezer Snow, John Goff, John Brown, Usual Goble, Cornelius Lowe, Gershom Livesay, Hezekiah Mead, Aries Hodge and others whose names escape me now. They resided in that portion of Big Flats known as 'Sing Sing.' On the left of us was Eleazer Owen, Clark Winans, Henry Farr, father of Valentine, John, W. H., and James E. Farr, Aaron Cook, Judah Mead, Ira Mead and John Mead, sons of Hezekiah Mead, Colonel Van Valen, Salmon Beard, Salmon Rowley, Doctor Thesus Brooks, John Winters, William Miller, Robert Miller. Robert Miller owned the farm east of the village of Big Flats. North of the village were Frederic Vaughan, David Trumble Vaughn, Samuel Minier, John L. Sexton, William H. Reeder, James Jackson, better known as "Old Hickory," John White, John S. Miller, Joseph Deates and still further north up Gardiner creek and on Hooker's and Reeser's hill were Robert P. Owen, Cornelius Harrington, Michael Shea, Justus Luce, John Baker, Anthony Reeser, William Ellison, senior, William T. Hooker, Austin Hooker, Daniel Reeser, and northeast from Big Flats were Giles Allard, Jacob Dorn, Ami Carrier, Lewis Pound, Henry Fuller, Darius Bennett, Telman N. Bennett, Ansel Carlton, Thomas Buck, Henry Minier, Frederic Wolcott, Charles Frye, John Silsby, Joseph Pound, Hezekiah Beebe, James Farr, Paul W. Breed, and to the southeast of the village, on the River Road to Elmira, were John

McNulty, Hezekiah Woodruff, Judson M. Park, Nathan Reynolds, Caleb L. Gardiner, David Reynolds, Levi Lovell, Reuben Lovell, Smith, Joseph Rhodes, Christian Minier, Joseph Parks, Simon Hawes, and across the river near the Elmira township line, were Orson H. Fitch, Daniel K. Fitch, Colonel John Hendy, Jr. I declare, Harry, here we are at Big Flats station! Where shall we go?"

"O, we will go to the hotel erected by Charles Reynolds fifty years ago. There is no omnibus running to it, but we can walk down into the village."

"The depot at this place. Uncle Jonas is located upon the premises formerly owned by your old friend John Winters, or "Pap Winters," as he was familiarly known. This schoolhouse was erected during the year 1854, during the official *terra* of John L. Sexton, Jr., as town superintendent of schools. There was considerable opposition, but the friends of education were in the majority, and the old red schoolhouse which stood near the road southeast of the village was abandoned. The grave-yard or its cemetery on the left has been enlarged, the original space given by the late Robert Miller having been fully occupied. It is the oldest grave-yard in the town, the first interment occurring over eighty years ago. The church (Presbyterian) was erected about fifty- five years ago, and has since been remodeled in its interior. The church here to the left of us is the Episcopalian, and has been erected for about twelve or fourteen years. The Episcopalians erected a church west of the village over fifty years ago; but after using it for twenty years it was sold to the Baptist, and in the year 1852 it was removed to the village, remodeled and is now in use by that denomination. The Methodist church was erected in the year 1865. When we get to the hotel. Uncle Jonas, we will talk these matters over. They arrive at the hotel and are conducted into quiet rooms by the landlord, Mr. Relyea. After they were comfortably located, Uncle Jonas said to Harry: "This hotel was erected about fifty years ago by Charles Reynolds, now deceased, father of S. T. Reynolds, of Elmira. Charlie Reynolds, as he was familiarly known, was one of the most enterprising and public-spirited men in the country. When I was a young man, Harry, he was engaged in the mercantile pursuits, and in purchasing grain and shipping the same in arks to the southern market on the Chemung and Susquehanna Rivers. His store stood on the opposite side of the street from this hotel, a little farther to the east. When the Chemung river was high he was enabled to load his ark with grain from his store, in that creek (Gardner Creek) and float it down through the meadows to the river. He built this hotel and the residence next to the west of us. Although he was so very energetic, still his health was not very good. Consumption had marked him as a victim, and he died in March 1837, in the prime of life, and when he had surmounted all financial obstacles which stood in his way. John Minier soon thereafter leased or purchased it, and was keeping it when I left for the west in the year 1841. These old hotels are landmarks, not always the scenes of debauchery, but the homes of the traveler, and the place where public and private business is transacted."

"That is very true, Uncle Jonas. Since you left this county, this hotel, upon the whole, has been specially well kept. Its landlords have been men of character and standing. I recall the names of John Minier, Captain William Dunn, William and George Edminster, Judson, M. Park, Waterman Park, Mrs. Mary Gardner, Isaiah J. A. Jones, John Relyea, I. P. Jones, A. S. Fuller, and the present occupant, John Relyea, Jr. Until a few years since it had a room set apart as a 'court room.' In that room, the justices' courts were held, as were also the town and state elections. There is a ballroom attached, and for many years, during the winter season, dancing schools were held. Those schools consisted of thirteen lessons, given once a week, usually ending by a public exhibition of the progress made by the pupils in the terpsichorean art, at which invitations were extended by the master or teacher and pupils to their friends. These public dances generally called forth the elite of the village and surrounding country, and was an occasion upon which every lady and gentleman particularly placed themselves upon the order of their good behavior. The utmost order and decorum prevailed. No dissipation or vulgar language was tolerated either in the hall or about the house. The pupils were taught polite manners and many accomplishments which fitted them for good society."

"I have no doubt of it, Harry. I have always been in favor of schools of deportment and dancing, regarding them, if properly conducted, as being a healthy and innocent amusement, and well calculated to impart good manners to their pupils. Now, Harry, I want to talk about some of the businessmen here of forty-five years ago."

"Well, Uncle Jonas, the first merchant here was John Huey, from Dauphin County, Pennsylvania. He engaged in farming west of here in the town of Corning, and was killed by the cars at Corning, September 1, 1854, aged sixty-three years. John M. French, another early merchant, removed from Big Flats to Rochester about the year 1838, and a few years since died there at an advanced age. He established a foundry and machine shop in that city. William A. Tuttle and Lauren A. Tuttle, who carried on business for many years here, are dead. Samuel C. Gibson is also dead. Your old friend, Benjamin Farwell, who for many years was engaged in the manufacture of furniture at this place, died recently at Painted Post, aged eighty-four years."

"I know his son, Harry. He is a prominent merchant of Chicago."

"Zachariah Clearwater, Moses Rumsey, Nelson Hotchkiss, Jacob Dorn, blacksmiths, are all dead. Lorenzo Brown, Captain David Brown, wagon makers, are still living, I believe — Captain David Brown in Elmira and Lorenzo Brown in Schuyler County. Dr. Thesus Brooks, for many years a resident of Big Flats, died in Elmira a number of years ago. Drs.

Corbett Peebles, William Woodward, and T. W. Reed are still residing here and practicing their profession. Dr. Peebles has resided in Big Flats over forty-five years, Dr. Woodward, about forty-one years and Dr. T. W. Read about thirty years. The Masonic lodge under the new dispensation, Uncle Jonas, was chartered July ll, 1855, with Dr. Corbett Peebles as W. Master; George Wolcott, Senior Warden, and Ebenezer L. Hoffman, Junior Warden, You recollect you told me about your initiation at Captain Gardner's in the lodge room in the garret. The lodge organized in 1855 before alluded to has upon the whole been exceedingly prosperous. It owns that large building known as the Town or Masonic Hall, and has a very fine lodge room upon the second floor, well carpeted and furnished. It would give me great pleasure, Uncle Jonas, to enter more particularly into its history, but there are so many things to tell you that I fear I cannot dwell upon the matter longer. Joel Rowley and his good wife, 'Aunt Becky' died many years ago at a ripe old age. Your friend John Minier, who married Emily Beard, daughter of Salmon Beard, is living here in the village and owns the George Gardner farm and the house in which you were made a Free Mason. His son, Samuel A. Minier and John R. Minier are engaged extensively in the sale of merchandise at the store formerly occupied by L. A. and W. A. Tuttle. The ancestors of John Minier, no doubt, were the earliest settlers in the Chemung valley, locating about halfway between this place and Elmira, on the "river road, "long before Colonel John Hendy settled at Newtown. I have. Uncle Jonas, been several years looking this matter up, examining records of Bradford County, Luzerne County and Northumberland County, in Pennsylvania, and the records in the land department at Harrisburg, and I have become thoroughly convinced that white men were in this valley long before the revolutionary war, and at the proper time I will give you my reasons for making this assertion."

"Harry, Big Flats does not seem to have increased much in population in the last forty-five years, if I recollect aright."

"That is true. Uncle Jonas. But the agricultural interest has been developed. Then there were few settlers on the hills north, south and east of here. Now there are splendid farms on Hawes' Hill, on Hooker's and Reeser's Hill, and south on the hills adjoining the town of Southport, in Chemung County, and number one, or Caton, in Steuben County. Then John L. Sexton had two or three miles on the creek where he settled fifty-five years ago and who was succeeded by. Paul W. Breed. John Silsby had a sawmill on the same creek; several steam sawmills were subsequently in operation, one large gang mill on the island in the river, opposite the hotel, and all together employing- a great many men and teams, and creating active business operations. A very destructive fire occurred here about twenty-five years ago, destroying some seventeen buildings on the south side of the street, among them the Charles Reynolds and John M. French stores, the owners of which were not generally insured, together with stores, halls, and dwellings which have not been rebuilt. A grist and sawmill, however, have taken their place. There was a time, however, when the now abandoned Chemung Canal was in operation, and the building of the Erie Railroad was in course of construction and the locks on the canal were being rebuilt, that business was brisk and money and work plenty. John Haggerty, son of your old friend Patrick Haggerty, was associated with Nicholas Mundy and Samuel Minier in the sale of merchandise, the purchase of railroad ties and wood, and contractors for the rebuilding of twenty or thirty locks on the Chemung Canal between Elmira and Watkins Glen, and between Horseheads and Corning about twenty- five years ago, with headquarters in Big Flats, made this one of the busiest little hamlets in the country. John Haggerty represented this county in the assembly of the state in the year 1858 and was a man of broad views and an intelligent and energetic businessman. Samuel Minier was high sheriff in the county from 1841 to 1844, and member of assembly in the year 1851, a prominent farmer and businessman. Haggerty and Minier are dead. Nicholas Mundy is still living, and is one of the most prominent and extensive farmers in the southern tier counties of New York. He owns the homestead of his grandfather, Nathan Mundy, his father's, Reuben M. Mundy. He has added to his inherited estate the Martin Hammond and Jonathan Boyer farms, adjoining the Mundy estate, aggregating over 400 acres, of as line soil as there is in the state. You can perceive, therefore, Uncle Jonas, that the firm did not lack capital or energy. They invented and created business and when it dissolved and Haggerty went to Waterloo [NY] to get near the center of public works, Big Flats lost a valuable citizen, and his death a few years thereafter was a great public loss. The business of the people has changed. About thirty years ago, the culture of tobacco was commenced at Big Flats, the first successful effort in the Chemung Valley. It has annually increased, until now there is scarcely a farmer in the town that is not engaged in its growth or indirectly interested in the business. From this point the cultivation extended up the rivers Chemung, Conhocton, Canisteo, Tioga and Cowanesque, and down the valley of the Chemung into the Valley of the Wyoming in Pennsylvania, and along the valley of the east branch in Binghamton and up the Chenango as far north as Utica on the Mohawk, and westward into Onondaga counties. Big Flats was the pioneer tobacco-growing town. Its cultivation in all the sections I have named was subsequent to its first cultivation here in the year 1850."

"Curtis Elmer, from the state of Connecticut, raised the first crop of tobacco for the market upon the David Reynolds farm on the banks of the Sing Sing Creek at the lower end of the flats in the year 1850. This proving a success, Reuben and George W. Lovell and John Parks, in the year 1851, raised several acres successfully. Their success stimulated other farmers in the town to engage in its production, among whom were

George W. Van Gorder, Orrin Wing, Hiram Hammond, John McNulty, David H. Bonham, James Hughson, Samuel Minier, John L. Sexton, Jr., Nicholas Mundy, Archibald Gates, John Minier, Martin Hammond, and many others. Thus in a few years, the industry spread wider and wider until it has covered the territory I have named. That is the supper bell. Uncle Jonas. We will go down into the dining room, the place where so many fine meals have been eaten in years gone past on private and public occasions. Many distinguished men have dined in this house, among whom I recall the Hon. Hiram Gray, the Hon. James Dunn, Hon. Amasa Dana, Hon. Andrew B. Dickinson, Hon. Alexander S. Diven, Hon. Robert Campbell, Hon. John Magee, Hon. Aaron Konkle, Hon. Andrew K. Gregg, Hon. Theodore North, Hon. C. C. B. Walker, Hon. Stephen T. Hayt, Hon. David B. Hill, Hon. Horace Greeley, Hon. Martin Grover, Hon. Thomas A. Johnson, Hon. James Hughson, Hon. Samuel Minier, Hon. George B. Guinnip, Hon. John Haggerty, Hon. Samuel G. Hathaway, Hon. William C. Rhodes, Hon. James Woods, Hon. Joseph Darling, Hon. James Pumpelly, Hon. Francis Granger, Bishop Delancey, and many others distinguished in public life and social position. I sat Uncle Jonas, at the table in the dining room in October 1852, with the Hon. Horace Greeley of New York, George W. Brown of Elmira, Judson M. Park, Lauren A. Tuttle, Nelson Hotchkiss of Big Flats, the Hon. A. B. Dickinson of Hornby, and the Hon. George W. Buck of Chemung. Mr. Greeley had made a speech at Corning on that day and was driven in the carriage of I. R. Brown, of Elmira, from Corning, accompanied by the Hon. A. B. Dickinson and the Hon. George W. Buck. Judson M. Park kept the hotel at that time and was a warm political and personal friend of Mr. Greeley. It so happened. Uncle Jonas that I was here and with Messrs. Tuttle and Hotchkiss were invited to dine with the party."

"It is with a great deal of pleasure, Harry, that I visit these old land-marks and listen to your recital of their history."

After partaking of a well-prepared supper. Uncle Jonas and Harry take a walk about the village. They first visited the former residence of Joel Rowley and Captain George Gardiner, which they find altered and remodeled, and their return and meet at the post office, which is in the store of the Minier Brothers, many of the present villagers and townsmen, among whom were Judge Ambrose, S. Fuller, George W. Lovell, Philander J. Brown, the Rev. C. L. Bacon, John L. Sexton, Dr. Corbett Peebles, Dr. William Woodward, Jacob Markle, Orlando Groom, E. W. Gardiner, Joseph Scofield, John Farr, Simeon Wormley, Simeon Hughson, Martin Hammond, Jr., Seeley Reeder, Patrick Elwood, David Quackenbush, Charles Quackenbush, Abram B. Minier, Joseph B. Lowe, Jerome Allard, Nicholas Mundy, James E. Farr, W. H. Farr, John R. Minier, Samuel A, Minier, David Churcher, Charles Hammond, and many others, and spent an hour or more in social conversation recalling old-time scenes, talking over hunting, fishing, barn raising, lumbering, rafting and local incidents of the past. Through the courtesy of John K. Minier, Uncle Jonas and Harry were permitted to look through the masonic lodge rooms of Big Flats Lodge Number 378 of Free and Accepted Masons. Returning to the hotel, they were introduced to a number of young men who had met to make arrangements for holiday amusement, and the evening passed off pleasantly and quickly. In the morning, a fine team and carriage were at their disposal, and they took that opportunity of driving up the river, passing the Rowley and Gardner homesteads, the late residence of the Hon. James Hughson, the old homes of Patrick Haggerty, Jonathan, and Samuel Boyer, Martin Hammond, the present elegant residence of Nicholas S. Mundy, driving out of the town of Big Flats into the county of Steuben near the present residence of A. J. Wormley, and the old home of his father, the late Jacob

Wormley, and passing the residence of Lucius Tuttle, John Storms, the old residence of John W. Durham, now the elegant home of John M. Burt, and viewing the residence of A. D. Huey, and the old residence of the pioneer merchant of Big Flats, the late John Huey, now occupied by his son Grant Huey, and on westward beyond the residence of Henry B. Noyes. After passing the residence of Mr. Noyes, they turned about and were returning to Big Flats, when opposite his house they were met by him and invited into his hospitable home where they spent an hour talking over reminiscences and bygones. Many were the pleasing and happy incidents recalled of his father, the late Thomas Noyes, and his amiable wife.

On their return to Big Flats, each one of the old residents of forty-five years ago, that lived along that beautiful highway were spoken of by Uncle Jonas and dwelt upon with interest. From the feeling manner in which Uncle Jonas spoke of some of the old families along that route, Harry half suspected that at some time in Uncle Jonas' early life, he might have been matrimonially inclined towards some of the fine daughters of those early settlers. Whether such was the case or not, it was certain, that no little trip had he taken with Uncle Jonas, which had seemingly given the old gentleman more delight than the one that morning. He dwelt upon the hospitality and culture of the Gardiners, the Reynolds, the Boyers, the Owens, the Mundys, the Hughsons, the Hueys, the Storms, the Wormleys, the Miniers, the Beards, the McNultys, and early citizens generally of Big Flats. Surely, they occupy a warm place in the old man's affections.

CORNING'S HISTORY.
THE VETERAN TRAVELER VISITS HIS OLD FRIENDS
AND RENEWS OLD ASSOCIATIONS.

Uncle Jonas and Harry dine at the hotel and prepare to leave Big Flats. They are driven over to the depot by Mr. Relyea in time to take a westbound train on the Erie for Corning. Away they speed up through as delightful a valley as there is in the middle states. Before arriving at Corning, Harry said to Uncle Jonas:

"I think while we remain in Corning, we had better stop at the Dickinson House. The Dickinson House was erected in the years 1850-51 and dedicated by a grand reception and ball on September 24, 1851. The house was named in honor of the Hon. Andrew Bray Dickinson, whom you well recollect as a prominent farmer of Hornby, in Steuben County, and a distinguished Whig politician, who represented this district in the state senate and who was appointed by President Lincoln as Minister to Nicaragua. The citizens of Corning at that time took a great interest m the erection of the hotel, and a committee consisting of its prominent business-men sent out special invitations in all portions of the southern tier to their friends to be present at its formal opening and dedication. The committee of invitation was the Hon. Andrew Bray Dickinson of Hornby, followed by citizens of Corning, Daniel D. Comstock, W W. Hayt, J. M. Hawley, Stephen T. Hayt, W. Halliday, Jason K. Snooks, William M. Mallory, Dwight Atwater, George W. Dyer, William Irvine, J. Maynard, H. Turner, Hiram W. Bostwick, Charles C. B. Walker, Jacob Lansing, Alexander Olcott, J. M. Goodrich, and A. J. Howell. Its reception and dedication will long be remembered as one of the great social events in this valley. Since its opening, nearly thirty-five years ago, it has entertained some of the most distinguished men in the country, those that have been prominent in civic, political, and military life, as well as the travelers and citizens generally. For ten or twelve years after it was opened, it had several landlords, among whom was the late Major A. Fields, who enlarged it. He was succeeded twenty years or more ago by D. A. Fuller, and he by his sons, George W. and Dwight L. Fuller, who, since 1865, have owned and controlled it, enlarging and refitting it from time to time, until it became one of the most noted hotels in southern New York. Its location adjacent to the Fall Brook depot and within a square of the New York, Lake Erie & Western depot, and in the business center of Corning has contributed to its popularity. It has become historic as the place of holding senatorial and congressional conventions of all parties, and the place for holding railroad and other business meetings. If you think best, Uncle Jonas, we will make it our headquarters. At the same time, we talk over the history of Corning, the New York, Lake Erie & Western Railroad, the Corning, Cowanesque & Antrim Railroad, the Syracuse, Geneva & Corning railroad, and other lines controlled and operated by the Fall Brook coal company and the surrounding country. Here we are at Corning. Here is the Dickinson house porter. Give him your check, Uncle Jonas. Here we are at the hotel. This, Uncle Jonas, is Mr. George W. Fuller, and this is Mr. Dwight L. Fuller. Gentlemen, we have come to your house to spend a few days while we look up old acquaintances and talk over things of the past."

"Happy to receive you, Mr. Lawrence and Mr. Sampson, and shall be glad to entertain you. Porter, show Uncle Jonas and Harry up to the double room upon the first floor above."

"I declare, Harry, you have the good luck or faculty of selecting the very best hotels in the country. This easy chair just suits me, and the room is so warm and comfortable this winter afternoon."

"I am glad you are pleased with your quarters, Uncle Jonas, and I think we shall have no cause to regret our selection. I was speaking of the committee of invitation that dedicated this house when we arrived at the depot. To continue: They were probably unknown to you, with the exception of the Hon. Andrew B. Dickinson; still, you ought to remember William W. Hayt and Stephen T. Hayt."

"Yes, Harry, I do."

Daniel D. "Comstock was a businessman. He came to Corning from the county of Otsego. Jason K. Snooks was also a businessman, engaged in the manufacture of harnesses. William M. Mallory was a banker, second son of Laurin Mallory. Dwight Atwater was a lumber merchant and shipper, now a resident of Elmira. George W. Dyer was an energetic and enterprising businessman of Corning, who, among other enterprises, erected a block of stores and a hall known as the 'Dyer Hall.' William Irvine was a learned able and successful lawyer who represented this district in Congress and distinguished himself during the rebellion, commanding a regiment of Union soldiers, and who went to California after the close of the war, and established a very lucrative law practice, and when in the zenith of his success, was taken suddenly ill and died a few years ago. He is interred in Woodlawn in Elmira; J. Maynard was a young lawyer; H. Turner was a merchant; Hiram W. Bostwick was a prominent citizen and banker, president of the bank of Corning; Charles C. B. Walker was engaged in the hardware business, has since represented this district in Congress and is now known far and wide as a most successful businessman; Jacob H. Lansing was a jeweler and since distinguished himself in the late rebellion, and was clerk of Steuben County at the time of his death a few months since; Alexander Olcott was a prominent citizen engaged in the foundry and machine business, and who still resides here one of the solid and substantial businessmen of today. This house, Uncle Jonas, stands upon the site of the first hotel erected here, known as the Corning House. Among the landlords who kept the Corning House, I recall those of Major Denton, Samuel

H. Maxwell, Nelson Somers, and Marvin Clark. It was destroyed by fire, and soon thereafter, the house was erected. We are seated so comfortably, Uncle Jonas, suppose we remain in our room, and I will give you a brief history of this enterprising village."

"Very well, Harry, go on."

"You will recollect, Uncle Jonas, that the Chemung Canal Feeder was constructed and finished to a point on the Chemung river about a mile below here in the year 1833. One of the great levers or arguments used to induce the legislature of the state of New York to pass the bill authorizing the construction of the Chemung Canal and feeder was, that south of this point there were inexhaustible semi-bituminous coal fields in Pennsylvania at Blossburg and vicinity, which together with the great forests of white pine, oak, Norway pine, and other valuable timber, would furnish tonnage for the canal. The terminal point of the canal having been located at the entrance of the Chimney Narrows, forty-two miles distant from the coal-fields, some other means of transportation had to be contrived whereby this tonnage of coal could be secured. The state of New York did not wish to engage in the enterprise and left it to individuals or companies to develop. The Hon. Erastus Corning, Sr, of Albany, Thomas W. Olcott and others of the same city, together with enterprising men in this county, organized a company known as the Corning Company about the year 1835 and purchased land at this point, and soon thereafter, in connection with capitalists of Philadelphia, obtained a charter from the respective states of New York and Pennsylvania empowering the companies to build a railroad from this point up along the Chemung and Tioga Rivers to Blossburg, the center of the coalfield. As soon as this project became known, the company laid out lots in this place, which then were covered with timber or stumps, and purchasers came here and located. The construction of the railroad commenced about the year 1836 and was finished in the year 1840. Railroads were then in their infancy, not more than one hundred miles were in operation in the United States, A few months before the completion of the Corning & Blossburg Railroad, the New York and Erie railroad company expended six million dollars in driving piles, building bridges upon their line between Piermont and Lake Erie, without completing but very few miles of connected railroad. You will recollect the mistake and how it drove the company into bankruptcy. Corning, however, profited largely by the expenditure of large sums of money in this locality and assisted in giving this young village a boom in wealth and population.

In the year 1839, a bank was chartered, under the title of the Corning bank, with a capital of about $100,000, secured by bonds and mortgages upon real estate, and securities of the state of New York. Many of the farmers of Steuben and Chemung Counties took stock in the concern and mortgaged their farms, which twenty years thereafter suffered severely for their confidence in its management. The establishment of a bank in this growing village with such men as Hiram W. Bostwick, Laurin Mallory, and Philander Mallory as officers, and John McBurney, John Patterson, Benjamin Patterson, Jonathan Brown, Frederic Woolcott, John L. Sexton, William Wambaugh, Thomas A. Johnson and others, directors or stockholders, gave Corning a standing in the monetary circles of the country and enabled it to put on airs and set forth its claims to distinction. The Steuben County bank at Bath, managed by the Hon. John Magee was the only other bank in Steuben County, and the Chemung Canal bank at Elmira, managed by the Hon. John G. McDowell, the Hon. William Maxwell and the Hon. John Arnot, the only bank then in Chemung county. So, this infant village, only five years old, had facilities for banking purposes equal to the older towns of Bath and Elmira, which had been founded for half a century. Corning had advertised itself through the Albany and New York newspapers, and speculators and *bona fide* settlers came thronging in from Albany, Utica,

Schenectady, and the counties of Schoharie, Otsego, Delaware, Broome, and Chenango. Corning was a forest queen sitting in her palace at the head of canal navigation and at the initial point of a railroad, which penetrated the valley of the Tioga and to the rich coal fields of Tioga county and the forests of valuable timber. The Chemung, Conhocton, Canisteo, Cowanesque, and Tioga Rivers, also bore upon their waters fleets of square timber and millions of feet of manufactured lumber, which directly or indirectly paid tribute to her."

NEWSPAPERS AND BUSINESSMEN.
SOME OF THE PIONEERS AND PRESENT
MANAGERS IN CORNING'S ENTERPRISES.

"About the time of the establishment of the bank of Corning in the year 1839, a company erected a bridge across the Chemung River and canal about three-quarters of a mile west of the John Shoemaker or McCormick tavern stand. This bridge connected with a highway that led past the residence of the late Judge Steele, the farm now owned by Mr. Erwin. This enabled the people of Big Flats to visit Corning at all seasons of the year, whether the river was high or low, instead of depending upon the uncertainty of fording at Gillett's, a mile below. This bridge was kept up until the state had made improvements in the Chimney narrows, and thrown up a towing-path which, for some years, was used leading from the old Post town road, at the mouth of Post creek, along the McBurney Flats and across the river on the old Erie Railroad bridge into Corning. The state for several years spent large sums of money annually in rebuilding the canal dam across the river and in blasting down the rock chimneys, making a permanent highway and towpath, constructing docks, etc., a large portion of which ultimately reached the pockets of the citizens of Corning. Some evil-minded people had the audacity to denounce the laboring men, and businessmen and contractors as "state robbers." But these epithets evidently were made in jest or prompted by envy at the good fortune of the citizens of Corning. The hard times of 1841-43 had its influence upon the young village, but she rallied and continued to increase in wealth and population.

In the years 1840-50, the Erie Railroad was being permanently constructed, and for several months during the year 1850, Corning was its western completed terminus. This added to the immense trade in lumber, and the shipments of coal from its docks contributed to its continued prosperity. Schools, churches, and mills were established within its limits, and progress was marked upon its every action. A terrible fire swept over it in May 1850, but it soon recovered from the shock. In the year 1852, the first division of the Conhocton Valley railroad was opened to Corning (now under control of the Erie, and known as the Rochester branch,) and about the same time the Corning & Blossburg Railroad was re-laid with iron. Its management placed in the hands of wealthy and energetic men. All these things contributed to build up Corning and attract population and capital to its borders.

As early as 1840, a newspaper had been published in Corning, entitled the *Corning & Blossburg Advocate*, edited by Charles Adams. It, however, did not prove a success, and in 1841 it was sold, and the press and fixtures removed to Bath. But in the year 1849, the Corning *Journal* was established by Thomas Messenger, and in 1851 it was purchased by A. W. McDowell and G. W. Pratt, and the next year (1852), G. W. Pratt assumed the entire control of it, as editor and proprietor. With the exception of a year or two, when Mr. Pratt had a partner, he has, for the past thirty-four years, controlled its columns and sat in the editorial chair and wielded a pen guided by one of the clearest intellects in the southern tier. As a weekly family newspaper, it has few equals and no superiors. It is a journal that can safely be taken into the household and the family circle, and nothing in its columns has been found to offend the good taste or corrupt the morals of the community. It has done much under Mr. Pratt's guiding and controlling hand to build up the prosperous village of Corning. For a third of a century has he nobly stood at the helm, giving his readers wholesome literature and interesting reading. In the year 1853, Mark M. Pomeroy, who had served an apprenticeship in the office of the *Journal* under Dr. George W. Pratt, and who has since distinguished himself as an editor of much force and ability, with P. C. Van Gelder published a newspaper entitled the Corning *Sun*. In the year 1851, the Rev. Ira Brown purchased the office and conducted it as an agricultural paper for two years.

"In 1857 Charles T. Huston and Frank B. Brown issued the Corning *Democrat*. Frank B. Brown, in a short time, purchased Mr. Huston's interest and, for the past twenty-eight years, has conducted it with ability and profit. About eighteen months ago, he established a daily which is meeting with good success. Thus, you see, Uncle Jonas, Corning has two weekly newspapers and one daily to fight the political battles and assist in developing the local resources of this prosperous village."

"In the year 1848 Corning was incorporated as a village. Its population then was estimated at about 1,800. Subsequent amendments have been made to its charter. It was taken from the town of Painted Post. A few years later, the town of Corning was formed obliterating the name of Painted Post as a township, leaving the village of Painted Post the heritage of that historical name.

We flew so rapidly through the country today that we passed the residences of many of the old settlers along on the river below here before I had an opportunity of pointing them out to you. But I will name them, and no doubt they will be recollected by you — "

"Oh, I know, Harry, who lived along the river this side of Thomas Noyes. There were Silas Gorton, Abram Bennett, Isaac Watrous, Asaph Rowley, Alva Rowley, Washington Rowley, John Shoemaker, Abram and Henry McCormic, Henry Burt, on the north side of the river. Joseph Gillett, Sylvester Gillett, Judge Steele, the Gortons, Calkins, and Wolcotts on the south side."

"Yes, that is very true, Uncle Jonas, but you have missed several old settlers, which we will look upon our return. Immediately succeeding the building of the Erie Railroad and the Conhocton branch, a new bank was established under the management of George W. Patterson, Jr., and John N. Hungerford, a foundry and machine shop and other industrial establishments were established, new churches were erected or enlarged, public halls were built. Masonic and Odd Fellow lodges organized, and Corning was placed upon a solid and permanent business foundation.

"Among the citizens and corporations who were prominent in building up the business interests of Corning, I recall the Hon. Erastus Corning and Thomas W. Olcott, of Albany, and at Corning, Hiram W. Bostwick, Laurin Mallory, P. J. Mallory, the Hon. John McBurney, the Hon. Thomas A. Johnson, Benjamin W. Payne, Robert Olcott, Alexander Olcott, Stephen T. Hayt, Charles C. B. Walker, R. E. Robinson, Jonathan Brown, John N. Hungerford, George W. Pratt, Frank B. Brown, L. C. Kingsbury, the Fall Brook Coal Company, the Erie Railroad Company, the Tioga Railroad Company, the Chemung Canal, the Corning Glass Company, Preston & Hermans, F. N. Drake, Austin Lathrop, Jr., Nelson Somers, J. M. Smith, Henry Goff, George W. Patterson, Jr., the Hon. Henry Sherwood, Lewis T. Fuller, General Jacob Lansing, Quimble Wellington, Dr. William Terbell, Hiram Pritchard, Charles G. Denison, and among the old business and professional men, I recall Dr. Joshua B. "Graves, Dr. Nelson M. Harrington, the Hon. George B. Bradley, the Hon. Charles H. Thompson, General William Irvine, Charles Douglass, William Walker, Zerah Todd, C. E. Corbin, William H. Brown, Fuller &, Gamman, Truman S. Pritchard, Edward Pier, Charles R. Maltby, C. G. Howell, A. T. Cochran, Rawson & Thatcher, Charles Freeman, Frank D. Kings- bury, John Hoar, Sr., A. Houghton, C. F. Houghton, Edward Clisdell, Thomas G. Hawks, Daniel F. Brown, A. L. Kendall, George Hitchcock, the Hon. George T. Spencer. Many of those I have mentioned, Uncle Jonas, are dead, but they contributed largely during their active lives to the prosperity of the village and should be gratefully remembered. Those who have gone to their long homes are

The Hon. Thomas A. Johnson, Laurin Mallory, Philander J. Mallory, Hiram W. Bostwick, Dr. Joshua B. Graves, General William Irvine, the Hon. Henry Sherwood, Benjamin W. Payne, Lewis Fuller, Robert Olcott, Jonathan Brown, John McBurney, A. T. Cochran, John N. Hungerford, Henry Goff, Dr. Terbell, and General Jacob PI. Lansing. It is nearly half a century since the Corning company was organized, consisting of Erastus Corning, Joseph Fellows, Thomas W. Olcott, Watts Sherman, Hiram W. Bostwick, William A. Bradley, and Lorin J. Gillis. All these have passed away, but the work they planned has gone on, and Corning, the child of the wilderness, has prospered and every year added to its wealth and population and made some new improvement or erected some new industrial establishment. It is now supplied with water and gas and Belgian pavements. Its railroad facilities are good, reaching north and south, east and west. Its banking facilities are ample, the press is in the hands of intelligent and public-spirited gentlemen, its churches are well supported and attended, its schools rank high, and its free academy compares favorably with any in the state, its industrial establishments are prosperous, the railroads centering here are doing a large and profitable business, and, indeed, the village of Corning, Uncle Jonas, is making rapid strides towards a city. A few more years of prosperity, and this will be accomplished. It is now the half shire of Steuben County.

"The large interests which the Erie Railroad, the Corning, Cowanesque & Antrim, the Syracuse, Geneva & Corning and their connections with the New York Central and Jersey Shore & Pine Creek Railway and the Delaware, Lackawanna & Western, coupled with the glass manufacturing, foundry, and machine shop, the agricultural works, the car and repair shops of the Fall Brook Coal Company, will surely and certainly place Corning in the front ranks among her sisters of the southern tier in a very few years. Its population is rapidly increasing, and the population have come to stay and make this their permanent home."

"Harry, look out of the window, there is an illuminated clock."

"Yes, Uncle Jonas, the clock tower, and the clock is the gift of the Hon. Erastus Corning, Jr., to the village of Corning. It is located in the center of Dickinson House Square, which has recently been laid with Belgian blocks, in a very substantial manner. The citizens of Corning highly appreciate the generosity of Mr. Corning in providing them at all hours of the day and night, the reliable time.

"Now, Uncle Jonas, I have rattled away upon the early history and present prospects of Corning until you must be weary. It is near tea time, and suppose we go down into the general reception room until after tea, and perhaps meet with some of the old citizens."

A RAILROAD CENTER.
DESCRIPTION OF THE FALL BROOK LINE AND
OTHER CORNING RAILWAYS.

The next morning Uncle Jonas requests Harry to tell him more about the Fall Brook Coal company, the Corning, Cowanesque & Antrim, the Syracuse, Geneva & Corning, and the Jersey Shore & Pine Creek Railways. Harry thus proceeds:

"There are several facts connected with the history of the Fall Brook coal company and these roads, which I have incidentally referred to before, but which to give you a clear and connected idea of the matter I will repeat. The first step was taken by the late Hon. John Magee, the founder of the Fall Brook Coal Company, towards engaging in the coal business, was in the year 1852. when he obtained the lease of the Blossburg coal mines at Blossburg and the railroad from Corning to Lawrenceville. His eldest son, Duncan S. Magee, was sent to Blossburg to oversee the mining and shipping of coal, and in the business, he was ably assisted by John Lang, who is now the treasurer of the company. In 1856 Duncan S. Magee, with the knowledge and consent of his father, the Hon. John Magee commenced exploring for coal upon lands of the late Christopher L. Ward, of Towanda, lying directly east of Blossburg. The exploration resulted in the purchase of those lands, about six thousand acres, and the incorporation of the Fall Brook Coal Company, April 7, 1859. The incorporators were John Magee, Duncan S. Magee, and James H. Gulick. The bill incorporating the company was passed in the legislature of Pennsylvania on March 12, 1850, and was vetoed by Governor William F. Packer. April 7, 1859, the bill was passed over the veto by more than a two-thirds majority. A railroad was built from Blossburg to these lands, during the summer and fall of 1859, and a mining town founded in the wilderness christened Fall Brook. The distance from

Blossburg to Fall Brook is about seven miles, some back switching being necessary in order to reach the elevation at Fall Brook. Mining has since that time (1859) been carried on there. The coal on its way to market at Corning passed first over seven miles of the Fall Brook Coal Company's road, then twenty-five miles over the road of the Tioga company, and lastly fifteen miles over the Fall Brook Coal Company's road from Lawrenceville to Corning. The Tioga interests were mining coal at Morris Run, and their outlet was over then- own road to Lawrenceville, and over the Fall Brook road to Corning. Some dissatisfaction grew out of this arrangement, and in the year 1866 explorations for coal were made by the agents or employees of the Fall Brook coal company on Wilson creek, south of Wellsboro, which finally resulted in the purchase of a large tract of land in that locality, and the final opening up of coal mines, the founding of a new mining town which was christened by Duncan S. Magee, Antrim. Of this, Uncle Jonas, we will speak more at length when we reach Antrim. In connection with the opening up of the mines at Antrim, a railroad was contemplated from Lawrenceville by way of Tioga, Middlebury, Niles Valley, Wellsboro to Antrim, and a company organized for that purpose with Humphries Brewer president, and James Heron secretary and treasurer. These two gentlemen were the chief engineer and cashier at Fall Brook for the Fall Brook company. Before it was constructed, the Hon. John Magee, Duncan S. Magee, and Humphries died, and the work of carrying these projects into execution devolved upon General George J. Magee, second son of the Hon. John Magee. He proved equal to the task, and by the year 1872, the railroad was completed from Lawrenceville to Antrim, under the immediate direction of General Magee and his engineer Anton Hardt, now chief engineer for all the roads operated by the Fall Brook Coal Company. About the same time, a railroad was projected from Lawrenceville up the Cowanesque to Elkland, and when it was completed, it was leased by the Fall Brook Company. The old road from Corning to Lawrenceville, the road from Law-renceville to Elkland, the road from Lawrenceville to Antrim, and the road from Blossburg to Fall Brook were consolidated under the general name of Corning, Cowanesque & Antrim Railroad. The Syracuse, Geneva & Corn-ing Railroad was soon thereafter projected, and in the year 1877 it was com-pleted. The Fall Brook Coal Company was interested in a large extent and became its lessee. The Jersey Shore & Pine Creek Railroad, which connects with the Corning & Cowanesque railroad at Stokesdale Junction in Tioga County, Pennsylvania, and connects with the Philadelphia & Reading at Williamsport, is now operated by the Fall Brook coal company, as well as a branch leading from Dresden to Penn Yan, and from Geneva to Lyons. The Cowanesque branch has been extended from Elkland to Harrison Valley in Potter County, near the head of the Cowanesque and Genesee Rivers. You can, therefore, form some idea of the magnitude and proportions of the Fall Brook Coal Company's interests in mining and railroading. We will call at their depot and look through the various offices. It is close at hand."

The extreme northeast terminus of the chain of railroads controlled and operated by the Fall Brook coal company is at Lyons, the county seat of Wayne County, in the very center of the land of the Six Nations. At that point, it connects with the New York Central Railroad, controlled by the Vanderbilts, and runs southeast to the foot of Seneca Lake, the site of the ancient Indian village of *Kane-de-saga,* now known as Geneva, one of the finest inland villages of the state. At Geneva, it connects with another branch of the New York Central, the Seneca Lake Navigation Company and a branch of the Lehigh Valley railroad. Geneva is the seat of Hobart College, a protestant episcopal institution, which was founded in the year 1826. It was also at that point that one of the oldest continued newspapers of western New York has been successfully printed for seventy-seven years (the Geneva *Gazette*), and for the past forty-seven years has been under the management of S. H. Parker, who has grown gray in its publication. It is also the oldest site of one of the oldest hotels in the county of Ontario, which has sheltered General Lafayette and many of the most prominent citizens of America, running up in the scale from the most humble citizen to the highest official in the land, including assemblymen, senators, canal commissioners, governors, United States senators, bishops, presidents, and those distinguished in every walk of life, civil and military — I allude to the Franklin House. Its commanding view of the noble Seneca, its ample rooms, its elaborate and well-furnished parlors, its commodious dining hall, have made it famous and historic. For a long period of years, it has been owned by S. S. Mallory, with Silas H. Remington lessee. From Geneva, the road runs along the western bank of Seneca Lake, through one of the most delightful countries in the United States. No wonder that the Red Man fought so desperately to retain this land, rich in all those attributes which were essential to their existence, and no wonder their warriors were eloquent, when they had been born and reared in a land of noble forests, sparkling streams and silver lakes, the streams and lakes filled with countless varieties of fish, and the forest teeming with deer, moose, elk and bear, and mounds of the busy beaver, and a soil rich in the extreme, producing golden ears of corn and fruit in abundance. At Dresden, it passes through a country made memorable by the universal friend, Jemima Wilkinson, and her followers. At this point, a branch diverges and ascends the outlet of Lake Keuka to Penn Yan, the foot of this beautiful lake, which extends westward to Hammondsport, and along whose sloping banks innumerable vineyards are seen. The road from Dresden to Penn Yan, NY is delightful. The waters of the outlet by the lake have cut a passage down through the salty formation for one hundred feet in depth until its bed rests upon a limestone basis. Commerce and industry have utilized the waters of this stream, whose descent is about forty feet to the mile, and a number of large and expensive paper mills are located in this narrow ravine.

From Dresden, the traveler has a fine view of the Willard insane asylum, which is situated upon the opposite side of Seneca Lake, about two miles distant. Leaving Dresden, the mainline proceeds to Himrod, gradually attaining a greater elevation above the lake, and thus enabling the passenger to obtain a broader view of the delightful country about him. At Himrod it crosses and makes connections with the Northern Central railroad, and then proceeds through the rolling and undulating country to Harpending's Corners, now known as Dundee, one of the brightest and liveliest country villages along the lake, containing two banks, two newspaper offices, several fine churches, a number of substantial business places, fine residences and a population of about 1,800 inhabitants. The passenger is still in the land once held dear by the Red Men of the Six Nations. The course of the railroad is still southward, crossing Rock Stream, passing through Reading Center, within three miles of the famous Watkins Glen. The passenger can now cast his eye to the eastward and feast his eyes upon a landscape rich in pastoral scenes. Away across the lake are seen beautiful farms, elegant farmhouses, fruitful orchards, and vineyards, while he is rolling along in a country grand in the extreme. At length, the famous Glen is reached. He has now reached the altitude of six hundred feet above the village of Watkins, and the chasm is crossed on an iron bridge four hundred feet in length and one hundred and sixty-five feet above the bed of the glen. This Glen stands second only to Niagara Falls in grandeur and public interest. Two hundred thousand people from all sections of America and Europe annually visit it. The railroad company have erected a large pavilion at its brink, and cut a stairway down through the rock, to effect an entrance at its western or middle outlet. Leaving this grand work of nature, the traveler is conveyed by the tireless engine, seated in well-upholstered and easy-riding coaches, southwestward to Beaver Dams, a thriving village situated nearly on the dividing ridge, between the points where water flows into Seneca Lake and southwestward into the Chemung River. If the passenger is so disposed when he is at Watkins station, or Glen Bridge station, he can alight and spend several days at Watkins, a beautiful village at the head of the Seneca Lake, and the site of the Indian village, Catharine's Town, made historic as being the home of that celebrated Indian queen, Catharine Montour; or he can continue from Beaver Dams down Post creek, made memorable in connection with the raid of General Sullivan in 1779, against the Six Nations, and the discovery of the celebrated Painted Post, an Indian landmark upon the banks of the Conhocton, passing Post Creek station, Ferenbaugh, and entering the valley of the Chemung, crossing the Chemung River and rolling into Corning. From Corning, its course is up the Chemung and Tioga Rivers, upon the great Indian path that led from Painted Post to the home of Tiadaghton upon Pine Creek, and the dominion of Shikelemy upon the west branch of the Susquehanna. In its route it passes through Erwin Center, Cooks, Lindley, reaching Lawrenceville at the state line. There one branch leads up through the valley of the Cowanesque, one of the finest valleys in northern Pennsylvania, touching at Nelson, Elkland, Academy Corners, Knoxville, Cowanesque and Westfield, penetrating a country rich in agricultural productions, thriving villages, and delightful scenery, and finally terminating at Harrison Valley, near the headwaters of the Conhocton, whose waters flow into Chesapeake Bay, and the Genesee, into Lake Ontario and the Gulf of St. Lawrence, and the Allegany, whose waters flow into the Ohio and the great Gulf of Mexico, while the mainline continues up the Tioga Valley to Tioga village, passing through Dunnings and Lathrops, then on the old Indian trail, crossing the Elkhorn and ascending Crooked creek to Hollidays and Middlebury, thence to Niles Valley and Stokesdale Junction, where the old line proceeds to Wellsboro, the beautiful county seat of Tioga County, surrounded by its rich and productive farming lands, a borough distinguished for the hospitality and refinement of its people, the home of United States Senator Hon. John I. Mitchell, General Jerome B. Niles, auditor-general of the state of Pennsylvania; the Hon. Mortimer F. Elliott, ex-congressman-at-large for Pennsylvania; the Hon. Henry Sherwood, ex-congressman and president of the Jersey Shore and Pine Creek Railroad; the Hon. Henry Williams, president judge of Tioga County; the Hon. Hugh Young, United States hank examiner; the Hon. Stephen F. Wilson, ex-additional law judge, ex-member of Congress and senator, and from thence away to the southeastward, ascending a steep grade until it reaches Antrim, the model mining town of Pennsylvania, while the mainline continues its course down through Marsh Creek Valley, a distance of about eight miles, and reaches the shores of the celebrated Tiadaghton, or Pine Creek, thence down Pine Creek through one of the wildest and most romantic gorges in the middle or eastern states, through a passage only wide enough to admit of the railroad and Pine Creek, with mountains lifting their craggy heads twelve hundred feet above the road-bed. Reaching Blackwells at the confluence of Babb's Creek with Pine Creek, the course is southward, still leading through mountain and valley scenery unsurpassed, until it reaches Jersey Shore on the west branch of the Susquehanna, from thence to Newberry Junction, where connections are made with the Philadelphia & Reading Railway. No person, Uncle Jonas, can adequately describe the beauty and variety of landscape scenery from Lyons to Newberry over the roads operated by the Fall Brook coal company. At times the traveler is rolling along in agricultural districts unsurpassed in loveliness. Again his eyes rest upon lakes, cascades, waterfalls, and chasms, then again river, valley, and rugged mountain views. The views are at every mile of the route interesting and attractive, and I am certain you will agree with me when we have taken the trip."

219

THE FALL BROOK COMPANY.
A VISIT TO THE OFFICES AND SHOPS —
THE MEN AND THEIR WORK.

Uncle Jonas and Harry take a walk over to the Fall Brook Coal Company's extensive freight and passenger depot and elegant offices, occupied by its various officials. Upon the second floor, facing the public square, they enter the office of the president of the company, General George J. Magee, upon whose shoulders the mantle of his distinguished father, the Hon. John Magee fell. Mr. Magee is a pleasant and affable gentleman about forty years of age, and no one would suppose from his bland manners and a genial smile that the cares and responsibilities of the Fall Brook Coal Company were controlled and managed by him. They found him dictating messages and orders to his private secretary and stenographer, L. P. Miller. Passing out of the president's room they enter the office of Vice-President and Treasurer John Lang, a gentleman who for more than thirty years has been connected with the Fall Brook Coal Company. Commencing his service at Blossburg for the Magee's several years before the Fall Brook Coal Company was organized — ever the same trusted vigilant and efficient official. In a room adjoining they met John H. Lang, assistant treasurer, and paymaster, who has for many years been employed by the company, and also met Charles K. Minor assistant paymaster John L. Lewis, Jr., chief bookkeeper, and S. J. Lang, Frank Osborn and W. J. Herman's clerk. After spending a few minutes with John L. Lewis, Jr., who is an old employee, they are conducted into the rooms of Daniel Beach, treasurer of the Morris Run Coal Mining Company, in which company the Fall Brook Coal Company are largely interested. Mr. Beach has been for many years, directly and indirectly, interested in the affairs of the Fall Brook Company and is one of the most pleasant and agreeable gentlemen connected with the company. The clerks employed in his office were L. P. Robinson, Samuel S. Denton, and A. I. Martin. They are then conducted into the room occupied by A. H. Gorton, general superintendent of all the lines operated by the Fall Brook Coal Company. Mr. Gorton has been for many years connected with the company. He commenced at the foot of the ladder, and by his skill and attention to business, he has risen to his lucrative, laborious, and high position. His assistant is George R. Brown, of whom we shall speak hereafter. The clerks are John Heron and Fred Leis. John Heron commenced his labors for the Fall Brook Coal Company a number of years ago, when his father, the late James Heron, was the manager at Fall Brook. Mr. Heron is eminently qualified for the position he occupies. They were next conducted to the traffic manager's room, where they found H. A. Horning, general traffic manager busily engaged in supervising the details of the immense business of the Fall Brook Coal Company's freight and passenger traffic personally, outlining correspondence and dictating letters and establishing rates of transportation to near and distant points. Mr. Horning has been many years a valuable employee of the company. The chief clerk in his office is John D. Lawton, who has been many years in the employ of the company, filling the position of the telegraph operator, station agent, and ticket agent, and in every position assigned him, he has discharged its duties with fidelity and satisfaction. He is assisted by C. S. May, W. A. Hyde, and Miss A. Fritts, who acts in the capacity of stenographer and type-writer. From the office of traffic manager, they went to the office of Auditor William Nicholson. They found him and his clerks busily engaged in auditing the accounts of the company with their various station and ticket agents, conductors, and shippers. His force consists of himself and D. F. Chandler, J. C. Collord, C. G. Cole, Ransom Pratt, F. A. Newton, and C. S. Day. From the rooms of the auditor, they next visited the office of the general purchasing agent. That position for a number of years was filled by Andrew Beers, now deceased. Mr. Beers was the first agent of the Fall Brook Coal Company at Corning when it first began the shipment of coal from Fall Brook twenty-six years ago and occupied that position for several years. A few years ago, he was chosen general purchasing agent and remained in that responsible position until his death. He was a careful, cautious, honest, and good man. The office is now filled by W. H. Chapel, assisted by his son, W. H. Chapel, Jr., and is conducted very satisfactorily. They next visited the car accountant's office presided over by J. B. Terbell, assisted by F. E. Sharp, Charles Gregorius, Frank Guernsey, A. H, Reynolds, and Robert Stere. They were well pleased with their visit and much interested in the work there performed. They then visited the well-lighted and cheerful rooms of Chief Engineer Anton Hardt. Mr. Hardt received them politely and kindly and a half an hour was agreeably spent in conversing upon the hues of railroads controlled by the Fall Brook Coal Company — examining photographs and draughts of bridges, trestles, coal schutes, and gaining much information in regard to railroading. Mr. Hardt has been in the employ of the Fall Brook coal company for about nineteen years. He surveyed and located the railroad from Lawrenceville to Antrim via Wellsboro, the Syracuse, Geneva & Corning, the Jersey Shore & Pine Creek Railroad, and has charge of all the railroads now operated by the Fall Brook Coal Company. He also has had for many years general supervision over all the company's mining operations in Tioga County, Morris Run excepted. He is a tireless worker and an able geologist, civil and mining engineer, and a graduate of one of the most scientific and popular schools in Vienna, Austria. He is ably assisted by H, A. Hernden, and H. H. Alber, W. J. Lynahan, son of William D. Lynahan, an old employee, is the private and confidential telegraph operator for the president, treasurer, and other officials. The visit of the chief engineer completed the offices on the second floor. Descending to the first floor, they entered the office of George R. Brown, assistant superintendent of the railroad, and superintendent of the telegraphs under the control of the Fall Brook coal company. Mr. Brown has been many years the laborious and careful train dispatcher and superintendent of the telegraph, performing his duties with signal ability and with commendable success. He has been ably assisted by John W. Lynahan, a gentleman equally painstaking and cautious. The great number of coal and passenger trains every day and hour of the day passing over their lines have required the utmost skill and attention. That it has received from Mr. Brown and Mr. Lynahan, They are assisted by Thomas McAvoy, H. Perry, F. J. Armstrong, and George C. Wade. Crossing the hall, they enter the office of C. E. Greenfield, station agent. Mr. Greenfield is a thorough and competent businessman and has the work at hand thoroughly systematized. The business at this office is simply immense. Mr. Greenfield, however, seems equal to the task of performing it with great satisfaction. He is ably assisted by C. B. Chandler, Clark Lockwood, and J. N. Purrong. Passing out of the station agent's office, they walk into the large and comfortable gentlemen's waiting room with the ladies' waiting room on the left, they pass out at the east door and walk into the large freight and warerooms connected with the depot, and like the main building substantially built of brick. Here they find Erastus S. Pier, Thomas Kennedy, William Grossman, Thomas Gill, John Kennedy, Sherman Derose, and William Painter, busily engaged in receiving and shipping freight, which has been transported over their lines, or is to be sent over them. There they saw freight of various kinds which had been shipped from New York, Philadelphia, St. Paul, Chicago, Buffalo, and intermediate points, and freight which was also destined to near and remote points, thus showing the many points reached by the Fall Brook Coal Company's roads and gave them a faint idea of their immense freight business, aside from the millions of tons of coal, both anthracite and bituminous that daily was hauled by their ponderous engines.

Leaving the freight room profoundly impressed with the immense freight business, they walk down to the immense car and repair shops of the Fall Brook Coal Company about three-quarters of a mile distant.

"These shops, Uncle Jonas, were established in the year 1862, while all the members of the original company were alive. About that time, the Hon. John Magee removed from Bath, NY, to Watkins Glen, at the head of Seneca Lake, the better to look after the increased coal trade. He had long been a resident of Bath, holding strong business relations with that town as well as having served Steuben County as sheriff and two terms as a member of congress during the Jacksonian administration. It was quite a severe loss to Bath, but a significant gain to Watkins Glen. He must have spent at least two hundred thousand dollars in Watkins building offices, docks, coal schutes, dwellings, and churches. The old superintendent of these shops was O. C. Patchell, who for over twenty years was the master mechanic, directing the repairing and construction of cars for the company. He died a few months ago, and his memory is cherished by a large number of mechanics and railroad men who, for years, had met him and been under his direction.

The present superintendent is W. A. Foster, a skilled mechanic, who is assisted by C. J. Butler, master car builder, with A. J. Etheridge as an assistant; A. Armstrong as a master boilermaker, William Adams, chief of supplies, assisted by William Buchanan, and Mr. Norwood as engine dispatcher. From time to time as business has increased, the company has enlarged its facilities for doing work until now there are about four hundred men employed in the various divisions and departments. Many of these employees have served fifteen, eighteen, and twenty years and regard the Fall Brook Coal Company as their very best friend. Many of the old engineers have pulled the throttle for the company from the earliest date of the coal trade. The longest engineers in continued service are Fred S. Bragg and Rod

Lounsberry. The oldest engineer is Deacon Lovejoy, but many years ago, he left the road and resided in Corning. The first engine on the road was named in his honor. It now belongs to the Blossburg Coal Company and about two years ago was placed by that company in the invalid hospital. Much of its machinery is excellent. It was used for five years on the Fall Brook branch and has drawn all the old members and friends of the Fall Brook Coal Company — The Hon. John Magee, James H. Gulick, Duncan S. Magee, John Lang, D. C. Howell, the Hon. Horatio Seymour, Daniel Beach, A. H. Gorton, R. J. Burnham, H. A. Horning, C. C. B. Walker, Austin Lathrop, Jr., A. J. Owen, Andrew Beers, and many others that I could enumerate. Its work is historical. Harry, have this large number of employees in any societies which they support or of which they are members? "

"Oh, yes, Uncle Jonas. The conductors have a society, and the engineers have one. The engineers have a division or lodge in Corning, and their organization is known as the Corning Division of the Brotherhood of Locomotive Engineers, No. 244. The division was organized on April 28, 1884, with sixteen charter members. Its officers were: James Roberts, C. E.; F. S. Bragg, F. E.; W. E. Clark, S. E; I. Switzer, T. E; George Marland, F, A. E.; Jesse Newell, S. A. E.; P. Helwig, C.H. Curtis, G. On the first day of October 1885, they had forty-seven members. The officers for the ensuing year are: F. S. Bragg, C. E.; W. E. Clark, F. E.; I. Switzer, S. E.; D. Robison, P. E.; George Marland, F. A. E.; Jesse Newell, S. A. E., Joseph Boyle, G. T. Shoens, chaplain; James Roberts delegates to the annual convention being held in New Orleans. It is a strong and commendable society designed to elevate and educate its members and exercising a wholesome influence upon those who have the lives of so many thousands in their hands."

"I might as well tell you now, Uncle Jonas, who are the principal employees of the road, as we are returning up Market Street to the Dickinson house. It will be a long list, but you must remember their names. It will

225

save me repeating them as we go over the road. We will commence at Lyons, the extreme northeast terminus of the route.

FALL BROOK FREIGHT AGENTS AND OPERATORS.

Syracuse, Geneva & Corning Railway. — Lyons— E. E. Kershner, freight agent; Miss A. Ransom, ticket agent; F. C. Burns, J. D. Engersoll, T. W. Townsend, F. S. Percell, E. M. Smith, operators.

Geneva.— T. W. Mills, freight agent; C. A. Baldwin, ticket agent; John Dodge, P. Gallagher, operators.

Earles. — James P. Hoose, agent.

Dresden. — B. F. Paddock, agent; Miss Hattie Harris, operator.

Penn Yan. — D. M. Hamlin, agent; J. W. Oberfell, operator.

Himrods Junction.— N. Jacobson, freight agent; E. T. Parks, operator.

Himrods. — L. G. Jones, agent.

Dundee.— W. E. More, agent; F. A. Dunning and E. H. Paddock, operators.

Rock Stream. — K. J. Vosburg, agent and operator.

Reading Center.— J. W. Warner, agent; Miss J. M. Warner, operator.

Watkins Glen. — D. S. Nye, agent and operator; J. J. Lane, baggage master.

Wedgewood. — James Wedge wood, agent.

Beaver Dams. — E. W. Hurd, agent; W. J. Maloney, operator.

Post Creek. — W. E. Ferenbaugh, agent.

Corning.— C. E. Greenfield, agent; C. B. Chandler, Clark Lockwood, J. N. Purrong, clerks.

Corning, Cowanesque & Antrim — Erwin Center. — T. J. Presho, agent.

Lindley. — E. D. Leggett, agent.

Lawrenceville. — J. H. Hitchcox, agent; S. M. McAvoy, C. 0. Roff, operators.

Tioga.— R. P. H. McAlhster, agent; V. D. McAllister, operator.

Holiday. — V. B. Hohday, agent.

Middlebury. — H. M. Lowell, agent; E. B. Mills, operator.

The New E. C. & N. Depot, Elmira, N. Y.

Niles Valley. — T, J. Purvis, agent; T. D. Rouse, operator.

Stokesdale Junction. — C. E. Fogg, agent; H. A. Bartholomew, operator.

Stokesdale. — Schieffelin & Co., agents.

Wellsboro. — H. J. Eaton, agent; T. W. Evans, operator.

Antrim. — U. Buckley, agent, and operator.

Nelson. — J. Bottom & Co., agents.

Elkland. — C. H. Benedict, agent.

Osceola. — D. Baxter.

Academy Corners. — M. V. Purple, agent.

Knoxville. — T. C. Campbell, agent.

Cowanesque. — A. B. Strang, agent.

Westfield. — E. S. Horton, agent.

Potter Brook. — William A. Ellison, agent.

Elmer— M. L. Haskell, agent,

Harrison Valley. — J. Bottom & Co., agents.

Fall Brook— F. G. Elliott, agent.

Pine Creek Railway — Ansonia. — M. B. Maynard, agent, and operator.

Tiadaghton. — G. B. Horton, agent, and operator.

Blackwells. — S. M. Kingsley, agent; Martin Dawson, operator.

Cedar Run. — J. G. Scarboroughi, agent; J. E. Degrote, operator,

Cammal. — B. A. Ovenshire, agent and operator.

Waterville. — C L. Ellison, agent, and operator.

Jersey Shore. — L. P. Willison, agent; John Walsh, operator.

Larry's Creek. — C. B. Riddell, agent, and operator.

Linden. — J. F. McLean, agent; J. F. McLean, Jr., operator.

Newberry Junction. — N. W. Peak, agent; E. M. Billiard, W. L. Strand, operators.

First-class conductors. — J. H. Way, T. D. Brown, E. A. Kriger, R. M. Richardson, R. Houghtaling, H. L. Daniels, George Weeks, L. F. Cowley, F. S. Winters, J. D. McGannon.

Second-class conductors. — J. D. Carlton, S. M. Copp, W. H. Doolittle, P. O'Brien, Edward Blair, C. K. Lathrop, John Wilson, William Brother, William Tullet, Ed. Garrison Pat. McGannon, John Driscoll, F. W. Pierce, R. E. Maleady, L. W. Kiff, H. D. Calkins, M. S. Melvin, Ed. Williams, E. A. Williams, J. T. Brown, J. G. Ryan, W. A. Pierce, John Ward, C. C. Cook, J. B. Brown, B. McCarthy, D. W. Weally, L. S. Husted, William Kirkham, Jerry Haley, George Ryal, George Winton, G. P. Gooding, R. E. Pierce, Pat Fleming, John Burke, Frank Withian, Robert Stitt, Fred Clarkson, W. H. Hyland, J. H. Hebe, N. Aldrich, A. F. Boyd, C. H. Bennett, James McCormick, George Weyer.

Engineers.— Henry Wheeler, F. S. Bragg, B. F. Burt, H. W. Lownsberry, C. H. Chapman, John Barber (twenty-four years), William E. Clark, John White, Jos. Boyle, James Richards, Jabe Orcutt, C. M. Reed, George Harris, James May, Leroy White. E. J. Patchill, C. L. Painter, J. T. Leavy, Hudson Phillips, Benj. Young. Isaac Switzer, Jos. Barber, W. E. Woolcott, M. L. Rice, O. L. Call, A. W. Smith, Yates Delancy, Peter Maxwer, R. J. Brewer, G. E. Brown, C. P. Wescott, James N. Robinson, James Green, A. Lamareaux, William Brewer, John Burgey, M. D. Robinson, Henry Earnest, Pat. Ready, D. B. Stevens, M. McMahon, M. J. O'Shoughnessey, O. C. Bennett, Z. T. Hall, Peter Helwig, John McCoy, C. D. Cool, George B. Cooper, J. J. Roberts, I. D. Wolcott, Henry Krebs, G. F. Brown, Jacob McCoy, A. J. Goble, David McQuade, Henry Veazie, Clark Keagle, Isaiah Johnson, R. E. Hathaway, J. D. Pease, A. Husted, T. H. Shoens, S. E. Pearley, M. V. Carey, John W. Baker, Chas. Doty, C. W. Smith, Abe Cowley, W. L. Keagle.

Baggage-masters.— John Shanley, W. H. Clawson, F. Bishop, F. S. Webb, M. Gleason, W. W. Gray, F. R. Fillman, Samuel Maxwell.

"Now, Uncle Jonas, you must be fatigued, and we will go into the Dickinson house and rest ourselves. Tomorrow we will go over the road to Wellsboro and Antrim."

CORNING TO WELLSBORO.
A PLEASANT RIDE DOWN THE FALL BROOK ROAD —
THE CHANGES OF A HALF CENTURY.

"There are two trains that go to Wellsboro in the morning, Uncle Jonas, one quite early that runs through to Williamsport, and one later that goes to Wellsboro and Antrim and at Lawrenceville connects with trains up the Cowanesque and Tioga valleys. I think we had better take the train that leaves about 10 o'clock, and that' will give us plenty of time here in the morning. We will not be hurried with our breakfast."

"I will leave the matter to you entirely, Harry."

"By the way, Uncle Jonas, I would like you to meet John H. Way, one of the oldest conductors in point of service that is employed by the Fall Brook Coal Company. Mr. Way commenced his railroad career about thirty years ago and has made many friends by his courteous manners and his care for the comfort and pleasure of the passengers who have been in his charge. He resides in a very pleasant cottage on East Church Street, and he has taken great care to make his home attractive. He is very clever with the brush and easel and has sketched many elegant landscapes, forest and stream views which are appropriately distributed in his parlors, sitting-room and library, making those rooms very attractive. His wife also possesses more than an ordinary skill and talent with the crayons and brush, and has produced a number of very fine works of art. But we shall not probably meet Mr. Way as he will take charge of the train that goes to Watkins Glen, Geneva and Lyons. Our conductor will be Thomas Brown, more familiarly known as Tom Brown. He, too, is a veteran conductor having been employed by the company for twenty years or more. Tom resides in Wellsboro and has a pleasant home. He is quite fond of the chase, and generally spends his vacations in Tioga and Potter counties in Pennsylvania, in hunting and fishing. He is a most excellent shot and when at leisure could relate some very interesting incidents of his experience in the wilds of those sections. But, Uncle Jonas, I will not weary you to-night with any further conversation, but will make the necessary arrangements for our trip tomorrow."

"This is the train for Wellsboro, Uncle Jonas, and this is Mr. Brown, the conductor, and this is Horace Lounsberry, the engineer."

"Gentlemen, I am pleased to meet you. Harry, my nephew, has told me about you, and I take it we will have a safe and pleasant ride. We will take seats on the right-hand side of the car, Harry, for I want to look out over the river as we pass along. Yonder, Harry, is the old residence of the McBurney's. I was well acquainted with the former judge, as well as his sons, the Hon. John McBurney and Thomas McBurney. Just above the bridge was the old residence of John Jennings, and the first home of Benjamin Patterson, the pioneer who subsequently removed two-and-one-half miles west of Painted Post. As you will recollect, Harry, Arthur Erwin, of Bucks County, purchased a township of the land of Phelps & Gorham, which included the site of the original Painted Post, and all the area skirting the Conhocton and Tioga Rivers for several miles. Arthur Erwin, the original patentee, was shot at Athens about the year 1790, but his sons came on here, settled, and became prominent and foremost citizens. I declare, Harry, we glide along so fast that I hardly have time to point out the old landmarks. Across the river, yonder was the former residence of John Evans, the learned and useful pioneer who came into this country from England about the year 1800 via Northumberland. Why I say he was so helpful was because he was a gentleman of regular and well-disciplined habits. He filled the position of teacher, accountant, land surveyor, clerk, justice of the peace. United States assessor, and revenue collector, when his district comprised what are now the counties of Allegany, Livingston, Steuben, Yates, Chemung, Schuyler, Tioga, Tompkins, Broome, Cortland, and Chenango. He was the very embodiment of accuracy, and his books, in point of everyday and elegant handwriting, cannot be excelled even by our modern professors in commercial colleges. Yonder is a lumber establishment which has become historic. I refer to Fox, Weston & Bronson. This Harry is 'Jacks Eddy,' named in honor of John Mullhollon, who was a pioneer settler and familiarly known as 'Jack' Mullhollon. The station here is named also after him. In that cemetery on the north side of the river is buried many of the old pioneers of this valley— Ben Patterson, Marcus Huling, Robert Patterson, and Ben Patterson, the second, with Jane E. Jones, his wife, are laid to rest there. Old raftsmen honor that point over yonder on the 'Canisteo turn,' on account of the abrupt and sudden turn in the river. We are now approaching Erwin Center. Forty-five years ago, Harry, this was an essential point for lumbering. It was the residence of the Smiths, Hoffmans, Messereaus, Redfields, and others. The renowned Captain Isaiah J. Jones, who fought the bear single-handed and killed her, resided here and owned the farm just above the station. Across the river are the famous 'blue banks,' well-known to old hunters as a 'run-away' for deer. Here, on the left, is the McCullough farm, and just beyond is where Abner Collins and Mat Paul resided. We are approaching now the homestead of the celebrated John P. Ryers and his son, Joseph A. Ryers, who was connected with the railroad in its infancy, and who removed to and died in Philadelphia. His brother, G. A. Ryers, died at the old homestead many years ago. They owned three thousand acres here of very valuable white pine and oak timbered land, which they sold to Fox, Weston & Bronson. At Ryers' Eddy was the home of an old pioneer, Hezekiah Kinney. Across the river were the homes of the Messereaus and Harrowers. Silas Cook was an early settler here, which has given the name of Cooks to this station. He was a son-in-law of Robert Patterson, the pioneer who, with his brother Benjamin, conducted General

Williamson's party in 1792 down this valley and to Bath, and who settled on this river a few rods above here in 1805. Patterson lived to see a railroad penetrate this valley, where fifty years before there was not even a highway or a settler. Frederic Heckart was an early settler in this vicinity as well as the Rev. David Harrower, Albert C. Morgan, Benjamin narrower, Porter Harrower, Eber Scofield, Abner Thurber. I told you about Mayor Lindsley and other old settlers of the southern portion of the town of Lindley when we were going up the valley of the Tioga, and will not repeat them."

After leaving Lawrenceville, Tom Brown, the conductor, found time to occasionally spend a moment with Uncle Jonas, pointing out old landmarks and making the hours pass pleasantly. Crossing the Tioga River at Lawrenceville, the railroad leads up on the west side of the river, passing the old home of Austin Lathrop, Sr., and keeping close under the base of the mountain until you reach the broad and alluvial flats upon which the village of Tioga is situated. At the latter point, the Elkhorn and Crooked Creeks unite and the course of the railroad is up through the valley of Crooked Creek, where thirty-five years ago lumbering was carried on very extensively, a plank road being constructed from Tioga to Wellsboro, where for many years a hundred teams per day could be seen hauling the product of the mills to Tioga for shipment either upon the river or the Corning or Blossburg railroad. At Holliday's, Middlebury and Niles Valley exciting and busy scenes were enacted. The great lumber firm of Phelps, Dodge & Stokes owned many thousand acres in this valley and contiguous territory and were employing a small army of men in the woods and mills. The descendants of those pioneer lumbermen own farms in this valley and are tilling the soil with full as much profit as their fathers hewed down the pines.

"Look at those beautiful farmhouses and outbuildings which show thrift and prosperity. The tanning business succeeded the white pine lumbering, and many thousand dollars have been invested in that industry.

"We are now approaching Stokesdale Junction, where the Jersey Shore & Pine Creek Railroad diverges. We will talk more about that road upon our return from Wellsboro. Among the prominent early citizens in this locality were Aaron Niles, father of General Jerome B. Niles, auditor-general of Pennsylvania; H. H. Potter and Jesse Locey. The train, however, is moving on at such a rapid rate that we shall have to recall those old settlers at a future time."

"Forty-five years ago, Harry, some of the finest hunting grounds in America, were in this vicinity. The forests were literally full of deer, elk, bear and smaller game. The streams were full of fish, which required very little skill to catch; in fact, it was the sportsman's *Eldorado*. I have been here when I could stop at Aaron Niles, Sheriff Potter, or Holliday's, and if necessary, take a wagon load of venison home with me. Or if it was in trout season I could pack in cans or tubs hundreds of as fine fish as ever swam in water. Crooked Creek, Marsh Creek, and Pine Creek were literally full of them."

"The next station, Uncle Jonas, is Stockdale. E. G. Schiefflein, son of one of the early pioneers, is largely interested in tanning at that point, and the little hamlet located there, is the outgrowth of the business of tanning, the dwellings being chiefly occupied by the employees of Mr. Schiefflein. You recollect, Uncle Jonas, when we were at Hoytville a few weeks since that I referred then to the magnitude of the tanning interest in Tioga County, and stated among other things that it required the hemlock bark from one hundred and fifty to one hundred and eighty million feet of hemlock timber annually to supply the tanneries of this county. At that rate the hemlock forests of this section of Pennsylvania, will in a few years, have been cut down. Here we are at Wellsboro."

"Wellsboro is the county seat of Tioga County and contains about three thousand inhabitants. We will take the Wilcox house omnibus, Uncle

Jonas, and go to that house, which is nicely situated upon the main street, near the public square and the county buildings. Its proprietor is Seth 0. Daggett, a grandson of Major Seth Daggett, one of the early pioneers and prominent settlers in the town of Jackson, in the northeastern portion of this county, and who looks attentively after the comfort and care of his guests. There are several other good houses in the borough, among which are the Cole house and Sandbach house, which are very handsomely kept. The reason I desire to stop at the Wilcox house is that I became acquainted with Mr. Daggett when he resided at Horseheads and promised to become his guest should I ever come to Wellsboro."

"Suit your own convenience, Harry, and I shall be content."

They step into the omnibus and proceed to the hotel, where they were met by Mr. Daggett and escorted to a room which commanded a view of the public park, was warm and neatly furnished. They prepare for dinner and go down into the dining hall, where a large number of guests are present from various sections of the country, enjoying their mid-day meal. After dinner, Uncle Jonas complained slightly of fatigue, and it was thought best by Harry that they should remain in their room for at least a portion of the afternoon.

THE FIRST SETTLERS.

The first settlers, Harry, in this vicinity located here about eighty-five years ago and were from Philadelphia, Maryland, Delaware, and Virginia. The first settler was Benjamin W. Morris, from Philadelphia. When it was a mere hamlet, it was christened Wellsboro by Mrs. Mary Wells Morris, wife of the first settler. Mrs. Morris was a sister of William and Gideon Wells, two early settlers. In the year 1804, Tioga County was formed, and in the year 1806, Wellsboro was selected as the county seat and has enjoyed the distinction ever since. But courts were not held here until about the year 1813. In the year 1830, Wellsboro was incorporated, John Norris being elected the first burgess or executive officer. At that time, there were less than fifty families in the borough limits. The great state road running westward from the county of Luzerne across the counties of Luzerne, Bradford, Tioga, Potter, McKean, and Warren, on the Allegheny River, was finished to Wellsboro about the year 1809. A few years before that date, a highway had been cut out, which reaches southward from Wellsboro to Newberry, upon the west branch of the Susquehanna, near the present city of Williamsport. Its course was over hills and mountains, and it was much used by the early settlers, who did business southward at Northumberland, Harrisburg, Philadelphia, and Baltimore. It would hardly seem possible, Harry, that the early merchants of this town hailed their merchandise with teams from Baltimore and Philadelphia, but it is true.

WELLSBORO, PAST, AND PRESENT.
EARLY SETTLERS AND THEIR GRAND WORK —
ENTERPRISING AND PROMINENT MEN OF TODAY.

"**A**mong the early settlers at Wellsboro were Benjamin W. Morris, John Norris, Samuel W. Morris, William Bache, Sr., William Wells, Erastus Fellows, William Eberentz, B.B. Smith, John F. Donaldson, F. Wetherbee, Elias Spencer, J. L. Robinson, Israel Merrick, Gates Wilcox, Josiah Emery, James Locke, Dr. O. L. Gibson, E. M. Bodine, L. I. Nichols, Samuel Dickinson, J. Kimball, D. Caldwell, E. M. Bodine, David Linsey, Doctor Wells, Samuel Mack, William Taylor, R. Christanot, who were residents here before the year 1835, or a little over fifty years ago. Some of those, of course, had made Wellsboro their home at a much earlier date. Several of the prominent businessmen of today, among whom are William Bache, Chester Robinson, J. L. Robinson, fifty years ago, had just commenced their business career. The Robinsons are bankers now, but they were merchants and lumbermen then. But a large number of what might be termed now as old citizens located here about thirty or forty years ago. Wellsboro developed slowly but surely. Her growth was not rapid or phenomenal. It was an inland town without any railroad facilities until the year 1872. You will observe. Uncle Jonas, that the dwellings and business places have a new and recently constructed appearance, although the shade trees along the streets and in the public square show that they have been planted many years. Several severe and destructive fires occurred here, and many of the best structures in the town have been erected since the railroad was completed. The courthouse was erected fifty years ago, but the county offices of the register and recorder, notary, county treasurer, and sheriffs are of quite a recent date and reflect credit upon the county. The courthouse is constructed of sandstone, which is peculiarly well-adapted to building purposes. It has withstood the frosts and storms of fifty years and yet looks fresh and substantial. There is a large quantity of the same kind of sand rock only a few miles to the south of us. The first store was opened here by William Bache, Sr., in the year 1812. However, several citizens had joined previous to that date in purchasing goods by the wholesale in Northumberland and Philadelphia, hauling them here and then distributing them among the persons who had invested in the enterprise. A few of the first settlers had taken the precaution to bring with them many of the necessaries of life to their wilderness home, and until several years had elapsed, and until stores of supplies were regularly established here, they had not exhausted their stores. Benjamin Wistar Morris was a Quaker and services in that faith were held in a log church or schoolhouse erected for that purpose.

Early in the history of the settlement of this vicinity, the Rev. Caleb Boyer, a Methodist minister, located here. He came about the year 1802 when there were only fifteen Methodist ministers in the United States. As the settlement increased in dignity and importance, the church organizations were made. The Episcopal Church was formed in the year 1838, the Presbyterian in 1843, and the Baptist in 1868. In the year 1817, an academy was located and established, which flourished for many years. In the year 1834, Wellsboro adopted the standard free school system, and soon thereafter took measures to erect suitable school buildings. The enterprise and public spirit of its citizens in the cause of education resulted in the erection of a central school building in the year 1875, which cost $35,000. Prominent among the friends of that enterprise were the Hon. Henry Sherwood, the Hon. H. W. Williams, the Hon. Jerome B. Niles, the Hon. M. F. Elliott, the Hon. John W. Bailey, the Hon. Hugh Young, the Rev. Dr. Charles Breck, the Rev. J. F. Calkins, the Rev. N. L. Reynolds, William Bache, James H. Bossard, Jerome B. Potter, the Hon. John I. Mitchell, the Hon. Stephen F. Wilson, J. L. Robinson, Chester Robinson. It was a public thing in which almost the entire community took a deep interest. The completion of the railroad from Lawrenceville to this point in the year 1872 brought in strangers, who located here and assisted in building up this beautiful village. It affected to increase the value of real estate, and whole farms were surveyed into town lots, readily sold and dwellings and business places erected thereon. For a few years, the tendency was toward an extreme, and the hard times came on and checked the growth of the town temporarily. But she has rallied from the depression and new buildings of all kinds and descriptions have been erected during the past year. Some of them are very fine in architectural design, notably the new opera house across the way built by Robert C. Simpson, and elegantly arranged in all its appointments.

"In the matter of the press, Uncle Jonas, Wellsboro has had many newspaper ventures. They have represented every political party since 1828. There are now two Republican and one democratic newspaper published here. *The Agitator* is the oldest. It was established in the year 1854 by M. H. Cobb, and has continued as the organ of the Republican party. A few months ago another paper was established by the late Charles G. Fairman, entitled the *Republican Advocate*. *The Agitator* is now and has been for a number of years conducted very ably and profitably by Messrs. Barnes & Roy, and the *Advocate* by J. H. Maston, and edited with ability. The democratic newspaper is the Wellsboro *Gazette*, and was established in the year 1874 by F. G. Churchill, of Elmira. It is now owned and published by Messrs. Wright & Conevrey. Wellsboro may well feel proud of its press. Three better country newspapers cannot be found in the state. In the year 1883 the Pine Creek & Jersey Shore Railroad was completed and connections made with the Corning, Cowanesque and Antrim Railroad at Stockdale Junction, as you observed today. This has afforded the citizens of this place a more direct route to Williamsport, Harrisburg, Philadelphia and intermediate points, and to receive newspapers published in those cities at a much earlier date. It has enabled them to do business with the merchants and businessmen of southern Pennsylvania, interchange products and hold communication with the people of the southern portion of the state. Until that very important railroad connection was made, they were deprived of that pleasure."

"I am rested now, Harry, and would like to take a walk about town."

Harry and Uncle Jonas make ready and go out visiting, first the park, or public square. "Those grounds are tastefully laid out, and much interest has been taken by the authorities in beautifying them and making them inviting. Wellsboro will soon have an excellent system of waterworks, and fountains will be erected upon the square, and seats will be provided where under the refreshing shade of the elm and maple, the weary can find a place to sit and while away the hours in hot summer afternoons. A pagoda or bandstand is already erected. It is also expected that a soldier's monument will be placed upon these grounds very soon. The soldiers from Tioga County upon the battlefields of the south, during the late rebellion, were many, and wherever the union flag floated, there they were found defending it and bearing it onward to victory. A million dollars was raised by the Tioga County and township officials to send these gallant men to those brave men to the front. Very many of them never returned. Others came home wounded, maimed, crippled, and broken down physically. It is very appropriate that some lasting memorial should be erected in recognition of their exceptional services for the perpetuation of the union.

"This fine building on the corner is owned by Henry Sherwood and Walter Sherwood, under the firm of Henry Sherwood & Son. They are prominent lawyers, and are officially connected with the Jersey Shore and Pine Creek Railroad, the father being president and the son one of the directors. All these buildings until you reach the church on the corner are occupied by gentlemen of the legal profession. There is the office of Jeff

Harrison, and nearby are the offices of John W. Mather, Henry M. Foote, S. F. Channell, A. J. Shattuck, General J. B. Niles & Son, Elliott & Watrous. General Niles is connected as attorney and agent for the Pennsylvania joint land and lumber company, which really is the old Phelps, Dodge & Stokes estate. This firm or company, in point of importance as regards the landed interest in Pennsylvania, stood second only to the Bingham estate and were among the most significant lumber manufacturers and dealers in the United States. Upon the east side of the public square standing back from the street and almost hidden by the shrubbery is the land office of the Bingham estate, which has for many years been represented by Robert C. Simpson, as agent or trustee. Mr. Simpson is a careful and sagacious gentleman, refined and polished, and ranks among the foremost citizens. He recently erected the elegant opera house I pointed out to you and has been prominent in the council of Free Masons. You will be pleased to meet him and perhaps we shall before we leave the town. Let us walk up past his office and take up towards 'Academy Hill.' You discover, Uncle Jonas, that there are many cozy and elegant residences hid away among the groves. That large residence with those beautiful grounds is the residence of William Bache. The grade is too steep for you, Uncle Jonas, and we will not go any farther in this direction, but take this street west to Main Street. They pass on their route up Main Street many splendid homes, and advanced far enough to catch a view of the southwestern portion of the street, as it leads toward the Delmar Hills. Many very fine residences adorn that portion of the town. Returning, they walk leisurely along, observing, not in an undignified manner, the very tasty, costly, and elegant dwellings with most carefully prepared grounds and excellent walks. They pass the "Robinson store," which was subsequently used as a bank and which was burglarized on September 16, 1874, and over one hundred thousand dollars of currency and bonds carried off. Harry briefly explained the history of the transaction, how the family of Mr. Robinson was seized, bound and gagged and the cashier, Mr. Eugene Robinson, compelled to go and open up the vaults of the bank, and to witness the plundering of the same, and how the affair became known, pursuit made and several of the robbers overtaken, returned to Wellsboro, tried and convicted and sent to the prison. Arriving at the county buildings, they go in and call on that veteran. General R. C. Cox, who for several years, has been the efficient notary of the county, and who did such gallant service in the union army during the rebellion. The general, among the bravest of the brave in the field of battle, is very modest regarding his exploits. They also met his son Henry, who has been connected with the office for an extended period. The general is a gallant older man, brave, civil, courteous, and polite. They next visited the office of George C. Bowen, register and recorder. He has served the county in that capacity for many years and is a very competent official. The office of Captain Horton, county treasurer, was next visited. The captain did excellent service in the union army during the rebellion and is a very genial and companionable gentleman, as well as a competent and reliable officer. The finances of the county are in safe hands when Captain Horton holds the key, disbursing the funds with accuracy and keeping a straight record of the same."

They next visited the county commissioner's rooms, where, through the courtesy of William H. Baxter, one of the county commissioners, they were shown through the entire building, and witnessed the admirable and convenient manner which its fireproof vaults, cases, pigeon holes, heating and ventilating apparatus was arranged and made. They met the recently elected sheriff Ferris, who kindly offered to show them through the jail. But Uncle Jonas declined, saying it was no pleasure to him to look at his fellow-man in confinement and disgrace. They passed out of the office, well pleased with their visit. They satisfied that the authorities of Tioga County, had provided a safe and convenient structure, where into keep their valuable records and those of its citizens.

They next visited the courthouse and called on Judge Williams, whom they found in his chamber, carefully looking up reference and authorities, but who found time to greet his callers with a hearty welcome. The judge has been about twenty years upon the bench, sixteen or more of which he has been president judge, a more significant portion of the time called to preside in Tioga, Potter, Mc-Kean, and Cameron counties. During these twenty years, he has been called upon to decide some significant cases involving many intricate points and thousands of dollars. He has upon the whole given most excellent satisfaction to litigants, based upon his fairness and impartial decisions. Notwithstanding his laborious duties, the judge is well preserved and the picture of health and contentment. He owns one of the finest residences in the town and is surrounded by very many of the comforts and luxuries of life, which he has well earned during a life of industry and sobriety.

Thus far, Uncle Jonas was delighted with his visit to Wellsboro. They leave the courthouse and call on the Hon. John I. Mitchell, United States Senator, who was home from Washington during the holiday vacation. They are kindly received by the Senator and his law partner, the Hon. David Cameron. Harry had, on a former occasion, when at Mitchells on the Tioga Road, given a brief history of the Senator, who was born at that place and shall, therefore, not refer to him at length today. In their calls that afternoon, they met the Hon. Stephen Wilson, G. W. Merrick, the Hon. B. B. Packer, Robert K. Young, Walter Merrick, United States Bank Examiner Hugh Young, J. H. Matson, District Attorney; Dr. W. W. Webb, Thompson and Shearer, Dr. M. L. Bacon, Charles C. Mather, a prominent merchant; F. K. Wright, a leading businessman; John W. Bailey, C. C. Van Valkenburg, C. M. Osgood, L. A. Gardiner, Frank Hart, James R. Cole, of the Cole House; Judge L. P. Williston, Squire Brewster, Judge Wheeler, I. M. Bodine, John R. Bowen, besides visiting the fire department rooms, the

Odd Fellows and Masonic halls, thus putting in full time for the afternoon, and returning to the Wilcox House in time for supper.

The evening was spent at their rooms at the hotel, where they were called upon by several older citizens, who related incidents connected with the early settlement of this vicinity and pleasant events which had taken place in the courts of the county, where important suits were tried, and the legal combats of the lawyers, the stupidity of the witnesses or jurors, and related many amusing anecdotes concerning the hotels thronged with litigants, jurors, and witnesses. There is always a particular atmosphere about county seats, especially if the county is large and thinly populated. Every county has a few eccentric characters who make it their business to attend every term of court, whether they have any business there or not. One of the callers on Uncle Jonas and Harry that evening was a particular judge who served many years at the bar of Tioga county as a lawyer, and who also was several years upon the bench, been a member of both Houses of the State of Pennsylvania, and served two terms in Congress. He had, therefore, been much in public life, had marked and could tell many ludicrous scenes in court, in the legislature, and Congress with a grace equaled by few. This judge, when the conversation turned to the old court scenes, refreshed his memory and, for two hours, kept Uncle Jonas' face bathed in tears from his immoderate laughter, caused by the judge's recital of his stories concerning the bench and the bar. At some future time, we may write them out for the benefit of the readers of the *Daily and Weekly Advertiser*, but for the present we must be excused as Uncle Jonas and Harry must go to Antrim tomorrow, and the next day visit Williamsport. Uncle Jonas begins to need a little quiet rest at Harry's home in Elmira. He has been six months today upon the road visiting and talking, and notwithstanding, he insists that he enjoys it. After we make this tour, which will take five or six numbers to write up, we will give the old gentleman rest until springtime.

WELLSBORO TO ANTRIM.
THE COAL INDUSTRY. — FAVORITE RESORT FOR
EXCURSION PARTIES,

Through the courtesy of a friend. Uncle Jonas and Harry were taken into a carriage and driven out by the residence of Dr. M. L. Bacon, the public school building, thence back to Main Street and as far north as the summer residence of Hon. Henry Sherwood, passing among other homes those of A. Hardt, chief engineer for the Fall Brook Coal Company, Fred. K. Wright, Mrs. Silas X. Billings, Walter Sherwood, Charles C. Mather, and Captain Niles. Returning they visit the agricultural fairgrounds which are annually made more attractive and convenient, and also the beautiful city of the dead which is so carefully guarded by those whose friends are therein entombed. The remains of those most prominent in the affairs of Wellsboro through all stages of its early settlements are resting therein. It is a historic spot, and well, do the citizens of Wellsboro honor themselves when they exhibit so much interest in the care of their dead. From the cemetery, they were driven to the depot, whereby good luck they found an extra train about to depart for Antrim and soon they were speeding away upon the Charleston Creek Railroad into the Charleston mountains — passing the Tioga County Poor House, one of the county's most deserving institutions. Round Top is at last reached — not that one made famous in the great battle at Gettysburg, but the peaceful round top of Charleston township in Tioga County, where flocks and herds graze undisturbed by wars or rumors of wars. We can look behind us and see Wellsboro nestled in the valley below us — her church spires gleaming in the sun and her dwellings and public buildings looking as fresh upon this winter's morning as if she had taken a bath in a May Day stream. Dr. Charles H. Williams, son of Judge Williams, was on board and entertained Uncle Jonas and Harry very much by his description of mountain scenery in various portions of the United States and Canada. The doctor is possessed of excellent artistic taste and rare skills in the use of a pencil, crayon, and brush.

"Here we are at the Summit and will soon begin to descend towards Antrim by what is known in railroad circles as "back switching." These, Uncle Jonas, are the same as those at Fall Brook, which I then explained to you. The engine has left us, and we are descending by gravity. Just watch Conductor John Wilson and see how carefully he manipulates the brakes. He is serving in the triple capacity of engineer, brakeman, and conductor. He is responsible for the safe delivery of this car at Antrim and trusts no one to do his work. He has been upon the road ever since it was opened in 1872, and had been employed several years before that time between Fall Brook and Corning and between Corning and Watkins on the Erie and Northern Central Railroads. Look, Uncle, we are rounding the point, and presently Antrim will be in view. Cast your eye to the westward and peer down into that gorge many feet below and see the stream dashing over the rocks and hurrying on to the Chesapeake Bay. There is a hamlet down there in that narrow valley known as Sand Run. A few years ago, these mountainsides were covered with an enormous growth of hemlock timber, which has been cut down for the lumber and bark it afforded."

"Is that Antrim, Harry, with its many painted dwellings, stores, churches, and school buildings."

"Yes, Uncle Jonas."

"Well, I expected to see a different town, one covered with coal dust, grim and smoky, and a lot of irregular tenements. I am happily surprised!"

"We will continue down to those coal schutes and then reverse and glide down to the depot, which you see near that fine stone church. There we will alight, walk down by the company's office and store, and a little further on we will find the Antrim hotel, whose proprietor is Mr. James D. Fish, son of ex-Sheriff Fish of this county. We will be kindly received there and well provided for."

The hotel is reached; the travelers are conducted to a cozy room, and soon dinner is announced. After dinner, they walk down to the schutes where the coal is received from the mines in small cars and shipped into larger standard gauge coal dumps and gondolas varying in capacity from six to twenty tons or more. From this point, Uncle Jonas and Harry obtain a view of the valley in which Hoytville, which they visited some weeks ago, is situated. It is at least a thousand feet lower than Antrim. These towns are only about three miles distant from each other — one located in the valley, and the center of an excellent tanning and lumbering industry, and the other situated upon a mountain about eighteen hundred feet above tide and an extensive mining town.

"Were it not, Uncle Jonas, for the pleasure of going down on the Jersey Shore and Pine Creek from Ansonia to Blackwells, we could go down to Hoytville by stage and from there to Blackwell, a distance of about five miles, and thus save many miles of circuitous travel, but we shall have a fine trip through this picturesque country."

The travelers retrace their steps to the hotel and from thence to the company's store, presided over by W. W. Forest, assisted by a competent corps of clerks. They also visited the office of the manager and paymaster. They met Mr. William Howell, Jr., the manager, and Messrs. James B. Howell and Samuel Heron, chief clerk and paymaster, also James Pollock, the resident civil and mining engineer. It was payday, and they saw many of the employees of the company. Work had been good for the past three months, and the miners and other employees had made full and some of the extra time, and were consequently much encouraged. Many of the miners' wives or daughters came to the pay counter and received the amount due to their husbands or fathers for the reason that the men were at work and did not choose to lose any time.

After Uncle Jonas and Harry had taken a circuit of the town, they returned to the hotel and talked over the history of the town, from the facts gleaned from the old citizens:

"The first explorations for coal were made where the village of Antrim is now situated, in the year 1866, by Thomas Farrar and John Smith, in the interest of the Fall Brook Coal Company. These explorations resulted in the purchase of several thousand acres of land by the company, then an unbroken wilderness. In the year 1867, Titus Drainsfield moved his family into a cabin that had previously been used as a shelter for the explorers. He was, therefore, the first settler who pinned his faith in the permanent development of the place and took up his abode in this mountainous country several miles distant from the habitation of men. Steps were immediately taken after the land had been purchased, to construct a railroad from Lawrenceville, by way of Tioga, Middlebury, Niles Valley, and Wellsboro to these lands, which was consummated in the year 1872. In December 1867, Humphries Brewer, who was one of the reliable men of the Fall Brook Coal Company, who had been their chief engineer, both civil and mining, as well as manager, died. He was one of the principal officers in the new contemplated road. Hon. John Magee died a few months after, in the year 1868, and Duncan S. Magee one year later. Duncan S. Magee, however, in the year 1868, with a party of friends, among whom were Hon. Daniel E. Howell, of Bath, Gen. George J. Magee, John Lang, C. C. B. Walker, A. H. Gorton, John Magee, Jr., Anton Hardt, John Smith, Thomas Farrar, Charles Crawford, S.S. Ellsworth, R. F. Cummings, and James Hoffman visited the mine and christened it 'Antrim.' Contemporaneous with the building of the railroad was the erection of a sawmill, a store and offices, dwellings, and schutes so that by the time the railroad was finished, the mines were opened and coal ready for shipment. Among those who assisted at the opening of the mines and the founding of the town were: Thomas Farrer, Thomas Gaffney, Charles Prothero, Titus Drainsfield, John Hinman, Chas. Hinman, Charles Hoff, William B. James, David J. Davis, Thomas Burton, Samuel Strong, James Ketcham, E. H. Tremain, W.W. Lounsberry, William E. Butts, Isaac S. Marshall, David Cooper, Joseph Murray, D. D. Holliday, Jerry Austin, L. J. Stothoff, John Forrest, Theodore P. Whiting, D. M. Edwards, Andrew K. Fletcher, Michael Keating, Thomas McMahon, James Gardiner and James Gaffney, who were assigned various parts in the work, and who performed it equally well. In the year 1873, at the December term, the township of Duncan, which included the village of Antrim, was formed and an election authorized to be held for township officers in February following, and Thomas Gaffney and E. H. Tremain appointed commissioners to hold the said election. The vote was held February 17, 1874, and resulted in the selection of Thomas Gaffney and E. H. Tremain as supervisors; Isaac S. Marshall and J. Shumway were chosen justices of the peace; W.W. Lounsberry, constable; William E. Butts, assessor; a school board consisting of David Cooper, A. Lake, Dr. E. George, William P. Thomas, Joseph Murray; town treasurer, John Hinman; Thomas Farrar, Charles G. Hinman, George W. Rice, auditors; town clerk, W.W. Forest; judge of election, Jerry Austin; inspectors of election, D. D. Holliday and Charles Prothero. Schools were opened, churches were organized, lodges were instituted, and everyone went to work with a will to build up a community possessing a large number of the advantages enjoyed by older towns, and you can see. Uncle Jonas, today, how much progress they have made in a little over ten years since the township of Duncan was incorporated."

"It is impossible, Uncle Jonas, to relate to you in our brief visit many little incidents which have occurred in the building up of such a town as this. There are many things which I shall be obliged to omit for want of time. But I trust I have given you a fair idea of it. This is one of the most orderly and law-abiding towns in northern Pennsylvania, and will in time become a great summer resort, on account of its pure and bracing air and the most excellent springs of water. This town has already become famous as a point for excursions for the people living on the line of this Corning, Cowanesque and Antrim Railroad, and the Syracuse, Geneva and Corning road. To those who have always lived in the farming districts of Steuben, Yates, Schuyler, and Ontario counties in New York, it is a great novelty to them to come up here, look the town over, take their dinners at this hotel or bring their lunch baskets with them, and go into the mines which penetrate for miles beneath these mountains; then to witness the mode of mining, and see what a skillful yet difficult process it is, pleases those farmers and businessmen more than a trip to New York or the seaside. I believe. Uncle Jonas, the most delightful excursion party I ever met, came here several years ago from those counties to which I have just referred. Those little trains hauled by mules, dashing through the subterranean railroads, guided by a driver with a coffee-pot lamp, with the rattle of cars in those dark avenues, gave them great enjoyment. They were captivated by the excitement. I sat quietly in my seat in the car on their return home and hastened to their exclamations of delight and pleasure. It is not the country people alone who take delight in visiting the mines, but students and scientists, and highly-educated and refined people are yearly increasing in numbers, who wish to visit this town. There are many valuable things to be learned here. Then there is no danger connected with it. It is not like going down a thousand feet or more into the anthracite coal pits filled with harmful and inflammable gases. There is no more danger in going into these mines here, either drawn by a small locomotive or a mule than there is in riding on a first-class narrow-gauge railroad. There is nothing connected with a ride into these mines to frighten the most timid."

"I had expected, Uncle Jonas, that we would remain here overnight, but I am told that it will be better for us to go back to Wellsboro with Conductor Wilson now, as it is uncertain whether we can reach Wellsboro by train in the morning."

As they were going to the depot, through the politeness of Mr. William Howell, they were shown into Trinity Church, a beautiful edifice erected through the generosity of John Magee, Jr., and made of cut stone taken from the quarries in the vicinity of Antrim. It is a durable and costly structure and will long remain as a monument to his generosity. Trinity church was organized July 24, 1872, through the instrumentality of Rev. Charles Breck, of Wellsboro, assisted by such churchmen as John Hinman, Thomas Gaffney, and others. John Magee, Jr., died quite suddenly of pneumonia at Watkins, NY, April 26, 1873, aged 29 years.

The time has arrived for the train to start, Uncle Jonas and Harry stepped on board. They arrived safely at Wellsboro and were driven to their former quarters at the Wilcox House.

PINE CREEK AND JERSEY SHORE.
A TRIP THROUGH A DELIGHTFUL VALLEY TO
WILLIAMSPORT.

"**W**ell, Uncle Jonas, this is rousing us up pretty early, but then we will try and accommodate ourselves to the circumstances. Passengers must be ready when the time arrives for the trains to depart, or they must remain over until the next train, is the principle, and a very good one too, that is enforced in this railroad age."

In due time Uncle Jonas and Harry are seated comfortably in the excellent upholstered cars of the Williamsport high-speed line and are conveyed at the rate of forty miles an hour down the valley of Marsh Creek. This is a very sluggish stream that winds around in the valley between the mountains, its descent to Pine Creek being only about one foot to the mile. On the side of the mountain rocks project, which indicates the outcroppings of the coal measure.

Several hamlets and lumber districts, through which they are rapidly whirled, are known as Leach's, Matson's, and Marsh Creek. Then Ansonia is reached where the railroad first enters the valley of Pine Creek. At this latter station, the train halts for several minutes to take on passengers who have come down the valley from the townships of Shippen, Gaines, and the eastern townships of Potter county.

"Ansonia, formerly known as the 'Manchester Farm,' about forty-five years ago was the center of a great lumber industry, which was conducted by the late Hezekiah Stowell, Phelps & Dodge, Judge Robert G. White, Scovil & Babcock, and many others. Mills and lumber camps were scattered all along Pine Creek from this point up into Potter county, a distance of fifteen or twenty miles. The parties named here had extensive mills, as well as others higher up the stream. There were the Furmans, Rexford's, Billings, Phenix, and others who had mills also and manufactured lumber extensively. There, an idea has occurred to me while speaking of those localities above here on Pine Creek, that next spring when the trout season opens we will take a trip up the valley from here and look over the ground I have mentioned, and visit the locality where your old friend Silas Billings, father of Silas X. Billings, fifty years or more ago was so extensively engaged in business."

"I think that would be a good plan, Harry, for I am informed that there are many points of interest in that direction."

"Josiah Furman was the first settler in this locality in the year 1804. He came up from Northumberland in a boat, and soon after planted several orchards, the trees being also conveyed here in a boat propelled by hand power up the stream. While lumbering was going on here so extensively, a little church was erected on the banks of Marsh Creek, and a graveyard laid out adjoining it. Many of the old settlers of this locality are buried there."

"But, Uncle Jonas, before the timber was exhausted in this locality, a company was formed at Williamsport which constructed a great boom and proposed to make Williamsport the great manufacturing center for lumber for the West Branch of the Susquehanna and its tributaries above that point. In that project, they succeeded to a large extent. Millions of feet of logs are now cut in this region and above here on Pine Creek, which is floated in the water to Williamsport, safely secured in their large boom and then manufactured into lumber, lath, shingles and kindling wood. The signal has been given, and away we will go down into this great Pennsylvania canyon."

PINE CREEK CANYON.

The waters of Pine Creek and the railroad occupy every inch of available space between the mountains for a distance of about sixteen miles. The course is not a straight one by any means. At every revolution of the driving wheel of the locomotive, it seems as if it was departing upon a different tangent. However, strange as it may seem, the rails are laid upon the highest principles known to the most experienced civil engineers, and no unpleasant feeling is realized by the passenger, as he whirls along at a rapid rate. Nor would he be cognizant of the fact that he was traveling in such a serpentine course if he did not observe objects through the car window or rear door of the hindmost coach. The passenger experiences no different sensations than he does over an ordinary road. But the views are grand, surpassingly grand. Here the waters of Pine Creek almost in reach of the hand from the car window, while fifty feet westward across the stream is a mountain which towers a thousand feet above the passing train, its sides denuded of timber, huge rocks projecting outward over which dashes a silvery flow of water, running, leaping, falling with a thousand sprays over the coach and into the more significant stream. Then again, another and larger stream is seen dashing down through miniature gorges, running rampant. By a series of cascades and waterfalls, it reaches the famous Tiadaghton or Pine Creek. Or again, the traveler observes water, which in the summertime, drips down the mountainside, but in winter is solidified, and huge icicles formed in every conceivable shape are suspended, which glitter in the sunlight like polished silver. Then again huge forest trees are seen standing upon projecting rocks, their roots bare but still clinging to the stone with the tenacity of a leech, their half dead and half alive branches swayed by the wind which sometimes sweeps with great fury along this grand and awe-inspiring canyon. Such is a description of the route for sixteen miles through which the Pine Creek and Jersey Shore Railroad, now controlled or leased by the Fall Brook Coal Company.

For years this mountain chasm stood as an insurmountable barrier in the way of constructing a railroad to the northward from the West Branch of the Susquehanna up Pine Creek to the northern tier counties of Pennsylvania. And so it would have remained for years had not General George J. Magee, Henry Sherwood and the late William H. Vanderbilt took the matter in hand, and by their skill and that of their coadjutors and assistants — wealth and perseverance — demonstrated that a railroad could be constructed, which would form a tremendous connecting link with the Corning, Cowanesque and Antrim, the Syracuse, Geneva and Corning and the New York Central & Hudson River Railroads, over which millions of tons of coal, lumber and other freight could be transported, as well as thousands of passengers.

The stations along this mountain canon are Darling Run, Four-Mile Run, Tiadaghton, and Rail Island. At Blackwell's, the road opens into a broader valley. At this point, a considerable stream flows into Pine Creek, known as Babbs Creek. Pine Creek is here crossed by the railroad by a substantial iron structure.

"At Blackwell's, Uncle Jonas is where the half-breed French and Indian chief one hundred and fifty years ago had his mountain home, and contemporaneously with Shikelemy, watched and guarded this pass and retreat, while Shikelemy held sway about the confluence of the north branch of the Susquehanna, with the west branch at Northumberland. When the ancestors of Enoch Black- well, after whom this station is named, came here nearly ninety years ago, there were still remaining portions of that old Indian town, and Mr. Blackwell has shown me relics of a French and Indian character, which he found at this point and which he still preserves. Implements which were made in France, conveyed to Canada, while it was

255

yet a French province and from there distributed to the Indians of the Six Nations. Tiadaghton is said, by well-authenticated tradition, French and American history, to have been a Canadian half breed, whose father left France, want to Canada, and married an Indian princess. Tiadaghton was the Tall Pine of the upper waters of the Susquehanna, fearless in the chase, brave in battle and skilled in travel and Indian diplomacy. His dominion extended west to the Alleghany and the Ohio line and as far north as Presque Isle."

The romantic scenery along the route does not by any means terminate at Blackwell's but extends along the entire line until the traveler reaches Williamsport. Uncle Jonas and Harry pass Woodhouse, a small station, and are soon at the mouth of Cedar Run when Harry briefly related that it was at the headwaters of Cedar Run that Silas Billings, the senior, about forty years ago erected a steam sawmill in the wilderness, cutting a road from Gaines up Elk Run, over a high mountain and descending again into a small valley through which Cedar Run flowed, and also constructed a plank road, nine miles in length, over which to transport his lumber to Pine Creek. He also stated that the village of Leetonia, where a large tannery is situated, is located upon lands formerly owned by Mr. Billings. They have now entered the county of Lycoming, and the valley of Pine Creek gradually begins to widen, and farms and farmhouses are more frequently seen. Some flag stations are passed, when the train halts for a moment at Waterville, and again dashes onward towards Jersey Shore. Evidence of thrift and plenty is observable upon either side. The stations of Ramsey, Tombs Run, Safe Harbor, Harris, Jersey Shore Junction are passed when the train arrives on time at Jersey Shore, one of the oldest towns upon the upper waters of the West Branch. They are now in the broad, beautiful, and fertile valley of the west branch of the Susquehanna. This is a valley replete with historical events, which it would take volumes to rehearse, and which would require the skilled pen of a Maginnis, a Watson or a Lloyd to portray. But we will say in passing that Jersey Shore was incorporated in the year 1826. While its progress has been slow in point of population, it has continued to increase in wealth and the robust and substantial character of its citizens. It has recently received a great impetus to its prosperity by the construction of the Jersey Shore and Pine Creek railroad, and the Beech Creek, Clearfield & South Western railroad.

"If it were possible, Uncle Jonas," remarked Harry, "I would gladly spend months along this valley with you talking over ' bygones' and referring to the very many distinguished men and women who have lived and are now living in this valley. My object in having you visit this locality was to view it today, not through the eyes of retrospection."

"Well, Harry, I was familiar with this valley many years ago, before the West Branch canal was constructed, and soon after the Newberry and Coudersport Turnpike was built. There were no railroads then. The population was comparatively small at Williamsport, at Newberry, and this place. West at the mouth of the Bald Eagle, my old friends, the Dunns and Hannas lived, and I would prefer now, Harry, to enter this valley, view its prosperity, observe its public improvements, note its industrial establishments, its public and private buildings, and mark the general characteristics of its present population."

While Harry and Uncle Jonas were engaged in the preceding conversation, several stations had been passed, and they were approaching Williamsport at a rapid rate. In due time they reached Williamsport and were safely domiciled at the Hepburn House.

WILLIAMSPORT.

After resting and refreshing themselves, the travelers went out and called on Mr. Maginnis, of the *Gazette and Bulletin*, with whom they spent a few minutes very pleasantly. They also called on Ex-Mayor William F. Logan, Col. F. E. Embick, Mr. Prior, of the Lumberman's Exchange, who gave them the statistics of lumber, lathe, shingles, etc., manufactured during the year 1885, which aggregated several hundred million feet. They also called at the Sun and Banner office, went into the Lycoming County courthouse, an imposing structure, and then took a carriage and were driven about the town, calling on Edgar Munson, Esq., an extensive lumberman, and manufacturer. From thence over to Fourth street, as beautiful a street as any inland city of the state can boast of, skirted with elegant and stately mansions. They passed by the Episcopal church, erected by Williamsport's former distinguished businessman, Peter Herdic, and had the pleasure of meeting that irrepressible gentleman, whom no reverse in fortune can put down, and who is always buoyant under the most disastrous circumstances. They rode around to the Park Hotel, formerly known as the Herdic House, and made the acquaintance of its genial Scotch landlord, and after having been driven about the city for two hours or more, returned to the Hepburn House. During the evening, they had the pleasure of meeting the Hon. H. H. Cummin, president judge of Lycoming county, the Hon. John J. Metzger, the Hon. Theodore Hill, Ex-Mayor S. S. Starkweather, and others, and a little later dropped in again into the Lumber-man's Exchange, and met many of the active lumbermen of the city and heard the outlook of the lumber trade discussed, and the future destiny of Williamsport.

From what they had seen during the day and learned from representative businessmen of various occupations, they were favorably impressed with the city of Williamsport as it is now, and of its "bright prospects for the future. It now contains a population of twenty-five thousand, is provided with extraordinary railroad facilities, and all the social, religious, and educational advantages which any community could desire. Its press is well conducted and seems to be well sustained, its banking privileges are ample, the means of obtaining cheap rates of transportation are more than ordinary, and with the prospect of other manufacturing companies locating there, in addition to what it already possesses, it would seem that Williamsport's future was bright. What adds more force to this conclusion is the public spirit manifested by its citizens of every vocation. Of course, the chronic grumbler inhabits Williamsport as well as any other city or town, which is disposed to detract from the public spirit of its citizens, by cynical and objectionable remarks. Of this latter spirit, they observed that Williamsport was comparatively free, and on the other hand, the sense of progress seemed to permeate the community, and they were disposed to look on the bright side. They were told, "we are going to have a large and expensive post office, with chambers for the holding of United States courts."

We are going to have many new industrial establishments, and other levers to prosperity." This seemed the spirit that manifested itself everywhere, and such a sense as this prevailing, we reassert that the future of Williamsport is secure.

WILLIAMSPORT TO ELMIRA.
DESCRIPTION OF THE BEAUTIFUL COUNTRY
ALONG THE NORTHERN CENTRAL RAILROAD.

Uncle Jonas and Harry decided to return to Elmira by way of the Northern Central railroad — one of the well-managed and equipped first-class roads that lead from the south, northward through the states of Maryland, Pennsylvania, and New York to Elmira, Watkins Glen, Penn Yan, Canandaigua, Rochester, Niagara Falls, and Buffalo, and which is run and managed in harmony with the interest of the Pennsylvania Railroad Company, and one of its great trunk or branch lines. Its initial point is Baltimore. It follows up the grand old valley of the Susquehanna to Harrisburg, Dauphin, Halifax to Sunbury, and from that point, it uses the track of the Philadelphia & Erie, passing through Milton, Watsontown, Muncy, in the valley of the west branch of the Susquehanna to Williamsport. At Williamsport, it leaves the west branch valley. It continues northward up the valley of the Lycoming through Cogan Valley, Trout Run, Ralston, Roaring Branch, Canton, Alba, Troy to Elmira, and from that city, as we have stated, to Rochester, Niagara Falls, Buffalo, and the lakes. It is well officered and equipped, and its rolling stock is in most admirable condition, its trainmen skilled in their work and gentlemanly in their deportment, and courteous and attentive to passengers.

At about eight o'clock Uncle Jonas and Harry bid goodbye to mine host of the Hepburn house, and step into a streetcar which passes the hotel door and are soon at the depot, a significant and substantial brick edifice which is used by the Philadelphia & Erie Railroad Company, as well as the Northern Central. Admirable arrangements are made by the officials in charge, that no passenger takes the wrong train. The doors fronting the railroad are kept locked, except when trains are arriving and departing, and the officer in charge calls out the stations to which the train is destined, unlocks the door, and personally directs the passenger which car to take a seat in. When this system was first introduced, early in the history of the road, there were a great many people who objected to its adoption and enforcement, and particularly the lumbermen and raftsmen who had come down the river from the upper waters of the West Branch, and who did not like the idea of having the front doors locked and the gate fastened so that they could not go out and promenade at their leisure up and down the depot platform. For several years the regulation was looked upon with very great disfavor. Some did not relish the idea of "being fenced and locked in," and many imprecations were hurled at the officers enforcing the rules. In time the people became familiar with the regulation and acquiesced in it, believing it conducive to the safety of the traveler who is not familiar with the trains, and a preventive of mistakes by those who are able to take the train, which runs in a different direction from that which they desire to go.

At the proper time, the doors were unlocked, and Uncle Jonas and Harry stepped aboard of the train headed for Elmira, with many pleasant thoughts concerning the lively lumber city of Williamsport. After they were comfortably seated and were rolling along up the valley of the Lycoming at the rate of forty-five miles per hour, Uncle Jonas reminded Harry of the contrast between the speed they were making then. That made by the thousands of raftsmen, who forty and fifty years ago, thronged this valley in the "rafting season."

"This was the route," said Uncle Jonas, "which the raftsmen took when on their return from a trip down from the Chemung, Conhocton, Canisteo, Tioga and Cowanesque Rivers. At first, away back in the years 1820, '25, '30, and '35, the raftsmen were obliged to walk most of the way from tidewater to the upper waters of all the branches of the Susquehanna. It was a long and tedious tramp, and yet the men seemed to enjoy it or did not complain very much even when their feet were blistered and their ankles chafed by the friction of their coarse, sturdy boots. I have seen half a regiment of raftsmen leave Williamsport and turn their footsteps northward over the very ground that we are traveling now, clothed in rough apparel, with bundles of goods slung over their shoulders upon a stick, purchases that were made in Baltimore, Wrightsville, Columbia, Harrisburg, and Northumberland, which they were carrying to their homes away up, perhaps, to the head of the Canisteo, near the present populous town of Hornellsville, or Elkland and Knoxville on the Cowanesque, or to Covington, Mansfield, Tioga, and Lawrenceville, or to Bath, Painted Post, Big Flats or Elmira on the Chemung. Those bundles might contain a new dress or shawl for the wife or daughter or some souvenir of the goodwill of that hardy class. By and by, the Pennsylvania and North and West Branch Canals were dug, and a 'horse railroad' was built from Williamsport to Trout Run, and the lumbermen and raftsmen had fewer miles to walk. But then some took the trip on foot, claiming that they could not afford to ride and that they could earn good wages by walking."

Cogan Station has been passed, and they arrive at Trout Run, a small village about fourteen miles distant from Williamsport. This village contains about three hundred inhabitants and is quite an industrial center for lumbering and extracting of tanning liquids, etc. "It was at this place, Harry, the old raftsmen, left the valley of the Lycoming and ascended Trout Run, crossed the summit of the Laurel Ridge mountain and followed the Williamson road to the Blockhouse, and from thence down to Blossburg, near the head of the Tioga valley. A few years later, the first railroad was completed about ten miles farther up to Ralston, and soon after, a new path was cut across the mountains, which left the Lycoming valley at Roaring Branch. This was known as the 'Yankee path,' and also terminated at Blossburg. When three or four hundred of these raftsmen took to this narrow path that led up the mountainside through the forests, ascending higher and higher until an altitude of over two thousand feet were obtained, carrying miscellaneous bundles, hallooing, shouting and singings they were indeed a wild and boisterous crew. I am not, Harry, losing sight of the grand scenery along this road — those towering mountains, covered with a high growth of timber, while the rocks, denuded of soil, stand out in terraces, and distinctly outlining the outcroppings of the semi-bituminous coal measures of Lycoming, so closely allied to those of southern Tioga and Bradford. Nor have I neglected to note, as we flew rapidly by, the many pleasant homes, nor failed to keep in sight the Lycoming, with its ever-varying course as it flows through meadows, leaps over dams which the hand of man has placed in its way, to utilize its power in turning the wheel, and making the hum of industry resound through this valley. Nor have I failed to observe the secluded spot, underneath those willows and alders, where the speckled trout delights to dwell. All these things, Harry, have not escaped my attention, notwithstanding I have been speaking of other matters."

Ralston is at length reached, twenty-four miles north of Williamsport and two hundred and two miles from Baltimore. Ralston is a little hamlet with an excellent hotel, which in the summertime is usually filled with guests from the south, who desire to enjoy the hunting and fishing in the vicinity, but more especially to obtain quiet and rest and breathe the pure mountain air of that locality. About a half-mile distant is another small hamlet, known as. McIntyre. At this place, they observe the McIntyre plane, whose base is on the level with the Northern Central railroad, and whose summit is about one thousand feet higher. It connects with the semi-bituminous coal mines, which are located on the top of the mountain, but which are not visible from the window of the car on the Northern Central.

"For a number of years, Uncle Jonas, mining was carried on at McIntyre extensively. The village at the mines contained twelve or fifteen hundred inhabitants, but now is almost entirely deserted, and its former inhabitants are mostly residents of Clearfield County. Passengers on the Northern Central, thousands of them, from time to time, have watched with great interest the descent and ascent of coal cars upon the McIntyre plane. A powerful engine was located upon the summit to control the force acquired by the gravity of the loaded cars on their descent, to haul up the unloaded coal cars or full freight cars. Two tracks were used; one for those going up the incline and for those descending. It was a fascinating sight to witness."

Uncle Jonas spoke of Matthew C. Ralston, Esq., of Philadelphia, and his engineer, William P. Farrand, who nearly fifty years ago were prominent in the construction of the railroad from Williamsport to Ralston, which in 1854 became a portion of the Elmira and Williamsport Railroad, and later passing into the control of the present company.   Our travelers are now thirty miles or more from the mouth of the Lycoming, where it discharges its waters into the West Branch near Williamsport, Iron ore is found in that locality to a considerable extent, and several furnaces were at one time in blasting in the valley. Every revolution of the car wheels since they left Williamsport has been propelling them higher and higher above sea level. The Lycoming, which at first was a respectable river in size, is now only an ordinary creek, but noisy and saucy as a petted child. Roaring Branch is reached, a village of four or five hundred inhabitants, a portion of which is located in Lycoming County, and another portion in Tioga county. Lumbering is carried on to a considerable extent. At this point, the Lycoming receives the last prominent tributary of its upper waters. Five or six miles farther to the Lycoming has disappeared from the valley and is only traced in rivulets as they hide away in the meadows and hills.

Carpenter's and Groover, two lively villages are passed, and Canton, one of the principal stations on the line between Williamsport and Elmira, is reached, distant two hundred and eighteen miles from Baltimore. The dividing line which separates the waters of the Lycoming flowing southward, and Towanda Creek flowing eastward, has been passed. Canton is beautifully situated upon undulating grounds with the Armenia Mountain towering one thousand feet above it on the west, and sheltering it from the violent west winds of winter. Its elevation above tide is twelve hundred and sixty-one feet, and with drainage tending eastward and northward, its sanitary condition cannot fail to be everything that is desirable. It is the most desirable place for a summer residence. Miss Fanny Davenport and Frank Mayo have elegant cottages at Canton.

Canton contains about two thousand inhabitants, with an excellent graded school, a bank, a newspaper office, magnificent dwellings, substantial business places, neat and comfortable churches, and is one of those bright and saucy northern Pennsylvania towns which resemble a spirited youth, full of glee, entertainment, and business, who has just washed his face after violent exercise, and with a twinkle in his eye is ready for the next adventure. Canton looks new, dressed in tasteful and cheerful colors, with its well-lighted streets, fine yards, and splendid shade trees.

"It is just the place, Harry," said Uncle Jonas, "where if I was twenty-five years of age, I should like to step off and go into business. I like its clean face and general appearance. Its early inhabitants were old friends of mine — the Geres, Griffins, Spauldings, Grantiers, and some of them had seen service in the war of the revolution and came here in the wilderness to fight in the second war, that of cutting down the forest and making for themselves homes in this new country, fresh from the hand of nature. Many a time, I have no doubt, have they stood on the Armenia mountains west of us, and turned their faces to the east and north, and surveyed the country

between here and the Susquehanna at Towanda, and dwelt with pleasurable emotions upon the beautiful landscape before them, and conjectured the picture that the generation of today would witness — farms and farmhouses, fruitful orchards, herds of cattle and sheep
grazing in rich pasture lands, and a happy and industrious people, pursuing their peaceful occupations, their granaries filled to overflowing with the plenteous fruits of their labor, while villages and towns with their shops and places of business, bear evidences of wealth and refinement; their church spires, pointing heavenward, their schools and academies, filled with happy youth, anxious to climb the ladder of fame and make their mark in the history of their country, either upon the battlefield, in the peaceful arts, or the forum, senate or executive chair."

While Uncle Jonas had thus been speaking, Minuequa and Alba had been passed, and they were whirling along towards Granville and Troy at a rapid rate. Referring to Troy, he said:

"Troy was a hamlet with only a hotel, a blacksmith shop, and a few scattered dwellings when I first saw it. I have no doubt she has changed very much for the better since then, for I am told that it is now the half shire of this grand old county of Bradford."

"Yes, Uncle Jonas, Troy is the most important borough in western Bradford county. It is distinguished for the wealth and refinement of its people, its manufactories, schools, churches, lodges, fire department, and the beauty and elegance of its buildings, business places, hotels, and the tone of its press. There are two newspapers printed there, and edited with ability. Several publications have been published there from time to time, with varied success.

The Gazette and *The Register* are permanent institutions. A. C. Hooker, of the *Gazette*, is a smooth and polished writer and an accomplished gentleman. *The Register* is younger in years than the *Gazette* and is fast gaining a substantial footing. Since you were at Troy, Uncle Jonas, not only has it developed into a vibrant and prosperous borough, but the country surrounding it has kept pace with the march and progress of events. Along the entire route from Troy to Elmira, on the old stage line from Elmira to Williamsport, are evidence of the same forward movement and development. Here we are at Troy! Look out of the car window, Uncle Jonas, at the town, and see if you think that I have overstated the matter about this beautiful borough of western Bradford and northern Pennsylvania!"

The twenty-five miles intervening between Troy and Elmira are quickly passed over. Columbia Cross Roads, Snedeker's, Gillett, State Line, and the Southport shops are seen in quick review, and the cars roll up to the union depot at Elmira. They take the streetcar, and are soon at their cozy home on West Water street, well pleased with their trip from Elmira to Big Flats, and thence to Corning and over the lines operated by the Fall Brook coal company and the Northern Central railroad company. At their quiet home for a few weeks, they will rest from their travels while they discuss social, political, industrial, and historical events concerning northern Pennsylvania and southern New York.

POLITICAL HISTORY.
UNSETTLED CONDITION OF THE COUNTRY AFTER
THE REVOLUTION — THE WORK OF ORGANIZATION.

"I have rested well, Harry, and feel very much refreshed. I will read the newspapers this morning, and this afternoon I want to have a 'long talk,' as the old Indian chiefs would express it. We have been looking over old landmarks, speaking of pioneers and their families in a so-cial manner and dwelling upon their trials and triumphs over the residents of the forests, hewing down the wilderness, and letting in the sunlight to accelerate the growth of grass, grain, and the products of the soil generally. It occurred to me last night that it might be well for me to give you an idea of the political influences, the public men and incidents connected with the development of southern and western New York and northern Pennsyl-vania before you came to know personally of those influences."

"Believe me, Harry, it is not my intention to speak from a partisan standpoint nor give any political party credit for accomplishing the most significant things, nor the blame for the failure of needed and wise mea-sures. I want to show you that it was not altogether the men who melded the ax and followed the plow, who deserve all the credit for the develop-ment of this country. They did their share and did it nobly and many times in a double capacity, both as pioneers and public men. Many of the men who guided and directed the affairs of state in those days belonged to the latter class, and consequently, double honors should be given them."

"Great battles were to be fought in local matters at the county seats, in the state legislature, the halls of Congress and in the executive chair, and clear heads and strong nerves, combined with intelligence, were in demand. And such men came forth at the call. I want to speak to you about these things, while yet they are fresh in my memory, and I think this afternoon would be an appropriate time to enter upon their discussion."

"It will give me great pleasure, Uncle Jonas, to listen to what you may have to say upon those topics."

After dinner, Uncle Jonas and Harry retire to the sitting room, and when they are comfortably seated, the old gentleman proceeds:

"You will recollect, Harry, that the revolutionary war closed in the year 1783, and peace was proclaimed between the American Colonies and the government of Great Britain, the sovereign and ministry of that country acknowledging the thirteen original colonies, who had entered into a confederacy the better to resist the mother country, to be free and independent states. The war closed as I have stated and left the American Colonies victorious but sadly demoralized in their internal affairs and burdened with heavy liabilities. By many, that era is regarded as the most dangerous to the perpetuity of a republican form of government that has ever occurred in the history of this country, the late rebellion not excepted. But I will not dwell at length upon that period. Patriotic, generous, and enlightened statesmanship brought order out of confusion, framing, and adopting a national constitution, which has since withstood all the attacks made upon it, proving an anchor and compass, directing and holding the American people in conservative paths. At the same time, they safely have sailed over many a billowy sea into the haven of peace and prosperity. At the time of the conclusion of peace with the mother country (1783), all of northern Pennsylvania, southern and western New York was a wilderness, under the control of the red man. The prior claim of all western New York was held by the Indian, supplemented by a claim of the colony of Massachusetts, who based their title upon a royal charter. Across the line in Pennsylvania, a similar state of affairs existed. The state of Connecticut held claims and a royal charter, which conflicted with the great charter of King Charles the second to William Penn, in the year 1682, and by subsequent concessions. The red men presented their charter or title from a more ancient and greater power, the great Father of the Universe, to lands now composed of some fifteen of the northern and western counties of that state. General Sullivan, in 1779, with his army, had penetrated this valley and fabulous stories were circulated by his soldiery upon their return home, concerning the alluvial soil and productive valleys of the upper Susquehanna, the Genesee and Allegany Rivers, and the crystal waters of the Seneca, Cayuga, Keuka, Canandaigua, Otsego, and other lakes. The war had closed, but the white man dare not enter and possess himself of the territory described without the permission of the red man. He still watched and guarded his inheritance. War had been resorted to during the revolution, but when it closed, the Indians still held their lands and denied admittance to the pale face. What war had failed to accomplish was left to diplomacy to perform. Peaceful means were resorted to, and in the year 1784: Pennsylvania made a treaty with the Six Nations at Fort Stanwix, NY,whereby they ceded to the commissioners of that state, all the territory described in northern and western Pennsylvania. That treaty relieved the Pennsylvanians, and similar treaties were made by the authorities of New York. The conflicting claims of Massachusetts finally settled, and the lands in question opened up to settlement. The Indians were not, however, removed, and for many years they held the right to hunt and fish at will over the entire domain. Later, New York gathered them upon reservations and confined them to certain localities."

"The Indian title extinguished, the difficulty with Massachusetts and Connecticut adjusted, this whole region was soon occupied. Settlements were made on the Chenango, Unadilla, the east branch of the Susquehanna, at Binghamton, Owego, Chemung, and at Newtown (now Elmira), and all along the courses of the rivers from here up the Chemung, Conhocton, Canisteo, Tioga, Cowanesque, upon the Genesee, around the lakes, Seneca, Cayuga, Keuka and on the shores of lakes Ontario and

Erie. Northern and western Pennsylvania was also rapidly covered. White men pushed their boats from Northumberland up the West Branch and its tributaries as well as the North Branch. These things occurred under the national administration of Washington, Adams, and Jefferson, and under the state administration of George Clinton, John Jay and Daniel D. Tompkins, in New York, and Benjamin Franklin as president of the Supreme Executive Council of Pennsylvania, and by the governors, Thomas Mifflin, Thomas McKean, and Simon Snyder. The representatives in congress from New York, who were particularly interested in this locality during the period stated, were John Lawrence and John Hathorn, but later such men as John Patterson, Erastus Root, Oliver Phelps, John Cantine, Reuben Humphreys, Uri Tracey, Daniel Cruger, Benjamin Ellicott, Jonathan Richmond, David Woodcock, Samuel Lawrence, John Magee, Thomas Maxwell, Jonas Earll, Jr., Robert Monell, Millard Fillmore, Gamaliel L. Barstow, Nathaniel Pitcher, Grattan H. Wheeler, Samuel G. Hathaway, Sr., Francis Granger, Stephen B. Leonard were in congress from the region described in New York and did much to bring the attention of the people at large to this section. The representatives in the state legislature of New York from this section were, of course, numerous, but not always unanimous in their wants and the direction of public policy to be pursued. General Charles Williamson, among the earliest members of assembly from Steuben county and especially the Pultney estate which covered an area of one million two hundred thousand acres in Steuben, Ontario, Yates, Livingston and Seneca Counties, had his own interest to look after and was naturally jealous of any project instituted by the citizens of Chemung, Tioga, Broome, Chenango, Tompkins and Cortland, which might in any degree conflict with his interest or the estate he represented. Emanuel Coryell of this district was a perceptive and able representative in the state legislature. Hon. Samuel Tinkham was a man of influence, as well as Hon. Edward Evans, Caleb

Hyde, of Tioga, and Obadiah German, of Chenango, which county, up to the year 1804, had looked after the wants of the settlers east of the Pultney estate, including the Chenango and East Susquehanna Valley. A few years later, Hon. John Miller, of Broome and Tioga, made his debut in public life and was contemporaneous with Obadiah German, of Chenango; George Hornell, of Steuben; Israel Chapin, of Ontario; Chauncey Loomis, of Genesee; James Pumpelly, of Broome, afterward of Tioga; and Oliver C. Comstock, of Seneca, and Eleazer Dana, of Broome. General Charles Williamson had located at Bath, in the year 1793, as an agent for the Sir William Pultney estate, representing unlimited capital and resources. He was a foreigner who had served in the British army. He at once became a naturalized citizen by taking the oath of allegiance; organized a court and caused himself to be appointed judge of the same; built hotels, dwellings, stores, mills, and boats to ply upon lakes Keuka and Seneca; caused himself to be elected member of the assembly of the state of New York, and was instrumental in the formation of the county of Steuben from Ontario. By some, in the eastern portion of the state and in this locality, his energy and presence have deemed a menace to American liberty. This, of course, was not so.

He, it is true, was ambitious that the estate he had in charge should become a profitable investment. Justice to his memory requires this to be said and admitted. But those who were in one sense his rivals, who owned vast tracts of land in the present counties of Chemung, Tompkins, Schuyler, Tioga, Broome, Otsego, Chenango, and Cortland were jealous of his power and influence; and even the old patrons of Delaware, Schoharie, Albany, Montgomery, and Rensselaer kept a watchful eye upon the skilled diplomat who had enthroned himself, as they termed it, in the land of the Six Nations, and was acquiring a foothold by the use of British gold that the mother country could not obtain by the force of arms. The Knickerbockers of the Hudson never had a kindly feeling towards the English, and Williamson was an Englishman, though I think of Scottish birth. Had he hailed from Amsterdam, the case would have been different. I only refer to this matter to show you that even in those early days, there were rivalries and jealousies, and the public current did not run as smoothly and serenely as a meadow stream."

"Many projects planned for the construction of turnpikes and state roads through the sparsely settled country when the war of 1812 was declared and held in abeyance. At times during the war, the party spirit ran high. Old feuds which had slumbered since the revolution were revived, and state rights parties organized to baffle the administration of James Madison. I would not refer to that matter were it not for the reason that the bad blood stirred up during that period extended up to as late as 1840 or 1850. It is not entirely forgotten now. The war is over, new projects were agitated, such as the digging of canals and utilization of our rivers as a means of inland, slack-water navigation. The insufficiency of roads during the war had demonstrated the necessity of some more elaborate methods of inter-communication between the waters of the Hudson River and Lake Erie, The Erie Canal was projected, and simultaneously with that grand scheme, localities not on the line of that proposed route began to agitate their claims for lateral canals which would become feeders to that trunk line. Our neighbors over the line in Pennsylvania had also caught the fever. Hon. James Ford, Hon. Samuel W. Morris, Asa Mann, Esq., Justus Dartt, Dr. William Willard, Silas Billings, Aaron Bloss, Hiram Beebe, Ira Kilburne and others of Tioga County, and Judge Edward Herrick, Samuel McKean, and hundreds of others in Bradford County were besieging their legislature and counseling with citizens of this state for a canal that would connect the waters of the Susquehanna with those of Seneca lake. On the 31st of March, 1815, the legislature of the state of New York passed an act entitled 'An act for opening the navigation between the headwaters of the Seneca lake and the Chemung River.' At a meeting of the president and directors of the Seneca and Susquehanna Lock Navigation Company, at Harris Hotel, in the village of Geneva, County of Ontario, in the state of New York, on the 2nd day of December 1815, present, John Nicholas, Wilhelmus Mynderse, Samuel Colt, Frederic A. Dezeng, Herman H. Bogert, Abraham Dox, Joseph Fellows, it was resolved, that Frederic A. Dezeng, one of the commissioners appointed by law to receive subscriptions to the stock of the company, be authorized to apply to the legislature of Pennsylvania to subscribe to said stock."

"In pursuance of said resolution, Mr. Dezeng did apply to the state of Pennsylvania as directed and accompanied his application with an elaborate statement setting forth the mutual benefits to be derived by the states of Pennsylvania and New York by the construction of such a work. The original document, Harry, is now in my possession. Mr. Dezeng and his coadjutors were not successful in obtaining subscriptions or material aid from the state of Pennsylvania. But the subject was agitated until the state of New York authorized, about fourteen years later, or in 1829, the construction of the Chemung Canal and Feeder."

"In the meantime, the population of the section under consideration was increasing at quite a rapid rate, which led to many projects for the formation of new counties and the location of the county seats. If possible, there was a greater diversity of opinion upon these topics than any other local question which had attracted the attention of the people since the days of General Charles Williamson."

FORMATION OF COUNTIES.
HOW THE COUNTIES OF NORTHERN PENNSYLVANIA
AND SOUTHERN NEW YORK WERE ERECTED.

"Soon after the close of the revolutionary war, the division of the twelve original counties, as they were termed, began. Montgomery County had been taken from Albany in the year 1772, three years before the battle at Lexington, and extended southward and westward as far as the limits of the state. Ontario was formed January 27, 1788, a little over four years after the close of the war, and was the first significant territory of which mother Montgomery had been deprived. The province of Ontario extended west from Geneva to the lake at Buffalo, and south to the Pennsylvania line. The remaining portion of Montgomery County included the present counties of Herkimer, Oneida, Madison, Chenango, Cortland, Otsego, Onondaga, Tompkins, Schuyler, Broome, Tioga, Cayuga, Lewis, Hamilton, St. Lawrence and considerable other territory which has been subsequently added to counties whose lineage is traced to the upper and lower Hudson river counties. Tioga County was taken from Montgomery, February 16, 1791, and on the same day, Herkimer and Otsego counties were formed, also taken from Montgomery. The erection of these four counties — Ontario in 1783, and Tioga, Herkimer and Otsego in 1791 — in the western and central portion of the state, maybe indeed said to have been the initial step which in a few years later developed into a popular cry for the division of counties. Chenango was formed on March 10, 1798, taken from Tioga and Herkimer, and had been preceded by two years by the formation of Steuben from Ontario, March 18, 1796, and one year by Delaware, which was formed from Otsego and Ulster, March 10, 1797. You will thus perceive, Harry, that the people from the Mohawk to the Delaware and Susquehanna and westward to the Allegany and the lakes must have been highly interested in these projects. Whenever there was a new county erected, the next thing to follow was the location of the county seat, and that stirred up local strife, called into requisition diplomacy, skill and wealth. Everyone who owned a township or a thousand acres of land desired the county seat located upon his or their properties, as the case might be, and caused much excitement and dissatisfaction. When Ontario was divided, and Steuben formed from its territory in 1796, the inhabitants who had settled along the Genesee River and whose interests were affected, determined to have a county of their own and did not like to be compelled to ride over the mountains at the headwaters of the Canisteo and Conhocton and pay their respects to the English colony of General Williamson, at Bath, or Geneva, or Canandaigua. The matter was agitated and canvassed, and in less than six years, they accomplished their purpose by the erection of the county of Genesee, March 18th, 1802, taken from Ontario, Hon. Nathaniel King, Joshua Mersereau, Jr., from Chenango, Caleb Hyde from Tioga, Daniel Capin, and Peter B. Porter from the district comprising Ontario and Steuben, were in the assembly that year. Thomas Storm, speaker, and James Van Ingen, clerk. And in the senate from the interested territory was General Vincent Mathews, of this county, with his associates from the western senatorial district, Messrs. William Beekman, Lemuel Chipman, Isaac Foote, John Frey, Frederic Gettman, Thomas R. Gold, Moss Kent, John Meyer, Robert Roseboom; clerks, Abram B. Bancker, Henry I. Bleecker; Jeremiah Van Rensselaer, Lieut. Governor and presiding officer, and George Clinton, governor.

"The majority " and "balance of power " were talked of as freely then as now. For each new county formed in the west, an equal number was established in the east and north. But, Harry, I will not attempt to speak of all the changes made over the entire state. I confine myself to southern, western and central New York, and here let me remark, that our neighbors south of us, the Pennsylvanians, were not idle in the manufacture of new counties — Luzerne and Northumberland were the two great counties of northern Pennsylvania up to the close of the last century. Luzerne had been formed from Northumberland on September 25, 1786, and extended northward up the north branch of the Susquehanna to the state line near Athens. Ten years later, or to be precise, April 13, 1796, Lycoming was formed from Northumberland and extended up the west branch of the Susquehanna and tributaries, reaching westward to the Ohio line and northward to the state line at Lawrenceville, now Tioga County, PA. The speculators, landowners, and others interested in that territory in the year 1804 made a grand raid on the legislature of that staid old common-wealth. It secured the passage of an act, March 26, 1804, forming the counties of Tioga, Jefferson. Potter, McKean, and Clearfield.

This move had two objects: one, to counteract the formation of Erie, Crawford Centre, and other counties which had been formed in the year 1800, and two, to enlist the state in the project of building state roads, to reach these unsettled portions, whereby the lands of the great property holders could be reached. At the time of the formation of the counties of Tioga, Potter, and McKean, there were not two thousand inhabitants, covering an area of nearly three thousand square miles. Closely following the organization of the counties last-named the county of Bradford was formed from Luzerne and Lycoming, under the title of Ontario, which on February 21, 1810, was organized by an act of the legislature as Bradford county and commissioners appointed to locate the county seat, which they fixed at what was then known as Meansville, now Towanda. On the same day, viz., February 21, 1810, the county of Susquehanna was formed from Luzerne, thus curtailing the territory of that county materially. Still, she yet had an ample domain, covering an area of about three thousand or more square miles now known as Wyoming, Lackawanna, and Luzerne."

"Turning our attention again to New York, we see that Allegany county was formed from Genesee in the year 1806, and the same year the county of Broome was formed from Tioga, and two years later, or April 8, 1808, the county of Cortland was formed from Onondaga. Three years previous to this, the interest bordering on Lake Ontario and along the rivers entering that lake, had secured the passage of an act forming the county of Jefferson March 28, 1805, taken from the northern portion of Oneida. Previous to this, the county of Seneca was formed, March 25, 1804.

The spirit of the western part of the state, principally known as the "Holland purchase," was awakened. On March 11, 1808, three counties were formed, named respectively, Chautauqua, Niagara, and Cattaraugus, taken from Genesee County. The utmost limit of the western portion of the state was covered by these counties. One of them, Niagara, included within her border's the greatest cataract in the world, and one which I am pleased to learn has been taken in charge by the authorities of the state of New York. Its grandeur and magnificence made free to the admiring gaze of the millions who will hereafter witness its splendors without restraint."

"This was about the state of affairs when the war of 1812 commenced and, as I stated last night, interrupted many plans that were then in vogue to develop these regions. The war is over, the projects were many of them revived in new forms and assumed a degree of importance without a parallel in the history of the state — I mean internal navigation by the construction of canals."

"Another topic was also attracting the attention of the people. It was the manner of holding elections, the qualifications of voters, and the election of judicial officers by the voice of the people, instead of by a council of appointment.

A certain amount of real estate was necessary to be owned by the citizen before he could exercise "the prerogative of a freeman " and cast his ballot at an election. I will not discuss this subject at length, Harry, but will briefly state that the agitation of these subjects resulted in calling a convention to revise the constitution of the state and extend to the people more generally the privileges they demanded. During all this excitement, however, the subject of new counties was not lost sight of. In the locality which we have had under consideration, the county of Tompkins was formed, April 17, 1817, taken from Cayuga and Seneca. On April 11, 1823, the county of Wayne was formed, taken from Ontario and Seneca, and on the 5th day of February of the same year (1823), the county of Yates was formed, taken from the counties of Ontario and Steuben. The county of Livingston had been formed from the counties of Genesee and Ontario February 23, 1821, and on the same day, the county of Monroe was formed, also taken from Genesee and Ontario, and Orleans from Genesee November 12, 1824; Erie from Niagara April 2, 1821. There are only two more counties in which we are especially interested — the counties of Chemung and Schuyler. Chemung was organized March 29, 1836, taken from the western portion of Tioga, and Schuyler was formed from Chemung, Tompkins, and Steuben, April 17, 1854."

"Having carved out the counties to suit them, and located the county seats, the people turned their attention to the erection of dwellings, schoolhouses and churches, the digging of canals and the construction of plank roads and turnpikes, and finally to the building of railroads which run at every conceivable angle across New York, Pennsylvania, and all other portions of this great country. Covering a period from 1815 to now (the previous period having been alluded to), many distinguished men have come to the front in the social, political, professional, and industrial interest of the section of the country. Under consideration, in their financial positions, among the great moneyed men of the nation."

"I propose, Harry, before I discontinue these "long talks," to take up several counties and speak briefly of their location, the public improvements, the railroads, canals, and telegraphs, their industrial, manufacturing, agricultural interests, their schools, churches, lodges and whatever pertains to their present prosperity and prospects; to speak of their foremost men in all trades and occupations, and briefly describe the mountain scenery, their cascades and waterfalls, and whatever is calculated to please the tourist or interest the traveler."

"In the few weeks that I shall remain here in your cozy cottage, I shall endeavor to talk over all the matters of interest, which can as well be discussed here as upon the road, and when the genial rays of the sun have changed winter into spring, we will again sally out and take personal observations. What say you, Harry, to the program? "

"Oh! I think it is just the thing to do. I have been exceptionally well pleased by these "long talks " of yours. You have given me a great deal of information and presented many things in a different light from any that I ever had before; of men and measures, and particularly how you have presented the motives which actuated and governed the men years ago in the formation of the several counties surrounding us."

FAMOUS CAMPAIGNS.
HOW LOG CABINS, COONS, AND CIDER FIGURED AS
POLITICAL ACCESSORIES.

"It is well we came home from Williamsport when we did, for I see by the *Morning Advertiser* that there has been a terrible flood in the west branch of the Susquehanna, sweeping away millions of feet of unsawed timber, tearing up the railroad tracks in many places and making mischief generally. The storm seems to have been general, for the paper is full of dispatches from all sections of the country, detailing incidents connected with the great flood. I propose we walk down to the bank of the Chemung and see how she is behaving during the flood."

They go down to the river bank, and after witnessing for half an hour or more, the little Chemung swelled to a big Chemung, the banks full to overflowing with maddening waters that are sweeping wildly onward to the Chesapeake, covered with every possible kind of flood wood, fallen trees, and floating logs, they return to their homes, Uncle Jonas remarking on the way that he could relate some inspiring incidents, which occurred many years ago, when high floods prevailed in the Chemung River, when houses, barns, cattle, and human beings were swept away like chaff before the wind. Arriving home, however, he sat down in his comfortable chair and soon began to speak of the early political campaigns which distinguished the elections forty-five and fifty years ago.

"There were," continued Uncle Jonas, "few mass meetings or public discussions held by the people at any elections that I recollect before the year 1828. Previous to that time, although the people were as deeply interested in the result of elections as they have been at any subsequent period, the discussion was confined to private debates. The country or village tavern was the great forum where the people would congregate in the afternoon and evening and tally over the affairs of the government, the state county, and township matters, sometimes in a lively manner. The taverns or inns were much frequented in those days by the citizens, the businessmen, the traveler, and even by members of the church. It was not infrequently the case that church services were held in the sitting rooms of taverns, so necessary were these public places regarded by the communities in which they were located. But during the time schoolhouses, as well as churches, were being erected, the tavern seemed to be the town hall."

"During the election which occurred in 1828 party spirit ran high, and no one tavern or inn was large enough to hold the people who desired to hear the issues of the day discussed, and political meetings were held all over th3 country. In 1832 it was particularly observable that political issues could not be confined to bar-room discussions. A special cause for excitement then, which was a side issue, and which should never have been cast into the political cauldron, was the intense anti-masonic excitement. It had commenced several years before, but all the anger of the preceding years seemed to have culminated in that year, particularly in that portion of Tioga County, now known as Chemung. It came down from the presidential candidates to town and county officers. The anti-masonic party came into being in the year 1826 and had been increasing in strength up to the year 1832. It had entered into a coalition with both parties at times, and finally, in the year 1832, made an independent nomination of candidates for the presidency and vice-presidency. Locally, in New York, it was the strongest in the counties of Ontario, Genesee, Seneca, Cayuga, and Tompkins. In 1832 it seemed to have reached its greatest strength nationally, although, in localities, previous to that date, it had been much stronger than it was at the period named. The prejudices then engendered have nearly all been worn away by the hand of time."

"One of the most exciting campaigns up to that period was that of 1840. The anger in the canvass of 1832 was greater, as the general enthusiasm of the people was greater then than in any previous campaign. Still, it was conducted more in a spirit of good nature, and was made the occasion of more happiness, fun, and laughable transactions than had ever before occurred."

"Here in Elmira the Whig party, as it was then called, made many demonstrations. The candidate for the presidency of that party was General William H. Harrison, of Ohio, who had done distinguished service in the war of 1812 in the west and northwest, and especially at the Battle of Tippecanoe. He was an excellent type of the frontiersmen and had seen considerable service, both in a military and civil character. The candidate for the vice-presidency was John Tyler, of Virginia, a descendant and representative of the best families in the state. He had seen considerable public service as a civilian and legislator. The candidate of the Democratic party was Martin Van Buren, of New York. President of the United States, who had served his state in almost every civil capacity, ranging from assemblyman, senator, governor, representative in congress, vice-president, and president of the United States, and the successor of Andrew Jackson, the ideal soldier, and statesman of the Democratic party, who, it was claimed, had left the mantle of his great fame as a legacy to Martin Van Buren, Col. Richard M. Johnson, of Kentucky, then Vice-President of the United States, a gallant soldier, and a great orator, was the candidate for re-election on the Democratic ticket with Van Buren. I will not detain you, Harry, by going into a statement of the questions at issue. The Democratic party was entrenched in power with great patronage at their disposal in the shape of the distribution of public offices "where they would do the best," a phrase and sentiment which has since been coined. Suffice it, that the issues were made. One was in power, and the other wanted to be. Several elements entered into that campaign, which was new, novel, and unique, introduced by the Whig- party — Glee clubs that sang campaign songs in honor of their candidates and derision of their opponents. At the same time, grand processions with coon skins, log cabins, and hard cider traversed the highways, attracting the multitude to some convenient spot. There the rustic platforms were surrounded by the admiring and interested followers, who were harangued, feasted, and made happy. At the same time, songs were sung, cannons fired, and the first and pioneer scenes of the west were delineated in a thousand different ways."

"The Democrats were entirely unprepared for such an attack, and the campaign had been so well planned and executed all along the line that before they could rally and chargeback upon their opponents with a similar mode of warfare, the Whigs had won the campaign, leaving the ranks of the democracy entirely at their mercy."

"I have seen, Harry, three thousand triumphant Whigs, with glee clubs, banners, barrels of hard cider, raccoons alive, raccoons dead and dressed, assembled in the little village of Elmira, parading the streets and marching over to Clinton Island and there having a grand barbecue and mass meeting. The farmer would leave his plow, the merchant his store, the mechanic his shop to join in the procession. Tough old hickory or Jacksonian Democrats were even swept from their moorings into the ranks of that party, and before they were aware of it, were shouting for "Tippecanoe and Tyler too." It not only captured the rustic mind but such learned and polished gentlemen as Judge Theodore North, Judge Aaron Konkle, Hon. James Dunn would join the meeting, and, under the inspiration of the moment, mount the rustic rostrum and deliver stump speeches, and sit down in their rough log cabins and drink hard cider and partake of coon meat and cornbread. The late Hon. Andrew Bray Dickinson, of Steuben, took great delight in those demonstrations. Judge Hiram Gray, Col. S. G.

Hathaway, Jr., Thomas Maxwell, Lyman Covell, William Maxwell, and others of like the character did all in their power to arrest the stampede of the Democratic rank and file into the lines of their opponents, but with no avail. These proceedings were not confined to this locality, nor to this state alone. They were universal from Maine to Georgia. The times had been hard, and in their campaign songs they had the words " two dollars a day and roast beef" held out as one of the promises by which they caught thousands of laboring men, who gave "Tippecanoe and Tyler, too," then vote, expecting that their promises would be fulfilled."

"The Democrats sent their best men to the front in order if possible to counteract the effect of that log cabin and hard cider crusade. The spirit of the war of 1812 had not died out, and its events were fresh in the minds of the people. Col. Richard M. Johnson, the democratic candidate for vice-president, was a participant in that war and had done some splendid fighting in the west, in Ohio, Indiana, and Michigan, against the British and Indians. No doubt was the soldier who killed Tecumseh at the battle of Monravian Town. His prestige was great as a soldier and an orator. He vacated his seat as president of the senate. He went out to advocate the cause of the democracy at public meetings and relate in the most glowing language the incidents connected with the Indian campaigns in the west during the war. He came into this county. He called around him the few remaining soldiers of the war of the revolution, gathered the soldiers of the war of 1812, had soldiers preside at his meetings, and by almost superhuman efforts essayed to stay the desertion from the ranks of the democratic party and their enlistment under the banner of "Tippecanoe and Tyler too." He held meetings in Elmira, at Horseheads and Pine Valley, at the old Daniel Parsons stand, where the late Capt. William Mapes, of Big Flats, a revolutionary soldier who had served in the Continental Army for five years, and had fought Indians under Gen. Sullivan, presided.

Col. Johnson and Capt. William Mapes stood side by side upon the platform, their gray hair shining in the sun, While the gallant vice-president was speaking in his most impassioned and eloquent terms of the services of Washington, Jefferson, Madison, Monroe, and the hero of New Orleans, and relating his encounters with the Indians, and more particularly with that great chief Tecumseh. He also referred to and defended the action of the democratic party, spoke of the services of Silas Wright, Jr., from New York, senator in congress, to his country, the gallant and heroic deeds of Andrew Jackson, who had fought in the war of the revolution, and eulogized his later services in Indian wars, and the war against Great Britain, and the defeat of the British army under Packenham at New Orleans, pointed out his sterling qualities in the presidential chair, and stated his wishes which he had made known from his retirement home, the "Hermitage," and did everything, that a great mind could suggest, or an eloquent tongue express, to hold in line the democratic voters of the country. But his efforts were unsuccessful. The result was, the whigs literally carried the election by storm, electing their president and vice-president by the most popular and electoral majority and increasing their strength in the state legislatures and in the congress of the United States."

"On the 4th of March following, Harrison and Tyler took the oath prescribed and were duly inaugurated president and vice-president of the United States. The whigs were much elated. They were confident that the Bank of the United States would be recharted and money is plenty. The country would enter upon a career of prosperity unprecedented in its history. President Harrison selected an able cabinet, consisting of Daniel Webster, of Massachusetts, secretary of state; Thomas Ewing, of Ohio, secretary of the treasury; John Bell, of Tennessee, secretary of war; George E. Badger, of North Carolina, secretary of the navy; Francis Granger, of New York, postmaster-general; John J Crittenden, of Kentucky, attorney-general. On the 17th of March, twelve days after the inauguration, the president issued a call for a special session of Congress to convene on the 31st day of May, to take into consideration the currency and financial wants of the country. But the gallant president did not live to see it convene. One month after the inaugural ceremonies had taken place with such high hopes and bright anticipations, the president died, and the capital and the country were dressed in mourning, and the American people plunged in grief. Vice-president Tyler assumed the duties of the president and did not fulfill all the brilliant promises of success, which had been expected of the administration of "Tippecanoe and Tyler too."

A FAMOUS STRUGGLE.
THE PRESIDENTIAL CONTEST OF 1844 —
MEN, PRINCIPLES, AND INCIDENTS.

"Harry, I wish to have one more 'long talk' upon the subject of political meetings, and then I will turn my attention to another topic. I have spoken concerning the political campaign of 1840, and now I would like to give you an idea of the political campaign of 1844."

"I was young at that time, Uncle Jonas, and have principally learned the events of the period from histories or slips from newspapers of that time, and shall be very glad to listen to one who was a participant in that active and eventful campaign."

"I shall endeavor to make a plain statement of facts, not attempting in the least to influence you in your judgment regarding the two great political parties which entered into the campaign of 1844. It must make no difference with you whether I was a Jackson democrat or a Henry Clay Whig, or an abolitionist who supported James G. Birney, who was one of the men instrumental in laying the foundation for the formation of the republican party ten years later. My sole object is to portray how the political canvass was carried on during that year, without regard to which party was in the right, or the wrong, successful or unsuccessful, and shall only allude to the positions taken by each party to illustrate my description of the contest.

"You recollect that yesterday, in referring to the campaign of 1840, I stated that the whigs had promised the laboring men of the country ' two dollars per day and roast beef,' and general prosperity if they would assist in electing 'Tippecanoe and Tyler too,' and giving them a majority in both houses of congress. Well, Harry, the laboring men and others of the country rallied to the wing standard and placed the party in power by unprecedented majorities. But unfortunately, their president died within a month after his inauguration, and the vice-president assumed the duties of the president. Also, Congress had been called in special session to legislate upon the currency, the establishment of a significant financial institution to carry out the plans and promises which had been made. Congress did pass such measures, and President Tyler set up constitutional reasons for vetoing them. A bankrupt law was parsed under the pressing wants of the businessmen, and, instead of years of prosperity, 'two dollars a day and roast beef,' the country was in financial distress. This state of things was dilated upon by the democrats, and in many cases, exaggerated. The whigs in congress and out of congress were at variance with their president, whom, they declared, had basely betrayed them and blighted their hopes. The democrats were not slow in striving to make the breach wider and the cause of dissatisfaction greater.

Whig and Democratic National conventions had been convened, and candidates for president and vice-president nominated. The democrats had placed in nomination James K. Polk, of Tennessee, a warm personal and political friend of Andrew Jackson, and for vice-president, George M. Dallas, of Pennsylvania The Whigs had nominated Henry Clay, of Kentucky, and Theodore Frelinghuysen, of New Jersey. Henry Clay was the great commoner of the west. He had served long in Congress, been speaker of the house, and for many years one of the most distinguished members of the senate. He had also been minister abroad and had signed the treaty of peace between the United States and Great Britain at Ghent, at the close of the war of 1812. He was one of the most brilliant and persuasive orators in the land, a great organizer, and a man in every way calculated to be a great leader, who would restore harmony in the ranks of the discouraged whig party, revive their drooping spirits, heal their disputes and lead them to victory. Mr. Frelinghuysen was a polished scholar and an accomplished gentleman well qualified for the service, which would be required of him in case of an election. Although not in power, the Democrats held the vantage-ground in the contest. It was better for them that the administration was nominally in the hands of the whigs with such a president in the chair as John Tyler. Then again, they had learned a lesson in the campaign of 1840, and intended to steal, so to speak, the thunder of the whig party and adopt their tactics in the manner of carrying on campaigns. They changed the program, however, and, instead of sporting coonskins, hard cider, and log cabins, they had glee clubs, banners, processions, hickory pole raisings and mammoth mass meetings. It was generally conceded here at the north that Van Buren would again be the candidate of the democratic party. It is said that in anticipation of that event, the Whigs had tons of democratic songs and other campaign documents all ready to fire upon the public and scatter broadcast through the land. The nomination of James K. Polk, instead of Martin Van Buren, made this great expense and outlay on behalf of the whig party useless. More than that, it brought storms of ridicule upon them, when the fact became known by the democrats, and the committee who had the matter in charge was caricatured and charged with 'losing their ammunition,' of 'flashing in the pan' (a phrase peculiar to the use of old flint-lock guns), and sundry other ridiculous epithets were showered upon the disconcerted whigs.

"The nominations were made in June, and the message announcing the nomination of James K. Polk, instead of Van Buren, was sent over one of the very first telegraph lines in the world from the democratic convention at Baltimore to Washington. (Contemplate for a moment, Harry, the magnitude of the telegraph system now, after the lapse of forty-two years. It has conquered even the depths of the ocean, connecting distant countries, and is found in every village, hamlet, and city in the civilized world. Its lines are laid along the routes of every railroad, and it sends its messages with the rapidity of lightning from continent to continent! The nominations were made in June, and simultaneously with their announcements, the country was aroused from center to circumference. Bonfires, illuminations, pole raisings, barbecues, and processions were the order of the day. Meetings were appointed in some central place, when almost every man for miles around would turn out and form processions composed of four, six, and ten horse teams, hauling boats, mounted on wheels, with banners and devices of every conceivable kind. Young ladies, dressed in holiday apparel, were seated in those boats, carrying flags representing the different states, and singing campaign songs. In the procession might be seen older men and veterans, carrying little hickory or ash trees, to which were attached banners. There were farmers with a dozen or more ox teams hauling ponderous wagons, loaded with the products of the soil, their oxen gaily ribboned and clothed with devices which the spirit of the moment inspired. There were bands of martial music, many of the musicians being veterans of the war of the revolution or that of 1812. There were caricatures and placards suspended upon massive platforms resting upon wheels, which were drawn along by a dozen or more horses, all of the same color. The posters, if it were a democratic procession, represented in derision the promises of the whigs in 1840, of "two dollars a day and roast beef," their log cabins and hard cider, their coon skins, and other paraphernalia, and perhaps to give more emphasis and significance to their sentiments, would have chained on a platform a live raccoon with indices pointing to him with such words as "the thief caught at last," or, the "Coon Polked." Then, again a stuffed raccoon skin would be displayed conspicuously and labeled "the dead party." Trades and occupations Would be represented in the procession, the operatives at work with these words painted in large letters upon banners, "The promises of 1840 — two dollars a day and roast beef," and underneath: "Whig promises realized — sixty cents per day and beef liver." Again might

291

be seen a banner bearing this inscription, quoted from the whig platform: "A sound currency," and underneath it, "bankrupt notices." In a thousand different ways were the promises of the whig party of 1840 derided and made light of by the enthusiastic democracy. At the place for assembling, the processions would form in a circle and create a dozen rustic platforms, and speakers would hold forth to the thousands there convened. Arguments, sarcasm, and ridicule were each used to the utmost advantage.

Extensive meetings were held by the friends of Harry Clay and Frelinghuysen, but they were much in the condition or position instead of the democratic party in 1840. They had advertised to show a significant moral reform in 1840 and failed to perform what they had advertised, and while they made a gallant and heroic fight, the democratic party had them on the defensive. In 1840 they had sent out flaming double-elephant posters, so to speak, and had failed to perform even what was on the small bills. In the west, the wave of public opinion was from the first with the democrats. It was about even at first. The Democrats had taken the lead before the middle of September. Silas Wright, who declined the nomination for vice-president, was nominated by the democrats for governor of this state, and he and his friends had thrown their whole energies into the campaign. Col. Hathaway, Hiram Gray, John Gr. McDowell, of this county, Martin Grover, of Allegheny, Darius A. Ogden, of Yates, Amasa Dana, of Tompkins, Daniel S. Dickinson, of Broome, as well as Silas Wright himself, had taken the stump, and mass meetings and processions unparalleled in the history of the country. Many of the rank and file who had deserted the democratic party in 1840 came back like prodigal sons, and those who gave the Democratic ticket of that year their nominal support rallied in 1844 with enthusiasm. Monster mass meetings were held in Elmira, Owego, Binghamton, Norwich, Cortland, Ithaca, Geneva, Havana, Penn Yan, Bath, Painted Post, Angelica, Lawrenceville, and Towanda. There were pole raisings besides, where two, three, five hundred or a thousand people would assemble, raise a hickory pole, have music by their local campaign glee club, or be assisted by one or two from a larger town. I attended a mass meeting, which was held here in Elmira, where at least twenty-five thousand people were present. They came in from every town and village in this county, and in great numbers from Bradford county, PA, and Tioga, Tompkins, Yates, and Steuben in this state. The Hon. David Wilmot, of Towanda, was one of the speakers. I also attended a monster mass meeting of the democrats, held at Painted Post, in Erwin's meadow, where twenty-five acres of democrats were present, with every conceivable device, banner, and caricature. The Hon. Daniel S. Dickinson was one of the speakers, and Gen. Francis E. Erwin was president of the day. Delegations and processions were there from almost every portion of Steuben, the county of Chemung, and the valleys of the Tioga and Cowanesque in Pennsylvania. Some of them had traveled on horseback and in wagons over sixty miles. I also attended one at Geneva, and one at Penn Yan, where, among the speakers, were James W. Nye, of Madison county, Martin Grover, of Allegheny, and Darius A. Ogden, of Yates. I went down with a delegation from here and saw thirty thousand democrats rush in from all directions to Ithaca. They were there from every farm, hamlet, village, and crossroads in all that region. They came up in boats on the lake, and, arriving there early, I saw them in processions of miles in length wind down the hillside from Watkins, Havana, Ulysses, Trumansburg, Hector, and marching down also from the south was a procession, which, it was said, reached halfway up to Newfield. Then from the north, they came from Cayuga county, gathering seemingly everyone in Lansing and Groton, while from the east for two hours was a ceaseless stream flowing in from the direction of Cortland. I also witnessed large meetings of the friends of Henry Clay, but they seemed to possess less spirit and enthusiasm than the democratic meetings. I believe they felt that they were beaten, but like the democrats of 1840, they were bound to keep, as the phrase expresses it, "a stiff upper lip."

The recollections of these old political days are among the dearest memories of my life, and I like especially to talk of these great campaigns of 1840 and 1844. In 1840 the whigs had the advantage of the democrats and won. In 1844 the advantage was in favor of the democrats, and they won. I have no doubt there are many an old Democrat and many an old Whig who would like to sit down together and talk and laugh over those campaigns.

A CHARMING COUNTRY.
THE ADDISON AND NORTHERN PENNSYLVANIA RAILWAY
— FERTILE VALLEYS AND STATELY HILLS.

"We have had a rest of several weeks. Uncle Jonas, and as the weather is now pleasant, suppose we take a trip to-morrow morning over the Erie Railroad to Addison, and from thence over the Addison & Northern Pennsylvania narrow-gauge railroad?"

"It is agreeable to me, Harry, and I will make arrangements to go."

Accordingly, the next morning Uncle Jonas and Harry rise early and go to the depot in time for the fast train west. They glide along through the Chemung Valley, which we have heretofore described, halting for a few moments at Corning, and then away up through the historic village of Painted Post, crossing the Conhocton River, and roiling up into the valley of the Canisteo, to Addison. The American Hotel omnibus was taken, and Uncle Jonas and Harry were driven across the Canisteo to that admirable hotel, where breakfast was served them.

Addison is a neat and prosperous village situated on the north and south sides of the Canisteo, and as Uncle Jonas had many years ago a large number of acquaintances, he desired to remain until afternoon and look the town over and recall the names of those who were early settlers and residents.

"You will bear in mind, Harry," said Uncle Jonas, "that the Canisteo Valley in the early days was settled by a class of people who have generally engaged in lumbering and running logs down the river to the Pennsylvania and Maryland market. They were hardy pioneers, accustomed to severe labor, truthful and outspoken, firm in their convictions, warm in

295

their friendship, hospitable, and free-hearted. Many of them had moved in the best circles of society in Pennsylvania and the New England states. Still, when they made their homes in the valley of the Canisteo, with a vast forest surrounding them, they naturally lost some of that polish which had distinguished them in their former homes. This place was initially known as Middleton, but April 6, 1808, it was re-formed and named in honor of the distinguished English poet Addison. Several townships since that time have been formed from it, lessening its area: Troupsburg in 1808, Cameron and a portion of Woodhull in 1828, Rathbone in 1856, and Tuscarora in 1859. Thus you perceive, Harry, that the township of Addison extended up the Canisteo river several miles and south to the Pennsylvania line, covering an area whereon grow some of the most beautiful white pine, oak, and hemlock timber in the Southern Tier of New York. At first, conventional sawmills were erected, and the wood converted by a prolonged process, compared with that of modern times, into a merchantable product, which was rafted into the Canisteo and floated to the lower Susquehanna. In the few hours that we shall remain here, it will be impossible for me to tell you all about the scenes that were enacted here in those early times. Among the early settlers were Reuben Searles, Lemuel Searles, Wilham Wombaugh, Elisha Gilbert, William Baskins Jones, better known as 'Bass Jones,' George Goodhue, Col. Griff Jones, John Martin, Jonathan Tracey, Stephen Dolson, Elisha Searles, and Dr. Frederick Wagner. These men in parties used to go do down the river, and frequently landed their rafts at Elmira and took on supplies for their down-the-river trip. In that way, we became acquainted with them. A considerable reinforcement to the settlements upon the Canisteo was made about the year 1840 when the old Erie railroad company commenced the driving of piles upon which to establish their road-bed. Enterprising men with capital came here then and have contributed to the prosperity of the village.

"Since that time. Uncle Jonas, up to the completion of the Erie in 1851, and subsequently, there have been many accessions: The Gillettes, the McKays, the younger portion of the Jones family — Col. James E. Jones, H. Ross Jones and Henry Jones; the Paxtons, Curtises, the Baldwins, the Weatherbys, the Jenningses, the Mileses, the Farnhams, the Dininnys, the Horrs, the Delamaters, and others have made Addison what it is. They established foundries and machine shops, grist mills, tanneries, erected academies and churches, established printing offices and banks, erected hotels, organized fire companies, masonic and odd fellows' lodges, built plank roads and railroads, and contributed to the building up of this enterprising village, which is the second in size in the valley of the Canisteo. It has suffered severely at various times from fires, but the people rallied and erected better buildings than those which were destroyed."

"The building of the Addison & Northern Pennsylvania Railroad in 1862, which extends from here over into the valley of the Cowanesque and thence south into the valley of Pine Creek, has done much to secure trade from those points and placed them in communication with a region rich in agricultural, tanning, lumber, and mineral products. It is a narrow-gauge road to be sure. Still, no other kind could have ascended and descended the mountains intervening between the Canisteo and Cowanesque Rivers, or between the Cowanesque river and Pine Creek. When the construction of the road was proposed by Col. Henry Baldwin, Col. James E. Jones, Hiram McKay, John Hinman, and others, there was many a doubting Thomas who shook his head and wisely predicted that the feat could not be accomplished. It was performed, however, and in less than four months, forty miles of it was constructed, and engines and rolling stock placed upon it. We will now walk over to the depot and call on the officials of the road located here."

The officers of the road are Thomas C. Platt, president. No. 82 Broadway, New York City; William Brookfield, vice-president, New York City; James E. Jones, secretary, Addison; Frank M. Baker, general superintendent, Addison; and H. C. Hitchcock, auditor, Addison.

The directors are Thomas C. Platt, William C. Sheldon, Henry P. DeGraaf, William Brookfield, Edmond S. Bowen, Frank H. Platt, George R. Blanchard, Walter S. Gurnee, of New York City, and James E. Jones, Addison; Charles L. Pattison, Elkland, Pa.; James Horton, Westfield, PA; John W. Hammond, Osceola, PA, and Royal W. Clinton, Newark Valley, NY.

Closely associated with the Addison and Northern Pennsylvania railroad company is the Gaines Coal & Coke company, which is operating the mines at Gurnee. The officers of that company are T. C. Platt, president; W. C. Sheldon, treasurer; J. E. Jones, secretary; F. M. Balder, general superintendent; P. A. Jordan, superintendent of mines; H. C. Hitchcock, auditor. Directors: T. C. Platt, W. C. Sheldon, J. E. Jones, C. L. Pattison, G. R. Blanchard.

In a few moments Uncle Jonas and Harry reached the Addison and Northern Pennsylvania depot. They called on Mr. Frank M. Baker, the general superintendent, who received them courteously and introduced them to Mr. H. C. Hitchcock, the auditor, and Mr. C. P. Colgan, C. L. Miller, clerks in superintendent's office, and to Jean Baptist Hein, the clerk in the auditor's office. A half-hour was spent pleasantly m discussing the prospects of the road, the coal trade, and the gradual increase of business over their line, which was developing at the rate of about forty percent each year and explaining the details of transferring from narrow gauge to standard gauge of the Erie using "Ramsey's gravity hoist, under the direction and supervision of Mr. Samuel Patterson. Mr. Baker also gave them a list of the station agents, telegraph operators, conductors, and engineers on the line, together with the name of Mr. J. P. Wright, roadmaster.

The names of the several officials are, J. Boyer, an agent at Freeman, NY; H. M. Johnson, station agent and telegraph operator at Elkland, PA; Vine Crandall, Osceola, PA; George W. Fisk, agent at Knoxville, PA, and E. M. Stroud, operator; G. H. Tremain, an agent at Westfield, and E. Bliss, operator; M. B. Stebbins, agent, and operator at Sabinsville; H. T. Alba, agent, and operator at Davis Station; R. H. Wombaugh, an agent at Gurnee, and P. J. McGuire, operator; E. A. Mack, agent, and operator at Gaines; Hugh Ross, agent, and operator at Galeton.

The conductors are J. W. Parshall, passenger; O. R. Enos, coal train, and F. P. Dodge, freight and passenger. The engineers are Henry Maxson, William Nelson, O. L. Baker, and Fred Pomeroy. Baggage master, W. E. Morgan, and United States mail agent, C, W. Ingersoll.

The entire length of the mainline is fifty-one miles, giving employment to one hundred and thirty men, besides those engaged in mining and labor connected with the mines. The company has five locomotives and a full complement of freight and passenger cars. The Gaines Coal and Coke Company mines about three thousand tons of coal per month. It is shipped over the Addison and Northern Pennsylvania Railroad and is transferred at Addison to the Erie and distributed east and west. The route also has an enormous tonnage in lumber, hemlock bark, hides, leather, grain, and merchandise, which keeps all their rolling stock in active operation.

Having learned all these details, our travelers return to the hotel and prepare themselves for the trip over the Addison & Northern Pennsylvania Railroad to the famous valleys of the Cowanesque and Pine Creek. The weather was all that could be desired, and the fresh spring breezes, bright sunlight, the birds singing in the shade trees, and along the banks of the streams, the budding trees, and the smiling face of nature generally inspired them with pleasure. Uncle Jonas had never before ridden in a narrow gauge coach, and its miniature proportions pleased him very much. As they steamed out of the depot and crossed the Canisteo, his eyes glistened with delight. It was a great treat for him. They soon began to ascend the valley of Tuscarora Creek nearly on the course of the old Indian war and hunting trails of the Six Nations over the Tuscarora mountains. They passed the old homesteads of the Wombaughs and Rowleys and soon began to wind around the face of the mountains. Looking out of the rear car door they saw the busy village of Addison, skirting the banks of the Canisteo, with its church spires pointing heavenward, the elegant dwellings and business places outlined, while on the Erie a long train of passenger coaches was sweeping down the valley with the rapidity of the wind and several freight and coal trains running in close proximity to each other were coiling and running around the curves like huge serpents. Immediately beneath them in the valley were farmhouses, and sturdy farmers turning over the mold with strong teams and steel plows glistening in the sun and sending forth flashes of light as from an electric battery. Ravines are crossed upon high trestles, and the little locomotive hauls its train upon a grade of over one hundred and forty feet to the mile, struggling and puffing like a porpoise. They finally reach an altitude where they can look to the north-westward and see the outlines of mountains away beyond Woodhull, and turning to the eastward, and southward the mountain ranges of the Canisteo, Tioga, and Conhocton appear in the dim distance. A few minutes more, they have reached the summit and rounded a point where the valley of the Cowanesque for miles is spread out before them.

They are now many hundred above the valley, and the descent is to be made. Soon they approach a point where the village of Nelson and the lower Cowanesque are seen. Nelson was formerly known as Beecher's Island — Hopestill Beecher, one of the first county commissioners of Tioga county, PA, having settled there and erected mills. They also get a view of Farmington away to the south of Nelson, with its many beautiful farms, buildings, and orchards. Then casting their eyes to the westward along the valley, they rest upon one of the fairest landscapes in northern Pennsylvania, The Cowanesque River meanders through rich and alluvial meadows, dotted along on its banks with hamlets and villages and skirted by ranges of mountains that rise hundreds of feet above the bed of the stream. The Cowanesque Valley was one of the earliest settled in the county of Tioga and has ever been distinguished for the fertility of its soil and the wealth and enterprise of its inhabitants.

While the eyes are thus feasting upon those beautiful scenes, the cars are rapidly descending into the valley and reach it at Elkland, a busy and enterprising town with several important industrial establishments which have recently been founded. The town also has an excellent school building, a bank, a printing office, two hotels, and is fast increasing in wealth and population. This village was for many years the home of the late Joel Parkhurst, one of the wealthiest men in the county, who died recently at an advanced age. C. L. Pattison, his son-in-law, one of the directors in the A. & N. P. Railroad, also of the Gaines Coal & Coke Company, resides at this point and has recently erected one of the most beautiful residences in the valley. There were many historical incidents connected with this valley, which Uncle Jonas desired to relate, but which for want of time he could not do.

From Elkland, the Fall Brook Railroad and the Addison & Northern Pennsylvania Railroad traverse the valley westward nearby until Westfield is reached when the Fall Brook the road continues up the valley, and the A. & N. P. Railroad abruptly leaves the valley and runs south up Mill Creek to its summit and then descends Long Run to Pine Creek at Gaines and then follows up the Pine Creek Valley to Galeton, or better known as Pike Mills, in the county of Potter.

As they sped up the valley from Elkland, Uncle Jonas remarked the improved appearance of that region since he last visited it, nearly fifty years ago, when his old friends, the Knoxes, Billings, Tubbs, Seeleys, Freebonis, Bulkleys, Bozzards, and many other distinguished pioneers and early settlers inhabited the valley. Even the narrow gauge locomotives don't wait for long stories at stations but speed along at a rapid rate. Before they hardly realized it, they had passed Osceola, Academy Corners, Knoxville, and were approaching Westfield. That borough is one of the most important in the valley and is rapidly increasing in population. The construction of railroads to its borders in the year 1882, and the establishment of a mammoth tannery a few years previous have quickened it and developed it into a very prosperous town.

From Westfield the A. & N. P. Railroad train #11 leaves the Cowanesque valley and ascends the valley of Mill Creek through the town of Clymer, having quite a vital station at Sabinsville, a village in the township of Clymer. This township was named in honor of William B. Clymer, an agent of the Bingham estate and grandson of George Clymer, one of the signers of the Declaration of Independence. The lands are rolling on either side of the narrow valley and are under a good state of cultivation. After leaving Sabinsville for a mile or more, the country is more rugged and begins to show evidence of coal deposits. The little locomotive puffs away until it reaches the summit, and then brakes are put on and down through the valley of Long Run. The train takes its course, passing Davis station and several flag stations and also the spur which ascends to the "Barren" or the coal mines of the Gaines Coal and Coke Company at Gurnee. Uncle Jonas and Harry consult and conclude to continue to Gaines and stop at the Isaac Walton house, for so many years conducted by that excellent landlord and trout fisherman, "Hod" Vermilyea. As they stepped from the coach and walked a few steps to the hotel, the declining sun's rays were dancing over the back of the Big Elephant, a mountain on the south side of Pine Creek.

THE LAST TRIP, AND A FINE ONE.
OVER THE ELMIRA, CORTLAND & NORTHERN,
THE SOUTHERN CENTRAL, AND SENECA LAKE.

After resting a day at their home in Elmira, Uncle Jonas and Harry take the early morning train over the Elmira, Cortland, and Northern Railroad, formerly known as the Utica, Ithaca, and Elmira, which, under the presidency of Austin Corbin and the control of Manager A. A. McLeod has been dramatically improved in roadbed and rolling stock and is in first-class condition. They pass Horseheads, wheel to the right up Newtown Creek to Breesport, and speed their way up among the grand old hills of Erin and Van Etten — a delightful ride that beautiful spring morning. In their course, they cross chasms and climb and descend slopes. Passing through the village of Swartwood, Erin, Van Etten, and Candor, then turning northward, crossing a high trestle at Mott's Corners, they reach Ithaca on its eastern limits, from whence a splendid view of the valley beneath and Cayuga Lake is obtained. They spend a day or more looking over that charming city-like village, calling on descendants of former friends, visiting Cornell University, and the thousand and one points of interest. To say that the scenery in and about Ithaca is superb but meagerly expresses its loveliness. It is situated at the head of the Cayuga Lake, a sheet of water forty miles in length, and on an average, three miles in width, the banks of which, by gradual elevation, rise to the height of two hundred feet or more, and are under the highest state of cultivation, with some of the finest farms and farmhouses in central New York, and with waterfalls and cascades, with elegant public buildings, splendid private dwellings, costly churches and substantial business places, busy manufactures, forming a picture beyond the powers of the most proficient artist. Than university hill affords, no grander outlook can be obtained elsewhere in the state. The lake with its busy commerce, the railroads with their express and ponderous freight and coal trains, the sloping hillsides with their fields of waving grain, meadows, orchards, flocks, and herds, the dashing waterfalls and cascades, the noble structures dedicated to art, intelligence, and education, fill the measure to completeness of all that is beautiful in art, nature, and civilization.

Ithaca has a grand lineage. The township was organized in Onondaga County in 1794, and without changing its beautiful location has formed a portion since Seneca, Cayuga, and Tompkins. She has good blood in her veins. Her citizens from her earliest history have made themselves felt in all the private vocations of life, and have been honored by some of the most distinguished public stations. They have been senators, judges, congressmen, attorney-generals, state treasurers, and governors, and have acquired a state, national, and worldwide fame.

From Ithaca, our travelers resume their journey on the Elmira, Cortland, and Northern to Cortland, distant about twenty miles. It is one of the " loveliest villages of the plain," a model of neatness, cleanliness, and industry. While Ithaca excels in her sister villages in the beauty of the landscape, Cortland stands in the foremost rank in elegance and grace. But the reader must not infer from this that she does nothing but look after her toilet and appear gaily dressed, for at Cortland are some of the largest industrial establishments in the state, employing several thousand men in the manufacture of wagons, buggies, cutters, sleighs, chairs, wire cloth, etc. Beautiful lawns and floral gardens, palatial mansions and cozy cottagers, excellent hotels, costly school buildings and churches, court-houses, well-conducted newspapers, steam and streetcar railroads, all go hand in hand with the factories and make her grandly successful. Bright, animated, and wide awake is Cortland, and such were the impressions of Uncle Jonas after visiting the town.

They next visited Homer and look over the busy little town, full of industrial establishments, and then resume their journey northward, stopping off at De Ruyter for dinner. They have entered the great central dairy belt of the state. A hundred cows upon one farm are frequently seen, while creameries and cheese presses are in abundance.

The next train is boarded, and on they glide to Cazenovia, one of the fairest villages of Madison county, nestled cozily on the shore of Cazenovia Lake. It is an incorporated village of about five thousand inhabitants and is quite a summer resort. Its chief pride, however, is its seminary of learning, under the control and direction of the Methodist Episcopal church.

Realizing that their time was limited, Uncle Jonas concluded to run over into the Chenango Valley. That evening they took a train for Earlville, situated on the Chenango River and on the county hue between Madison and Chenango, between fifty and sixty miles north of Binghamton. They visit the villages of Smyrna and Sherburne. There they were indeed in the dairy belt.

They met there a few of the descendants of the early settlers, with such honored names as Guthrie, Sexton, Wilcox, Talcott, Collin, Hubbard, Hall, Lynde, Mudge, Rexford, Woods, Case, Kenyon, Gardiner, Smith, and Knowles. Then they passed on to Norwich, the county seat of Chenango County. The Chenango Valley has ever been distinguished for its pastoral beauty, its flocks and herds, soft meadows and rich pastures, and its fruits and orchard products. Never did it appear lovelier. Uncle Jonas was eloquent in his words of admiration of the scenery, the villages, and towns. He had formerly had acquaintances in very many towns in Chenango County at Smyrna, Sherburne, Norwich, Oxford, Greene, Bainbridge, and other localities, and many of the early settlers of Chemung and Steuben Counties in New York, and Bradford and Tioga in Pennsylvania were natives of that grand old county. Uncle Jonas made their acquaintances in business and social way. He recalled their names with much familiarity as those of his native county of Chemung. In addition to the names already given, there were the names of Tracy, Monell, Hubbard, Brooks, Boynton, Bush, Shepard, Weaver, Whitney, Bowen, Truman, Whittenhall, Root, Clark, Welch, Mitchell, Graves, Squires, Patterson, Warren, Olney, Campbell, Franklin, Hatch, Purdy, and a fist of others which might be continued indefinitely.

Norwich dates its organization and incorporation away back to the year 1816. Until the Chenango Canal was constructed, which occurred some sixteen years later, it was a mere hamlet with only the river and the typical wagon road as an outlet. The construction of the canal gave it an impetus, which soon, however, seemed to relapse. But being the county seat of a rich and populous county, it held its own and slowly but surely increased in wealth and population. It is now quite a railroad center, and being surrounded by a rich agricultural country, its future is indeed auspicious. Its population is now about seven thousand. They call on old friends in Oxford and Greene, Chenango Forks, and Bainbridge and spend a few hours at each place very pleasantly. They then go by way of Binghamton to Owego and at the the last site takes the Southern Central for Auburn. The Southern Central railroad's southern terminus is at Sayre, connecting with the Lehigh Valley railroad at that point. It runs eastward to Owego, and from thence almost directly northward to Lake Ontario via Freeville, Groton, Auburn, and Weedsport. The president of the road is the Hon. T. C. Platt, of 82 Broadway, NY. It is conducted in a reasonable manner. Uncle Jonas and Harry were comfortably seated, and away they sped over the high lands and valleys of northern Tioga, eastern and southern Tompkins, crossing the Elmira, Cortland, and Northern at Freeville, a few miles east of Ithaca, thence to Groton, one of the most enterprising incorporated villages in Tompkins county. The air was soft and balmy, and through the courtesy of the conductor, they were given favorable seats for observation. Uncle Jonas remarked that instead of becoming weary of these excursions it seemed that if the last he was to make was just as agreeable as the first, over eight months ago. It more firmly convinced him that there was no better way to spend a vacation than to do it on first-class railway trains by short rides. He should never again go to any more fashionable watering places and be crowded into narrow, over- heated ill-ventilated rooms, but should take to the railroads, stop at good hotels where he could be cared for comfortably and where the scenes of the day were varied and diversified and not one monotonous routine. They remained overnight at Groton, and during the evening, Uncle Jonas recalled many of the names of the old settlers with whom he was acquainted. Among them were Crittenden, Blodgett, Carpenter, Wright, Atwood, Ingall, Perrin, Williams, Clark, Leonard, Beach, Hinman, Luther, Whipple, Dean, Blood, Ladd, Hale and others. He also spoke of visiting Groton academy fifty or more years ago.

The next morning after partaking of a most excellent breakfast, they again take the Southern Central for Auburn — passing through the villages of Locke and Moravia, arriving at Auburn in due season. Auburn is now a city containing about 25,000 inhabitants and could Oliver Goldsmith again be called back to earth and view the city of Auburn in the year of our Lord 1886 and be told how his lines concerning the "deserted village" had been the cause for the christening a beautiful country village in far off America, which instead of becoming " deserted" had blossomed into a growing. Prosperous city, the odd Irish poet would "weep with joy." The conductor on the Southern Central had been very accommodating and kind to Uncle Jonas, and he very reluctantly parted company with him at Auburn.

After viewing from the outside the walls and structure of the Auburn prison, they strolled about the city for two hours or more admiring its elegant churches, seminaries, schools and public building and the cost-ly mansions, cozy cottages, industrial establishments, and spacious stores, they take a train on the New York Central and run up to Geneva, passing through Cayuga, Seneca Falls, and Waterloo.

At Geneva, they stop at the Franklin House, one of the historic hotels of the country, for dinner. Uncle Jonas wanted to take one more ride on the crystal waters of Seneca Lake. Therefore after dinner, they go down to the landing and step on board of one of the very elegant steamers that ply on that lake between Geneva and Watkins Glen. The trip was made in less than four hours. They were given a very convenient position for viewing the scenery on either side of the lake, and never did two men enjoy voyage better than they. They had been, as the reader recollects, over the line of the Syracuse, Geneva and Corning Railroad, operated by the Fall Brook Coal Company, which for some miles commands a view of the lake. Still, now they wanted to ride upon the lake and observe the landscape from the upper deck of the steamer. It will be remembered that the course of the lake is nearly north and south, and that like the Cayuga, the lands are cultivated down close to the shore. The banks rise from the shore until they gradually reach an altitude of two hundred and fifty feet or more two miles distant from the water. Nature could not have constructed a more convenient place for the planting of gardens and vineyards or the perfection of agriculture in all its various branches. Uncle Jonas was familiar with every point and re-lated his experience in navigating the waters of the Seneca fifty years ago or more. It seemed to him as if "the best wine for the feast had been reserved for the last," so well did he enjoy the trip. A gentle breeze was blowing from the west, but not so strong as to disturb the water to any extent, and the boat moved proudly upon the water. At times the old gentleman would be silent, gazing upon the beautiful, constantly-changing banks. Then he would narrate some incident, some Indian tradition or some fact connected with General Sullivan's expedition against the Six Nations, or perchance some story concerning the early boat captains who ran the *Richard Stevens* or *Canaseraga*.

They had chosen a propitious time. The apple, peach and plum orchards were in full bloom, the wheat fields and meadows were green, and the forest trees in the numerous small groves were clad in their spring attire. Beautiful farm-houses were half-hidden by the orchards and groves which surrounded them, while cottages were faintly discernible hid away among arbors and vines. It was like passing through fairyland, so soft and beautiful was the scene spread out before them. The sun and fleecy scattering clouds with the high vault of blue beyond lent enchantment to the scene and formed the setting of the picture. The boat was going nearly south. The sun had crossed the meridian, and the fleecy clouds swept leisurely across the lake from the west to the east for a few moments obscuring the sun from view. Then the long shadows would cover a grove, a vineyard, or a green field, which would change their appearance. By and by, the clouds would pass away, and the fields and groves which had been overshadowed would again appear in the sunlight more beautiful, if possible, than at first. 'Tis, thus in life. Fascinating characters are often overshadowed by clouds of reverses and misfortunes and many times by malice. Still, the sunlight of truth at length shines out, and they stand forth again in all their dignity and manhood.

At length, our voyagers land at Watkins Glen, and reach Elmira in safety, by the Northern Central railway, having enacted their program to the letter. After arriving home, Uncle Jonas and Harry were comfortably seated in the sitting room, when Uncle Jonas said: "Harry, you have been a kind and helpful nephew; you have accompanied me on all my tours for the past eight months or more. No period of my life have I passed away so pleasantly, and I may add so beneficially to my health, as the months spent with you. I must go to Chicago the day after tomorrow. I must call on some friends with whom I have met since I came here, and some whom I have not met, among the latter, Rufus King, esq., who I learn has lived here more than forty years and was a great friend of Col. Hathaway, and there are some others. I shall go to Chicago, as I state. These towns have furnished me food for reflection and will buoy

me up and stimulate me for some time to come, but I am not satisfied. A few of my old friends, I have neglected to call upon, not intentionally, on my part, but because their names had slipped from my memory. Forty-five years, Harry, is a long while, especially when added to the age of a man when he has arrived at thirty, and I want you to say to my old friends, wherever they may be found, that I thank them for their courtesies and civil treatment. If my health permits and God grant that it will, I shall return to the city and county of my birth and again go out over mountain and vale and seek for those whom I have overlooked. I shall expect you to accompany me, your business permitting."

"My dear Uncle, I am happy to know that you are well pleased with your visit, and should you come again, I shall hold myself at your service. I am under obligations to you for the opportunities afforded me to enjoy your conversations upon former times."

These letters, containing Uncle Jonas Lawrence's reminisces, created so much interest when published in the Elmira *Weekly Advetiser* that it was thought best to gather them in book form.

The date and the historical statements given in these accounts may be relied upon as correct, and therefore, as a book of reference, as well as general reading, it will be found in every library throught this section of country. It is possible, as intimated above that Uncle Jonas may at some future time renew his acquantiance with readers of the Elmira *Advertiser.*

More special edition reprinted books about Elmira from New York History Review

A Brief History of Chemung County, New York, 1779 -1905
by Ausburn Towner with new index

Harper's New York & Erie Railroad Guide Book of 1851

The Elmira Prison Camp
by Clay Holmes

Our Own Book : A Victorian Guide To Life

Historical Sketch of the Chemung Valley, New York
by T. Apoleon Cheney

A Soldier's Story
by Miles O. Sherrill

Diary of a Tar Heel Confederate Soldier
by Louis Leon

Zim's Foolish History of Elmira
by Eugene Zimmerman

The Great Inter-State Fair

www.ingramcontent.com/pod-product-compliance
Lightning Source LLC
Chambersburg PA
CBHW031237090426
42742CB00007B/234